Rehab

An American Scandal

Shoshana Walter

SIMON & SCHUSTER
New York   London   Amsterdam/Antwerp   Toronto
Sydney/Melbourne   New Delhi

Simon and Schuster
1230 Avenue of the Americas
New York, NY 10020

For more than 100 years, Simon & Schuster has championed authors and the stories they create. By respecting the copyright of an author's intellectual property, you enable Simon & Schuster and the author to continue publishing exceptional books for years to come. We thank you for supporting the author's copyright by purchasing an authorized edition of this book.

No amount of this book may be reproduced or stored in any format, nor may it be uploaded to any website, database, language-learning model, or other repository, retrieval, or artificial intelligence system without express permission. All rights reserved. Inquiries may be directed to Simon & Schuster, 1230 Avenue of the Americas, New York, NY 10020 or permissions@simonandschuster.com.

Copyright © 2025 by Shoshana Walter

All rights reserved, including the right to reproduce this book or portions thereof in any form whatsoever. For information, address Simon & Schuster Subsidiary Rights Department, 1230 Avenue of the Americas, New York, NY 10020.

First Simon & Schuster hardcover edition August 2025

SIMON & SCHUSTER and colophon are registered trademarks of Simon & Schuster, LLC

Simon & Schuster strongly believes in freedom of expression and stands against censorship in all its forms. For more information, visit BooksBelong.com.

For information about special discounts for bulk purchases, please contact Simon & Schuster Special Sales at 1-866-506-1949 or business@simonandschuster.com.

The Simon & Schuster Speakers Bureau can bring authors to your live event. For more information or to book an event, contact the Simon & Schuster Speakers Bureau at 1-866-248-3049 or visit our website at www.simonspeakers.com.

Interior design by Wendy Blum

Manufactured in the United States of America

10 9 8 7 6 5 4 3 2 1

Library of Congress Cataloging-in-Publication Data has been applied for.

ISBN 978-1-9821-4982-6
ISBN 978-1-9821-4984-0 (ebook)

For Miriam.

Contents

Introduction: America's Other Drug Crisis   ix

PART ONE: AN EPIDEMIC BEGINS

Chapter One: Chris Koon, Pineville, Louisiana, 2005   3
Chapter Two: April Lee, Philadelphia, Pennsylvania, 2001   15
Chapter Three: Larry Ley, Noblesville, Indiana, 2004   23
Chapter Four: Wendy McEntyre, Thousand Oaks, California, 2004   35

PART TWO: THE ROAD TO RECOVERY

Chapter Five: Chris Koon, Pineville, Louisiana, 2015   47
Chapter Six: April Lee, Philadelphia, Pennsylvania, 2014   53
Chapter Seven: Larry Ley, Carmel, Indiana, 2013   61
Chapter Eight: Wendy McEntyre, Skyforest, California, 2014   69
Chapter Nine: Chris Koon, 2015   83
Chapter Ten: April Lee, 2014   99
Chapter Eleven: Larry Ley, 2013   105
Chapter Twelve: Wendy McEntyre, 2014   113
Chapter Thirteen: Chris Koon, 2015   121
Chapter Fourteen: April Lee, 2014   139

Contents

Chapter Fifteen: Larry Ley, 2014 — 151
Chapter Sixteen: Wendy McEntyre, 2015 — 161

PART THREE: RELAPSE AND RECOVERY

Chapter Seventeen: Chris Koon, 2017 — 179
Chapter Eighteen: April Lee, 2016 — 187
Chapter Nineteen: Larry Ley, 2019 — 197
Chapter Twenty: Wendy McEntyre, 2022 — 209

Epilogue — 221

Acknowledgments — 227
Notes — 231
Index — 285

INTRODUCTION

America's Other Drug Crisis

On a bright morning in May 2014, an amateur search party stepped onto a crumbling cliffside studded with stinging nettles and rattlesnake-infested shrubs. In front of the crew was an endless expanse of blue sky and snow-topped mountains. Beneath them, a near vertical drop into the San Bernardino National Forest, and its canopy of towering, swaying Bristlecone pines. The search party skidded down the incline as brush, dust, and rocks dislodged from the dry sandy soil and hurtled into the canyon, a mile down below. They were looking for the remains of 21-year-old Donavan Doyle, presumed dead. In fact, he had last been seen outside a quaint 1940s inn perched on the top of the mountain where the searchers now stood. That inn had an unusual purpose—as a drug rehab facility.

Donavan's parents had heard all sorts of stories from Above It All Treatment Center in Skyforest, California, and none provided a clear picture of what happened the day their son went missing. The for-profit rehab industry was rapidly expanding to meet the growing demand for treatment

Introduction

services that were now covered under the Affordable Care Act, and with this expansion came a meteoric rise in business practices intended to maximize profits—often at the expense of patient care. Each week Donavan Doyle had been at Above It All he seemed to get worse. Unbeknownst to the Doyles, even the employees at Above It All had grown concerned about Donavan's treatment. Donavan had started wetting the bed. One employee thought he was being overmedicated and that Donavan needed more intensive treatment services, which Above It All could not provide. Donavan routinely begged his parents to pick him up and take him home—requests that were denied at the recommendation of the rehab's owner. But it wasn't until Donavan refused to attend group sessions—preventing the program from collecting all his insurance benefits—that Above It All decided to discharge Donavan from their program. By that point, about two weeks in, the rehab had already billed more than $14,000 for its services. That's when Donavan's counselor told him that he had to leave. A scuffle broke out. Then Donavan walked off, disappearing into the fog, without a trace. Eight months later, the Doyles were still looking for answers.

The crew descended the cliff carefully in a zigzag formation, carrying yellow caution tape to mark whatever they found. Donavan's father, Shannon, was among them. He was joined by a retired crime-scene investigator, but all the searchers were volunteers—mostly local townspeople who had worried for years about Above It All's expansion into their small town. At first, the locals were angry about the program's proximity to a school bus stop and the tattooed men they saw milling about. When they encountered the Doyles walking door to door, they had offered to help organize the search, more familiar with the rocky cliffside terrain than Shannon, a longtime truck driver from Fresno, whose heart thudded rapidly in the 90-degree heat. He carried only a plastic water bottle, squeezed into the back pocket of his pants, while he struggled to remain upright on the shifting soil.

While Shannon clung desperately to the mountainside, Donavan's mother, Cyndi, clung to another local volunteer, a woman named Wendy McEntyre. Wendy had joined the search party because she, too, had lost a

Introduction

son. The two women were a striking sight: Cyndi was short and round with a blond bob; Wendy was tall and lanky with a slight stoop and a frazzled blond coif. It had been almost ten years since Wendy's son had overdosed and died at a sober-living home. Following his death, she left her high-paying job as a mortgage broker, sold her suburban home in a wealthy Los Angeles suburb, and moved to this mountain community. She'd made it her mission to force a change in the rehab industry. She was so loving that she had cried with the Doyles at their first meeting. "You can tell how much she cares," Cyndi later told me. "When you're in pain, she's in pain." At the same time, Wendy could be so zealous in her pursuit of justice that—to bureaucrats and detractors—she could come across as unhinged.

Wendy didn't think they'd be able to find Donavan. It had been too long, and winters in the mountain were too extreme. But she knew her presence could help the Doyles accept whatever was to come.

The crew was almost 3,500 feet down when one of the searchers lost his footing. He cried out, the two hikers below him hurling themselves out of the way as he hurtled down the steep stope, clawing clods of loose dirt and rocks until he came to a stop. Covered in leaves and dust, the man rose to his knees and noticed something in the brush. It was a wallet. "Shannon," he called out. The father quickly confirmed it was his son's. They had bought it at an outlet mall on their drive to Above It All.

As Shannon stared at the wallet, the searchers continued on. Someone found Donavan's Nike sweatshirt, which was inside out with bite marks on it, as though animals had gnawed through it. They saw what appeared to be broken bones. And then they saw a skull, resting in a cluster of fallen trees. It was brown and gray, with several broken teeth—a detail that later stood out to Shannon because Donavan had always had beautiful straight teeth. The group marked the location of the remains with the yellow caution tape. Shannon swallowed down his growing panic, and the search party began the difficult climb to the top.

The San Bernardino County Sheriff's Office, which had already classified Donavan's disappearance as voluntary, declined to dispatch its homi-

Introduction

cide unit to the scene. The next day, the agency confirmed the identity of the remains and reaffirmed their stance: This was not a suspicious death. The medical examiner soon reached a similar conclusion. Donavan had been staying at Above It All "for drug-related issues," the examiner wrote. "Attempts have been made to speak with family regarding Donavan's social history and medical history. Due to poor telephone reception and other issues, we have not been able to make contact." The coroner ruled Donavan's cause of death as "undetermined," but said that "exposure to the elements [was] a distinct possibility." The case was closed.

For the Doyles and for Wendy McEntyre, however, it was just the beginning. Wendy was used to hearing drug-addicted people blamed for their own deaths. Her own son's death had been ruled an accident. But after years of digging, she was convinced that negligent care and a lack of oversight had contributed to his fatal overdose. To her, it seemed there might also be more to Donavan's disappearance.

How did a young man from a loving family living five hours away end up at a rehab in the mountains of San Bernardino? How had Donavan Doyle managed to leave this rehab—blindly, into the fog, without a trace? And why was Above It All allowed to continue operating without any further investigation?

The story behind Donavan's death would reveal a largely hidden world that reached far beyond Wendy's mountain town. It was almost exclusively populated by desperate and addicted people who had been lured to rehab with the promise of a cure for what ailed them, only to repeatedly falter and fail inside a system that treated them like dollar signs. This was the world of addiction treatment, with thousands of programs scattered across the country that were mostly shielded from public view. This system had been transformed and emboldened by federal policies, but was ultimately governed by a uniquely American approach to addiction treatment: a philosophy that lurched between personal responsibility and punishment, all while driven by the need for profit. The industry was shockingly underscrutinized, considering the scope of America's addiction crisis, which

Introduction

has killed more Americans each year than died in the entire length of the Vietnam war. The stark truth was that there would be no solving America's opioid epidemic unless the country developed an effective addiction-treatment system. And until a growing group of people like Shannon and Cyndi Doyle and Wendy McEntyre confronted a system that was broken. It was a system that all too often seemed to believe people like their sons—people struggling with addiction—deserved their fate, up to and including death.

MORE THAN A YEAR after Donavan Doyle's remains were found, in October 2015, then-President Barack Obama stepped up to a podium in a gymnasium in Charleston, West Virginia, and publicly acknowledged for the first time that the opioid crisis had reached epidemic proportions. "More Americans now die every year from drug overdoses than they do from motor vehicle crashes," Obama announced. "This crisis is taking lives. It's destroying families. It's shattering communities all across the country."

This speech reflected a marked shift in thinking, brought about by the deadliest drug epidemic in American history. In years past or present, the president might have pledged to unleash the full force of the police, to patrol lawless communities, to lock up drug dealers and users, to secure the border, and to cut off drug supplies. Instead, Obama took a different tack. He described the people buying the drugs as *people*. This was not a problem caused by minority communities overrun with crack and crime. This epidemic was universal.

"This could happen to any of us in any of our families," Obama said. "It touches everybody—from celebrities to college students, to soccer moms, to inner city kids. White, Black, Hispanic, young, old, rich, poor, urban, suburban, men and women. It can happen to a coal miner; it can happen to a construction worker; a cop who is taking a painkiller for a work-related injury. It could happen to the doctor who writes him the prescription."

Introduction

During the crack epidemic, drug users—predominantly Black and Brown, from the inner city—were vilified and arrested. Now, a new generation of users and their families—predominantly white—were demanding a different, more compassionate approach. And the political capital of white families could not be so easily ignored. Members of Congress in both parties began framing addiction as a disease and the people afflicted with it as "victims." The villain responsible for this epidemic was identified as Purdue Pharma, the pharmaceutical company behind the blockbuster pain medication OxyContin, which became the target of widespread activism, prosecution, civil lawsuits, and dozens of books and television shows, eventually leading the company to declare bankruptcy in 2019. Lawmakers pledged to fund solutions to the problem, and they promised to never let it happen again. For this drug epidemic, treatment seemed to be the near unanimous answer.

In the years that followed, some forms of that promise took shape. The country's drug-treatment system underwent an enormous expansion. First, the federal government—led by then-Senator Joe Biden—partnered with a pharmaceutical company to produce Suboxone, the country's first treatment for opioid addiction that could be prescribed from the comfort of a doctor's office. During the Bush and Obama administrations, a series of funding packages and additional rules followed, including a law requiring insurance companies to cover addiction treatment just like any other medical procedure. Then the Affordable Care Act expanded addiction treatment to millions of people. Today, addiction treatment is a $53 billion per year industry. Once solely the domain of the wealthy, rehab is now accessible to more people than ever before.

But meanwhile, the epidemic continued its steady climb. Year after year, it broke new records as the deadliest drug crisis in U.S. history, far outpacing the overdose death rate of all other high-income nations. In 2021, there were more than 6,100 overdose deaths involving illicit drugs in the entirety of the European Union; for that year in the United States, there were more than 107,000. Since the start of the crisis in 1999, overdose deaths have increased 541 percent. In total, more than 1 million people in the United

Introduction

States have died of overdoses. In just two years, the deaths caused by synthetic opioids like fentanyl alone were more than triple the casualties from the Iraq, Afghanistan, and Vietnam wars combined.

Everyone seemed to agree: People need treatment. So why hasn't it worked?

PURDUE PHARMA IS an easy villain to blame for the opioid epidemic. This book tells the story of America's *other* drug crisis—the one that has received but a small fraction of the attention: the profit-hungry, under-regulated, and all too often deadly rehab industry.

What began as a well-intentioned effort by lawmakers to stem the tide of overdose deaths instead became a key reason why today so many Americans remain mired in a cycle of relapse, addiction, and arrest. Lawmakers invested in finding a medical cure for addiction—Suboxone. But they created restrictive regulations that made Suboxone scarce during the most crucial years of the epidemic and enriched the pharmaceutical company behind it. Lawmakers passed the Affordable Care Act, creating greater access to treatment than ever before. But as the law came online, and for-profit rehab programs proliferated, both regulators and law enforcement failed to reel in unethical business practices that endangered lives.

Some of these practices had existed for decades, despite evidence they often did more harm than good. For example, at some rehab programs, patients worked full-time manual-labor jobs for free, classified as "work therapy." Other programs overmedicated patients to the point of impairment, then were all too eager to re-enroll those patients once they had inevitably relapsed upon release. Insurance companies erected barriers to coverage, preventing many patients from accessing any programs at all. But even patients who had access to "good" rehab programs were at risk. At their lowest and most vulnerable, with decreased tolerance, patients struggled and relapsed when the support of rehab evaporated. Studies

Introduction

show that patients are more likely to overdose and die after a 30-day stint in rehab than before it.

Rehab programs definitely help people recover. For the worst cases of addiction, some treatment is better than none. But the success of a program often hinges on what happens *after* people leave and what kind of support and opportunity patients have to fall back on. As lawmakers went all-in on treatment, these changes laid bare the gaps in our social safety net that left people—including those who attended rehab—even more vulnerable to relapse and death.

In the following pages, you'll find the stories of four people, each in a different region of the country, who represent the failures of our treatment system. Some of these people meet tragic endings, while others manage, through a combination of luck and miraculous tenacity, to survive the system and even thrive.

April Lee, a Black mom in Philadelphia, is a self-described "crack baby" who witnessed firsthand how the government's punitive response to the crack epidemic impeded her own mother's recovery. As a child, April knew she wanted something different for herself. She dreamed of becoming a lawyer or a cop. But after she became addicted and wanted help—was even begging for it—she couldn't get it.

Unlike April, Chris Koon, a young middle-class white man from Louisiana, got the chance to go to treatment instead of to prison. Yet the only program the judge permitted was one that forced him to perform backbreaking menial labor at for-profit companies. This was essentially his sole form of treatment, for which he received no compensation except one pack of cigarettes a week.

You'll meet Wendy McEntyre, a mother from a wealthy suburb of Los Angeles. She's the kind of clamoring and privileged constituent who has pushed lawmakers to treat this epidemic differently from the drug crises of years past. When Wendy's own son died of an overdose in a sober-living home, she began investigating the treatment programs unleashed by the Affordable Care Act that prioritized billable services over individual needs.

Introduction

Yet, law enforcement and regulators routinely ignored her warnings. And the rehab patients continued to die.

You'll also meet Larry Ley, a surgeon from Indiana who struggled with addiction, and who would eventually become one of the first Suboxone prescribers in the nation. But despite the medication's successful use in other countries to stem overdose deaths, the United States kept a tight rein on it, limiting its availability during a crucial time and enriching Suboxone's manufacturer in the process. And Larry, intent on finding ways to serve the many patients lining up outside his doors, soon drew the attention of the Drug Enforcement Administration, which launched an investigation of Larry and other doctors.

These four people do not reflect all the possible experiences of addiction, treatment, and recovery. Given the severity of America's drug crisis, it might sound like a turn toward more rehab is a good thing. When rehab works, it can save lives. It can mend families and be among the most redemptive narrative arcs in a person's life. People want to get better. Parents empty their bank accounts to put their children through rehab. People move across the country to escape the deadly grip of an addiction that controls every aspect of their lives. People struggling with addiction do need help.

But the treatment system we have today isn't working. Too often, rehab not only fails to help people but also contributes to a cycle of relapse that can prove deadly. Despite the rehab industry's many claims, there is no magical cure for addiction. As Obama, Biden, and countless other politicians have declared, anyone can get addicted. But in America, only certain people get the chance to recover.

Only by understanding this pattern and seeing how it plays out in our treatment system can we begin to understand how to do better—how as a nation we can actually overcome this epidemic, and the others to come.

Part One

An Epidemic Begins

CHAPTER ONE

Chris Koon

Pineville, Louisiana
2005

Chris Koon was 15 when he tried opioids for the first time. He was visiting his cousin's house, showing off on a three-wheeler. Then, one of his shoelaces got caught on the pedal, and he hurtled onto the pavement. He woke up splayed in the middle of the road, blood and gravel streaked across the side of his face. *How can I play this off?* he thought at first. Then he tried to stand, the adrenaline wore off, his ankle collapsed, and the pain kicked in. He realized his ankle was broken. Three surgeries later, he lay in bed, feeling useless. He took one pill, and it made his ankle feel better. He took two pills, and it made him feel better about lying around useless in bed. "I felt happy," he said. "Felt good."

Chris had always felt kind of lonely, and he longed to fit in. According to his grandmother Pat Koon—otherwise known as Granny, a sturdy no-nonsense woman and a believer in astrology—Chris was practically destined to be exploited. He was born in September of 1990; in other words, he was a Virgo. "Virgos are real kind-hearted people," Granny explained. "Easily taken advantage of. They help people at their own expense."

Rehab

Chris's parents had him young. In 1989, John Koon was in his second year of college and he went back to visit his old marching band teacher. Right there, in band class, was a senior who caught his eye. They began a courtship that soon resulted in a surprise. "I believe the exact statement was, 'You're what?'" John recalled. John's father had worked two or three jobs on and off his whole life, so John soon assumed the role he'd long seen his dad perform. He worked his ass off. Carrie and John moved in with John's parents while he finished college, and they both worked. In between shifts flipping burgers at fast-food restaurants, they played classical music for Chris while he was still in the womb and they dreamed of growing a large family.

It ended up being just Chris. When he turned four, his parents divorced and John graduated from college and began an overnight job at a mental health facility. Chris's grandparents became his caregivers. Chris was especially fond of his grandfather, who now had all the time in the world for his first grandson. They made cranberry sauce together at Christmas and listened to classical music. But then Chris's grandfather, too, moved on. He died when Chris was six. After that, Chris shuttled between Dad and Mom and Granny, switching houses and schools whenever he missed the other parent, got angry about something, or was just plain bored. His mom remarried and had two other sons, while his dad remarried and got a stepdaughter. They were two families, who saw each other full-time; Chris was part-time.

Chris's desire to belong led him to try many things, even when he knew he shouldn't. When he was 10, after his mother had remarried, Chris was hanging out with some older kids in the woods behind the house who were passing a blunt back and forth. "Eww," Chris said. "Smoking is gross." But they insisted it wasn't. This stuff was different. Try it. So, Chris did. Afterward, he went back to the house, swung open the freezer door, and consumed nearly all of Mom's leftover wedding cake. "They didn't know I had the munchies," he recalled. "They just knew my fat ass ate their cake."

Next, Chris tried Adderall. In junior high school, everyone seemed to have an ADD diagnosis and a prescription. Another time, an older boy in the neighborhood offered Chris and his friends some crack. No one seemed interested, so Chris decided to be the badass. This time, he was the first to try it, and then the others followed.

In high school, the only education Chris received about drugs was through DARE—Drug Abuse Resistance Education—a Reagan-era program that often deployed horror stories about drugs to scare teenagers away from trying them. That tactic didn't work for most kids. Studies had found that kids who learn "self-efficacy," who feel empowered to make their own choices, are also more likely to effectively deal with peer pressure, more likely to feel comfortable refusing drugs if offered, and more likely to talk to their parents about it. Of the schools that offered prevention programs, only 10 percent deployed these kind of strategies.

What Chris knew about drugs was this: They were fun. They brought people together. They alleviated anxiety and made people feel better. And the adults around him knew that, too. Pain pills were so ubiquitous in the parish that it was easy to find people willing to part ways with them. Procuring the pills made Chris feel like he had something to offer, like he was important and a little bit dangerous, a part of something greater than himself.

In his mind, this wasn't some kind of big criminal enterprise. He just tagged along with friends, met friends of friends, and neighbors of friends. Many of them were his parents' age and older, people who had worked for years in physically demanding blue-collar jobs, who easily obtained prescriptions for OxyContin and other pain pills, and now had more than they could possibly use. From 2006 to 2019, more than 2.6 billion pain pills were supplied to patients in Louisiana. For many of those patients, out of work or struggling financially, selling their pills on the black market provided an easy income stream.

Others traded their medicine for something that worked even better. Chris remembered meeting one woman who had been diagnosed with late-stage lung cancer. She didn't want money for her pills; she just wanted marijuana, which was illegal in Louisiana but helped with the pain and nausea in a way the pills never did. Even though she gave Chris almost her entire bottle of pain pills, she never asked for more weed than she needed. "Are you sure?" he'd ask, concerned. Chris grew fond of her and visited her often.

CHRIS'S ADOLESCENT DRUG experimentation coincided with a period of increasing inequality in and disillusionment with American working life. In 1960, the unemployment rate was about 4 percent. By 2009, a year into a national recession, the rate had more than doubled. Jobs were more unstable, and less likely to come with health insurance, while at the same time welfare benefits for families had plummeted. Amid the high rates of poverty and joblessness came higher rates of chronic pain.

A small, family-run pharmaceutical company best known for manufacturing pain pills for cancer patients cooked up the cure for what was ailing working-class Americans. In 1996, Purdue Pharma released OxyContin, an extended-release oxycodone pill that was twice as strong as other common opioid-based painkillers.

Over the next decade, Purdue Pharma invested heavily in transforming the hearts and minds of America's physicians and patients. There was an untreated epidemic of chronic pain in the United States. OxyContin, the company promised, would provide the cure: immediate relief without addicting people. Soon, other companies began marketing powerful opioid-based pills directly to the public.

The healthcare system was poised to embrace this pain pill revolution. Doctors, under pressure to see more patients, were spending less time with them, while insurance companies stopped reimbursing for more expensive, longer-term pain treatments. Purdue Pharma deployed a vast army of mouthpieces to sell physicians on OxyContin, claiming that it was specially designed to prevent misuse. Less than 1 percent of pain patients develop addictions from opioids, the sales reps said, citing an article from the prestigious *New England Journal of Medicine* that was, in fact, not a scientific study but, rather, a letter to the editor written by a single doctor. These pharmaceutical representatives all insisted the drug was impossible to abuse. Its extended-release formulation meant that, once ingested, the painkiller would be absorbed over time, not all at once in one powerful high, they said. Purdue also poured funding into patient advocacy groups, launched educational programs for doctors, and offered paid speaking gigs and freebies, from plush toys to CDs to training conferences at fancy resorts.

But people who took the pills noticed they didn't last as long as described. To ease their pain, some people took more than was prescribed. Others saw how easy it was to get around the extended-release coating. If they crushed the pill, they could snort the powder or mix it with water and inject it. The resulting high was powerful and immediate.

By 2002, six years after its release and while Chris was in middle school, OxyContin's sales were soaring. Purdue Pharma was selling roughly $1.5 billion worth of the drug every year, transforming the once fledgling family company into the biggest-selling pharmaceutical manufacturer in the country.

Meanwhile, deaths from the drug began to mount. At first, they were noted only by medical examiners in rural communities, but soon the numbers were impossible to ignore. When President Nixon had declared his war on drugs in 1971, annual overdose deaths were 6,771. By 2008, when Chris graduated from high school, the annual drug-overdose death toll had reached more than 36,000, soon surpassing car accidents as the leading cause of accidental death. Prescription narcotics were now killing more Americans than all illegal drugs combined, and joblessness seemed to increase the risk of these deaths. With every 1 percent increase in unemployment came a 3.5 percent increase in opioid-related deaths and a 7 percent increase in overdoses.

Rapides Parish, where Chris grew up, had once been a central hub for the slave trade, and following the abolition of slavery, home to a white community that thrived amid the brutal violence of Jim Crow. For decades after World War II, the federal government encouraged public and private investment in segregated white communities across the country, which was a boon for the white working and middle classes, who bought homes and found stable jobs in manufacturing and other industries, while Black towns and neighborhoods remained largely excluded from those benefits, sometimes violently. As parish leaders fought integration and school busing, Main Street in Pineville bustled with activity, a beacon of civic duty and commerce beside the bayous and pine forests. Then, in the 1980s, American lawmakers began to relax regulations on private capital. As employers closed plants or fled to cheaper pastures abroad, bleeding jobs from American workers, many white communities, too, began to feel the sting of capitalist betrayal and the pain of government neglect.

By 2008, amid a national recession, Pineville's Main Street had become mostly a series of dilapidated, empty storefronts. With so much industry now overseas, attracting major employers to a town or city had become a competitive sport, with offers of massive tax breaks to incentivize companies to relocate. But attracting new business to the parish was difficult because, in order to function, those companies would need functional workers, and it seemed to potential employers that most workers there could not pass a drug test. Developing a drug problem felt almost inevitable, especially for a young unemployed man, unsure of his purpose or his future.

ONE DAY, not long after he turned 18, Chris went to his dealer's house. He was about to buy some weed when he got a text from a friend, who told him to wait. "Be there in ten minutes," he said. Chris plunked down into a chair in the backyard. The dealer rolled a blunt, Chris rolled a joint, and they waited, listening to the symphony of frogs that echoed across the night sky.

Less than ten minutes later, Chris heard loud whoops, the barking of dogs, and the dreaded sound of police. *Oh, shit.* Chris threw away the weed, swung his hefty frame over the fence, and ran until he felt lightheaded and out of breath. He slowed down in a nearby cemetery and ducked behind a tombstone, panting. He thought for a moment. His truck was still parked outside the house, and it was registered to his mom. Sooner or later, the police would find out who owned the vehicle and call them. He again began running, got to a friend's house, and then called his dad.

"Where the fuck are you?" John Koon asked. "The cops are looking for you." It was the middle of the night, but John drove over and picked Chris up from the friend's house.

Chris's mother was out looking for her son, too. As Chris expected, the police had called her when they found his truck. Apparently, a young woman had been trying to drive off in it, claiming she was Chris's sister. Carrie told them that was a lie. But now the police knew Chris had been there and they wanted to arrest him. Carrie believed Chris needed to learn there were consequences for his actions. She wanted to bring Chris to the police. She called John. "Where are you?" she asked.

John, a prison guard, had no illusions about the criminal justice system. It wasn't a place for his son. He told Carrie where he was, and then told Chris to hide in the back seat. "I'm still looking for him," Chris heard John say when his mother pulled up alongside the car. "I ain't seen him."

"Well, he needs to turn himself in," she replied.

"Well, I don't know, I ain't seen him," John said. As soon as Carrie pulled away, John turned back toward Chris. "She's crazy," he said. "We're getting you a lawyer."

Chris was petrified at the thought of being handcuffed and interrogated, and taken off to jail. But as dawn broke, he felt even worse about putting his parents through hell. He decided to turn himself in.

Lucky for Chris, the cop at the police station saw a kid who had fallen in with the wrong crowd and was just experimenting. Chris walked out of the station with his car keys and a parking ticket.

Rehab

NOW OUT OF high school, Chris began to fill increasing amounts of his free time with drugs. He tried ecstasy, mushrooms, other hallucinogens. But pain pills were by far the easiest to find. He started eating pills—Dilaudid and Opana—and he didn't stop. He bounced from house to house, from his grandma's house to his mom's. He would do well for a time; he'd hold down a job, his parents would breathe a sigh of relief, and then he'd do something stupid. Like shoplifting two CDs from a Best Buy store. Or hanging out with a friend who swiped a girl's purse off the pool table at Riches. The sum total of these heists was about $43. Chris was 21 when he was arrested a second time.

Chris was an adult now, which meant he had to get a job. Work seemed to be in his family's DNA—he had grown up in a Czech immigrant community that prided itself on its work ethic. Also, he'd always loved to read—he and his dad shared a love of sci-fi and fantasy series—but his grades hadn't been great, and his broken ankle had ruined his high school football career along with any hope of a college scholarship. So, Chris had no idea what he wanted to do. He had a hard time imagining himself like his parents, working long hours to eke out a marginally middle-class life. Both of his parents had college degrees and they worked multiple jobs, his dad as a prison guard and his mom as a nurse. These were dependable jobs, they advised him. "Do what you gotta do now so you can do whatever you want later," John would tell Chris. He did try some jobs. There was an offshore job that ended with an oil rig explosion. An EMT trainee position that ended when he tested positive for weed. Nothing stuck.

By now, heroin from Mexico was beginning to flood into the United States, finding a ready customer base in users of OxyContin and other pain pills. Heroin was cheaper but it produced the same high—a bigger bang for the buck that was hard for a chronically underemployed person like Chris to resist. Before long, he injected heroin for the first time. Euphoria enveloped his body like a warm electric blanket, before spreading to his brain. "I couldn't do nothing but sit there and feel splendiferous," Chris said. "It doesn't matter if it was raining blood on you right then. You would be alright. You might nod out, might throw up. Who knows? It don't matter. Because you feel great and nothing can touch you." Chris sat there for who knows how long. He couldn't talk, he couldn't move. He was a fuck-up, he knew that; but using heroin made him feel like everything was alright.

ONE DAY, Chris was deep into one of his shame cycles when he ran into someone he knew who once had a heroin problem. He'd aways looked ragged and paranoid, but now he looked normal, even healthy. He told Chris that a doctor had prescribed him a medication called Suboxone.

Suboxone, a combination of the drugs buprenorphine and naloxone, is a maintenance treatment for opioid addiction, and a partial opioid agonist, filling the same receptors in the brain as illicit opioids. In essence, an opioid agonist moves into the same region of the brain usually stimulated by heroin or OxyContin, takes away the withdrawal symptoms that usually come with stopping opioid use, reduces cravings, and makes it difficult to continue to use a drug like heroin or OxyContin and get high. And unlike OxyContin or heroin, it has a "ceiling"; that is, if an opioid user like Chris took more than was prescribed—as he often did—it would have no effect.

Chris felt compelled to give it a try. He was the happiest he'd been in years, and lately the constant pursuit of heroin had begun to feel like more trouble than it was worth. At 21 years old, he was in love. The woman was a pretty brunette with two young kids, and Chris felt like he was fulfilling his dream of having his own family. He finally felt like he belonged. "So lucky to have found such a great woman to spend my life with," Chris wrote on Facebook. "Laying down with the kids just hanging out and dozing off—best high ever." Granny was not surprised. Even amid all his fuck-ups, she always thought he would make a wonderful father.

At first, Chris had trouble finding a prescriber, and he started buying it off his friend. Then he found a doctor. But Suboxone was expensive, and the clinic only took cash.

Rehab

Chris started working as a night cashier at a Circle K convenience store. He found the job bleak and boring. Every night, he would stare at the line of refrigerators filled with beer that was located along the back wall, waiting for customers to come in. He felt like he was treading water. "Gotta go to school and get a career," Chris wrote on Facebook one night. "I have about 30 years of working ahead of me so I might as well be doing something I like, am I wrong."

Then tragedy struck. His best friend died in a car wreck. A couple of months after that, the girl he'd hoped to marry broke up with him. He stopped taking Suboxone because it was too expensive.

By that time, Chris had gotten a job delivering pizzas for Papa John's. He found himself craving that high, and soon he was stopping by the Circle K to shoot up in the bathroom before continuing on his route. He started showing up late for work—or not at all. He lost that job and started spending all his time and energy searching for heroin. After a few months of this, Chris was shooting heroin several times a day. He kept using more and more of the drug, just to feel something and to stave off withdrawal symptoms. He knew it was only a matter of time before he overdosed.

Finally, he did overdose. He was at his friend Zach's house. He felt himself sinking into his own body, then sinking into the ground, and then he was floating above, watching himself below, frozen in terror and euphoria, unable to move. Zach noticed Chris lying there, like a corpse. He had a Suboxone tablet in his pocket and he gave it to Chris. Soon, Chris was puking his guts out, in the thick of withdrawal—but he was alive.

Chris thought that would be the last time. He'd almost died; why would he feel compelled to use heroin again after that? One day, he was at Granny's when he noticed a pile of papers on the kitchen table. They were an application for a burial plot—for him. "Shook me to my core," he said. It made him want to stop. But, of course, he didn't.

The Suboxone was but a brief reprieve. It was so hard to find, so out of the mainstream, that Chris didn't even think of turning to it again. If the

Chris Koon

drug had been easier to get—if there were more doctors prescribing it, if it was cheaper, or covered by insurance—maybe Chris could have stayed on Suboxone and off the pain pills and heroin. But the pharmaceutical company that made Suboxone, and the U.S. government itself, had made that next to impossible.

CHAPTER TWO

April Lee

Philadelphia, Pennsylvania
2001

In 2001, as the opioid epidemic was beginning its rapid ascent, a Black teenager in Philadelphia heard a knock at the door.

April Lee, 15 years old and newly pregnant, had just moved into the house two months ago. It belonged to her boyfriend's father, an old jazz musician with gnarled hands who primarily occupied a single bedroom, ten televisions deep. The man was a hoarder, and despite the limited space, April felt safe there, inside his fortress of stuff. She began picking her way through a maze of boxes and newspapers, old scrap metal and VCRs and model train sets, and opened the door to find herself face-to-face with the legacy of the crack epidemic: a gaunt woman, looking far older than her age.

"Hey, Mom," April said.

April couldn't believe how much her mother had deteriorated. Nadine had been addicted to crack since before April was born, in 1987; she had even used crack when April was in the womb. A lot of the time, when she wasn't hurting for supply, drugs seemed to quiet the hurt and

Rehab

doubt Nadine felt inside and made her more focused. In some ways, she was an even better version of herself. April had fond memories of her mother cleaning the house, taking the neighborhood kids on long walks to the Liberty Bell, and handing out food to homeless folks downtown. But when Nadine's supply dwindled, April suspected that her mother turned to prostitution to fund her habit. She would disappear for weeks at a time, reappearing only when her hunger was cavernous and her feet were cracked and bleeding.

To deal with all of this, April occupied her mind. Ever since April's Bible-loving aunt had taught her how to read, April had gulped down books from the library, a dozen at a time. Her favorite was Louis Sachar's 1998 novel *Holes*, in which the main character, Stanley Yelnats, is afflicted with an intergenerational curse of bad luck. As a result, 14-year-old Stanley is wrongfully convicted of a crime he didn't commit and is sentenced to a work camp, where he spends his days dodging poisonous lizards and digging holes to hunt for his oppressor's treasure. Only after fleeing and using his newfound strength to carry another kid up a mountain does Stanley lift his family's curse. That tale resonated with April, who always sought to find meaning in the shit she saw. *Sometimes you gotta dig holes for what seems to be no fucking reason at all*, April thought. *The more shit you gotta hold and carry up and down this mountain, the stronger you're going to become.*

The Lee family had long been afflicted with its own kind of intergenerational curse. For generations, the family had jumped from house to house within the sprawling 51-square-mile radius of North Philadelphia. As in Chris's hometown, structural racism had shaped the landscape of Philadelphia, making their neighborhood one of the most segregated in the country. Although the crack epidemic had officially passed, the crisis had left an indelible mark. It wasn't just the drugs that had debilitated so many, feeding on the poverty and despair that had settled into the area following the short-lived victories of the Civil Rights era. It was also the structural racism and discrimination that persisted. And it was the government's response to crack: a series of punitive measures that had made America one of the

April Lee

world's number one incarcerators, and had led to hundreds of thousands of children and babies placed into foster care.

The cycle of addiction and arrest destabilized the adults in April's life. Her uncle had been addicted to heroin and had spent many years cycling between Grandmom's house and homelessness, and prison. She remembered the game the kids used to play when her uncle nodded off while standing in the dining room—his jaw slack, his body slowly folding into itself until all it took was a slight jab of the finger to topple him over. As a kid, April often thought Grandmom was cruel. She refused to give the kids money, even when there was no food in the house, because she didn't want it to go toward drugs. But when her uncle wanted to stop using heroin, it was Grandmom who procured the drugs for him to ease his withdrawal symptoms—it was she who bathed him and caressed his head while he slept.

Crack addiction did not come with the same kind of physical withdrawal as did heroin, but it was just as addictive psychologically, and when Nadine wanted to get away from Grandmom's house, or find some other place to get help, there was nowhere for her to go.

During April's childhood, through the late '80s and into the '90s, the authorities were much more concerned with cracking down on crack usage than with treating it. In 1990, less than 1 percent of the federal funds for drug treatment were allocated for women. Despite the politicized concerns about "crack babies," most treatment programs refused to treat pregnant women, especially crack users on Medicaid. And most of those programs that would accept pregnant women or women with children were not providing the services their patients most needed: childcare. Given the childcare option, many women wouldn't choose it anyway, owing to their legitimate fears they might be reported as drug-dependent and their children removed by child protective services.

A mother of nine like Nadine could not take a timeout from child rearing to get better. When Nadine decided to stop using, she left Grandmom's house and took the kids to a homeless shelter, where drugs and alcohol were not

Rehab

allowed. But the shelter was not a permanent solution. Nadine still needed a place to live and a way to support her kids.

Welfare reforms passed by Congress during April's elementary school years only added to Nadine's challenges. These new regulations imposed work requirements and time limits on welfare recipients, pushing mothers into the minimum wage workforce. But without childcare, or adequate income, this program had become something like a trap, preventing many single mothers like Nadine from being able to financially support and raise their kids. Simply put, if Nadine worked, she couldn't take care of her kids; but if she took care of her kids, she couldn't work—and then would be denied government help.

The shame and despair of her addiction and these self-perceived failures always led Nadine back to drugs, and soon April and her eight siblings found themselves back with Grandmom. If it hadn't been for Grandmom's crowded three-bedroom row house in Philadelphia, crammed with 23 people, April doesn't know how they would have survived. But it was hard living on top of one another, sleeping on the floor or a couch, getting only five minutes in the bathroom, and absorbing or fighting off one another's pain.

Eventually, April ran away, and her mom didn't try to stop her. She was only 13 years old, but already 5 foot 10 inches tall, with breasts and hips, and chain-smoking Pall Malls. She carried herself like an adult, in part because of the responsibilities she'd long assumed at Grandmom's house. In the two years since she'd left, she had worked in a house full of strippers, found a boyfriend, then moved in with him and his hoarder father. April had survived sexual abuse, and now she was pregnant at 15, nearly the same age her Grandmom had been when she had Nadine.

April ushered her mother into her home, looking her up and down. Nadine had always been tiny but boisterous, with a loud, long laugh that took up the room and sent everyone else into fits of giggles. People in their old neighborhood had called her "Bamm-Bamm," after the club-wielding toddler in *The Flintstones* cartoons, because she liked to slick her hair back with a scrunchy into a tiny ponytail, which sprouted from the top of her head

April Lee

like a blade of grass. But now it was clear Nadine was very sick. She seemed weak on her feet. Her normally clear skin was mottled and gray. Even in her worst days of addiction, her mother had never looked anything like this.

April and her boyfriend moved the boxes and stacks of old newspapers out of a bedroom. Over the next few weeks, Nadine slowly began withering away. Halloween came, and April stole a wheelchair from outside an emergency room so her mother could come trick-or-treating with her and the kids.

April began bathing her mother, helping her in and out of bed. One day, her mother asked for some weed. The two smoked together, giggling into the folds of the blanket. Eventually, Nadine could no longer control her bowels. She became too weak to eat. April took her to the hospital, and she died within two weeks. At the time, Grandmom told April it was cancer—a brain tumor. It wasn't until a couple years later, when April ordered a death certificate, that she learned her mom had actually died of AIDS, likely contracted some time during the many years of sex work that had allowed her to support her family and fund her crack habit.

The time April had spent with her mother before her death was the most intimate they had ever been, and it brought April a kind of peace. "I'm not worried about you," Nadine had told April shortly before she died, "I know you gonna make it." But April had come to feel that addiction was a choice, and that her mother—and so many other members of the family—had made the wrong one. They had failed to heed the warnings of the cops who came around the projects at night, toting their displayed images of zombie-faced addicts who only later, April realized, bore no resemblance to her mother. Those were the same messages Chris Koon had received in DARE, and that so many others of their generation had grown up hearing on radio and seeing on television. It was the message: "Just Say No." As if it were that easy.

So, April decided she wouldn't make the same mistake.

Rehab

FOR A LONG TIME after her mother died, April did not have a drug problem. She hopped from guy to guy and found numerous ways to support herself and eventually her newborn son.

She did try a number of different drugs, usually introduced by a boyfriend, who was almost always much older. For a time, she used cocaine, and then she tried crack. Like her mother, April became productive when she smoked. She cooked and cleaned so fast that she even had time to begin prepping the next day's meal. It only backfired once, when she accidentally opened the pressure cooker too soon and the collard greens exploded everywhere, scalding her. One day, she looked at herself in the mirror and realized she needed to stop. "This is what got Mommy," she said to herself.

She stopped using everything. She got heavily involved at a church, she left her boyfriend, and she moved into church housing. She was mostly sober. But her abusive ex would not leave her alone, and when the church pastor sided with him, urging April to give him another chance, she left the church and slid back into her previous habit.

April was still functional, because none of the drugs completely took over her life. That is, until she had her second child. The birth had caused her back pain, and in response, a doctor prescribed her Percocet.

In April's mind, taking Xanax and Percocet did not make her an addict. An addict was her mother. It was someone who used street drugs, who was so far gone that everything else became secondary: kids, home, job, even something as simple as food or a shower. But April had a job and a home. She cooked and she cleaned; she even took the neighborhood kids to the playground. Further, these were prescribed medications—white-people drugs. In her mind, she was lucky to have them, and in a sense, she was—studies have shown that Black patients are far less likely than white patients to be treated and prescribed medications for pain.

But like many people who have been prescribed pain meds, the longer she took the pills, the less effective they became, and she soon found herself taking more than was prescribed, running out of her prescription early. By the time the doctor cut her off the meds, April was chewing the pills. Then

April Lee

she began buying them on the street and selling them to support herself and the kids. April still thought she was better off than her mother, though. She had an income and a roof over head. She had three children now—including a baby girl who was dependent on her. She now lived with that daughter's father, in an old row house they were fixing up for themselves. Yes, April had pain and trauma. But she was managing it.

One night, in 2012, April went out to a bar for a single drink and blacked out. When she woke up, she realized she had been raped. This was the third time in April's life that she had been sexually assaulted, and it broke her. She learned she was pregnant yet again, and though she didn't believe in abortion, she couldn't fathom carrying her rapist's child, so she ended the pregnancy. The medication she took to prevent the onset of HIV made her physically ill. She was offered a therapy session at a rape crisis center, but she couldn't imagine going to it, peeling open her grief and trauma, leaving it exposed, all the while supporting and caring for three children. April could barely leave the house as it was. There was no way. So, April leaned into the medication she knew would ease her pain.

A drug-treatment program that allowed mothers to bring their children might have benefited her, much like it might have benefited her mother. More than 70 percent of women in need of treatment have children; it's one of the top reasons women cite for not seeking help. Time and again, studies have shown that women who are allowed to enter drug-treatment programs with their children stay in those treatments longer and have better outcomes. Yet since the beginning of the opioid epidemic, the number of treatment programs that provided childcare or housing for families had sharply declined. By 2020, there would be only 397 residential programs, or 2 percent of all facilities nationwide, that allowed women to bring their children—a decline of 33 percent. And demand was so high for those programs that many had months-long waiting lists. Further, some states had no residential facilities at all for families.

April also could have benefited from a medication like Suboxone, which might have provided a physical or mental respite while she worked on

Rehab

changing other aspects of her life. Or from the visits of a care provider to her home. But, studies have shown that, perhaps because of the high cost of treatment, Black patients are much less likely than white patients to receive a buprenorphine prescription, and many such programs refuse to admit pregnant women or women with children. The array of options increasingly available to those with money or the right health insurance were not available to April. Her only logical choice was to use the Percocet to prevent withdrawal symptoms, so she could do what she needed to do: walk her children to school and make her daughter's bottle.

After a while, the pills were not enough. April began buying and taking more to get the same effect, and the costs were stacking up. She met a man who introduced her to heroin, a cheaper alternative, and soon enough she found she could not stop. She knew she was a mess, just one fuckup away from somebody calling child protective services. She knew she could not be what her kids needed her to be. She needed a reprieve—to get her life together and make sure the kids were safe.

April pursued the only option she had: She asked an old friend of her mother's to take the kids in. The older woman agreed to take the children, but not April. For two days, April shame-spiraled between heroin binges. She considered her options and called the rape crisis center to find a counselor. But when she returned to the woman's house two days later, her kids were gone. Child welfare authorities had taken them away. According to the city of Philadelphia, April had abandoned them.

April screamed. She broke windows. And then she gave up.

CHAPTER THREE

Larry Ley

Noblesville, Indiana
2004

Dr. Larry Ley was midway through a toasted English muffin with peanut butter when his phone rang. It was a sales representative from Reckitt Benckiser, the company that made Suboxone. He furrowed his bushy eyebrows. They were relentless, he'd give them that.

Since getting certified to prescribe Suboxone about a year ago, Dr. Ley hadn't done much with it. He was more focused on his career comeback. His addiction to alcohol had started as a way to deal with the pain from his degenerative spine condition, then over 30 years grew into an addiction that imploded his career as a surgeon as well as his marriage. The pain was still so bad he couldn't work full time. But Dr. Ley had gotten sober and found a new niche in addiction medicine, treating clients who had gotten into trouble for driving under the influence. Now, he was speaking at white-tablecloth luncheons, championing treatment to the press and the fancy businesspeople of Noblesville, a wealthy suburb outside Indianapolis. He was eager to put the miserable days of bourbon binges behind him and regain the social status he'd once had as a surgeon.

In the last year, Larry had heard regularly from Suboxone's sales reps, asking when he was going to put his new skills to use. They were as aggressive as any of the reps he'd encountered from Eli Lilly or Pfizer. "They were smooth talkers," he said. "Used car salesmen."

But this call was different. In a neighboring town, the rep said, a Suboxone-prescribing doctor had died from a sudden blood clot, leaving his 30 opioid-addicted patients cut off from their medication. Without a doctor to take over the group, the patients would suffer withdrawals and likely relapse, maybe overdose and die. Could Larry step in quickly to make sure the patients weren't cut off from their medication?

Larry agreed to take over the group. "I just rolled up my sleeves and said I'd go down and help out," he said. He viewed it as part of his mission as a doctor and a member of Alcoholics Anonymous, which he credited with his sobriety. He liked helping people, and he especially liked when people looked to him for help. But like Reckitt Benckiser, the company that manufactured Suboxone, Larry also saw a unique business opportunity. Amid the growing drug crisis, there was a huge need for treatment providers. Suboxone was in high demand but still hard to find.

The source of this scarcity was a problem of the country's own making. By the time Larry—and Chris and April—entered the world of opioids, many other wealthy nations had already dealt effectively with their overdose crises. In 1995, France had been facing a heroin crisis of its own, with skyrocketing overdose death and HIV infection rates, when the country made a drastic change. To stem the crisis, the country expanded syringe exchange programs and began permitting any doctor to prescribe buprenorphine—or bup, the drug underlying Suboxone—without special training or a license.

France framed these changes as an effort to minimize the harms of addiction, a strategy known as "harm reduction." It was a radical departure from its previous system, which much like the Reagan-era DARE program prized abstinence above all. Now, the goal was not necessarily to stop drug use but to stop so many people from dying. With the change in law, French primary-care doctors without any special training became the vast majority of bup prescribers in the country, instead of addiction specialists, psychiatrists, or treatment programs.

The result was striking. Within four years, overdose deaths in France declined by 79 percent. The number of people in treatment increased tenfold, with about half the country's heroin users receiving treatment. Some users also were diverting bup and misusing it, a problem that had elicited public concern. But by and large, the country accepted the fact that bup on its own was a far safer drug than heroin, with substantially lower overdose risks and a ceiling on any potential high. The benefits—keeping people alive—outweighed the public safety concerns. And as a result, more people had the option of treatment, leading more people to recovery. In the face of a public health crisis, the voice of law enforcement had been kept at bay, with positive results.

When this conversation came to the United States, the results were entirely different. Since the early twentieth century, federal law had barred doctors from prescribing a controlled substance to someone known to be addicted. Doctors had been continually investigated and arrested for treating addiction with narcotics. In the 1960s, when prominent researchers at the prestigious Rockefeller Institute began experimenting with methadone to treat addicted patients, federal agents infiltrated the clinic, stole records, and spread false rumors about their research results. "You'd better watch out," one agent said. Despite patients' high rates of success, law enforcement "had a sincere belief that the way to control the problem was to stamp it out," the lead researcher later said. "If it's not working, then the punishment is not severe enough." That was why methadone was dispensed through specialized clinics, under a system of surveillance more akin to law enforcement than to medicine.

But the epidemic—and its spread into white suburban communities—was shifting attitudes about addiction. Heroin, an "inner-city" drug, had "jumped the tracks and has been killing kids in some of our most prosperous suburbs," *Dateline NBC* warned in 1998. Instead of being a scourge, these troubled youth were framed as victims in need of help. In this effort, there was an unlikely ally: then-Senator Joe Biden, one of the primary architects of the nation's war on drugs.

Senator Biden had long supported finding a "medical cure" for addiction, working with Congress to create a special division of the National Institute on Drug Abuse (NIDA), which worked with pharmaceutical companies to develop new medications. NIDA proposed a partnership with Reckitt to develop and manufacture a medication for opioid addiction: Suboxone, a new form of buprenorphine that, according to Reckitt, would be difficult to abuse. Reckitt hired former Bill Clinton advisor Charles O'Keeffe as its president and CEO, and O'Keeffe worked with another former White House staffer to write legislation that would allow primary-care doctors to prescribe the medication from their offices. If passed, the Drug Addiction Treatment Act would create a new system of addiction treatment in America, supplied by primary-care doctors, instead of separate addiction-treatment programs, like methadone clinics. Biden threw his support behind the legislation and for the manufacturer behind it.

Congress convened a hearing on the bill, and from the outset, it proved a remarkable departure from previous drug policy debates. When Black communities—and Black mothers like Nadine—were the face of the crack epidemic, lawmakers had jockeyed to prove they were tough on crime, passing laws to lock up more people and expand prison sentences for drug possession. Now, the white face of the opioid epidemic was changing the politics of the conversation. Instead of declaring war, lawmakers were advocating for compassion. "It only makes sense to unleash the full powers of medical science to find a 'cure' for this social and human ill," Biden said during the hearing, which was marked by a complete lack of drug war rhetoric. "There is no other disease that effects so many, directly and indirectly. We have 14 million drug users in this country, four million of whom are hardcore addicts. We all have a family member, neighbor, colleague or friend who has become addicted." Addiction was now a disease, an epidemic, and an affliction.

Yet the same punitive policies remained in place. The bill did nothing to reverse or stop the unequal impact of the nation's drug laws on Black and Brown people. It did nothing to bolster the social safety net after decades of gutting by lawmakers. It would not address addictions to other substances. The bill would primarily benefit people with health insurance or with the money to pay out of pocket, the vast majority of whom were white.

Despite this reality, not a single speaker or lawmaker during the hearing mentioned race during the hearing. Instead, the speakers talked in thinly veiled racial terms about how the new law would make treatment more accessible and palatable to certain people, like suburban youth.

The existing treatment option for people with heroin addiction were methadone programs. But these programs, associated with the stereotype of Black and Brown heroin users from the inner city, were too scarce, too restrictive, and too stigmatizing. Dr. Larry Alexander, an emergency medicine doctor in Texas, testified that "it has been a shock to my suburb as well as others around the country to find that young people who have all the necessities and many of life's extras would wind up using heroin—some of them even dying from it." This new law would create a better option—for certain people. Bup is "expected to reach new groups of opiate addicts," said Donna Shalala, the secretary of Health and Human Services, such as "those who are reluctant to enter methadone treatment programs." The head of the National Institute on Drug Abuse added that bup would appeal to "those who may be reluctant to enter a methadone program; and adolescents and new heroin addicts who are unsuited to methadone."

In addition, the bill was missing key ingredients of France's successful opioid response. French lawmakers had considered bup an "opioid substitute." It was part of that country's broader network of social support and healthcare services. But in the United States, the lawmakers were framing bup as a pharmacological "cure," one that would take the place of a comprehensive treatment, healthcare, and social welfare system.

France expanded access to syringe exchange programs, while the United States' program had effectively banned them. France had nearly universal healthcare. Doctors who adopted bup typically were reimbursed 100 percent,

Rehab

and the patients could get it at any pharmacy—a process that substantially improved treatment access, retention, and success rates. Psychosocial support services were also covered.

But the U.S. poverty rate was more than twice that of France, while its public social spending was half that of France. In 2001, about 39 million Americans were uninsured—about 13 percent of the total population—and even among the insured, it was common to pay as much as a 50 percent copay for addiction treatment.

Another key difference remained: the influence of law enforcement. U.S. lawmakers simply couldn't ignore the demands of the Drug Enforcement Administration (DEA). Key to France's success was the policy that any doctor could prescribe bup to any number of patients without restriction. But under the DEA's influence, the U.S. bill became more restrictive. Congressional staffers saw no other way to get it passed. In the United States, doctors under the law would be required to go through an eight-hour training session and apply for permission to prescribe the drug. They would be limited to 30 patients and subject to oversight by the DEA. No other area of medicine, including the prescribing of pain pills, was subject to so many rules and restrictions. "Is it going to be diverted? Is it going to be sold on the street? Is it going to be doctor shopped?" Pat Good, who was then the chief liaison officer at the DEA, asked at the time.

This limit would be detrimental for U.S. patients, but for ensuring profits, Reckitt had a plan. O'Keeffe, the company's president and CEO, lobbied the Food and Drug Administration (FDA) for orphan drug status, a designation typically bestowed on medications to treat rare diseases that gives a pharmaceutical company seven years of market exclusivity—no generics allowed. O'Keeffe claimed the company qualified for that designation because it would lose money on bup. In fact, the FDA's own analysis of Reckitt's proposal found that in four of nine scenarios, bup would actually become profitable within its first seven years on the market. But FDA staffers were swayed by the novelty of O'Keeffe's proposal, and the Reckitt product. The FDA approved O'Keeffe's application, and soon—amid a burgeoning drug crisis—it granted Reckitt Benckiser sole permission to sell Suboxone, in a regulatory landscape that seemed almost deliberately designed to create scarcity. In other words, this was a recipe for massive profits.

In 2000, the bill passed both houses of Congress, enshrining into law two separate and unequal systems of opioid addiction treatment. One system was for poor people—disproportionately Black and Brown people—that was scarce, heavily surveilled, and stigmatized; and one system for those with access to doctors, who wished to be treated discreetly as medical patients, not as criminals. It was a treatment revolution—for some.

DR. LARRY LEY'S new patients were the kind of people those lawmakers had targeted with their bill—white, young, and middle class. And they were the people Reckitt began to court after the law's passage. In a way, the Reckitt ads seemed progressive, even somewhat radical, dovetailing with growing public sentiment and research. Addiction was a disease, they said, not a moral failing. People who struggled with addiction needed help, not punishment. And the best treatment for addiction—Suboxone—was not punishment but, rather, medication prescribed by a doctor. But in these advertisements, this newfound philosophy seemed to apply to only one demographic: white people.

Even though the rates of heroin use were almost identical among ethnic groups, Reckitt sought to distance itself from the stereotype of a heroin user—poor, Black, and from the inner city. The ideal patient, according to those marketing materials, was a victim, someone who had unwittingly become addicted to opioid pain pills and now needed help. On its website, the pharmaceutical company featured videos of patient success stories like that of Jennifer, a suburban stay-at-home mom who had become addicted to prescription painkillers following a tonsillectomy. Suboxone allowed her to return to a normal life, she said. All the people featured in the company's

Rehab

marketing materials were white. They had families and jobs. They had never tried heroin. They had never tried methadone or traditional drug treatments, nor should they. Like Jennifer, their addictions had started innocently, when they had become addicted to drugs prescribed for a legitimate medical reason. They were normal middle-class white people, unscathed by the traditional markers of poverty and structural racism, or by multiple encounters with police and the criminal justice system, or by the stigma of methadone treatment or a punitive drug rehab.

Reckitt's sales strategy was borrowed from the playbook of another well-known pharmaceutical company: Purdue Pharma, the maker of OxyContin, the drug that had caused the problem Reckitt Benckiser was claiming to solve. Reckitt even poached its salesforce from Purdue Pharma.

Among the original representatives hired from Purdue Pharma was Gail Groves Scott, a curly-haired suburban mom from Pennsylvania who had fallen into pharmaceutical sales years ago, almost by accident. Fast-talking and perpetually chipper, Scott immediately took to sales. She was good at it. But at Reckitt, she felt a higher calling. Her job title was not "sales rep" but, rather, "clinical liaison." And she had a lofty mission. Her role wasn't just to sell Suboxone but also to convince the medical system and the country that addiction was a medical disease that could be treated with a pharmaceutical. Further, that addiction should not be stigmatized or criminalized, but instead should be treated by medical professionals.

Many insurance plans at the time did not pay for addiction treatment or for medications like Suboxone, so this was an uphill battle. Gail had a sales territory, and every day she went out to visit doctors, take them to lunch or dinner, and educate them about Suboxone. "It's very high pressure," she said. "You're taught constantly . . . How do you analyze each doctor's style? How do you influence them?" And like Purdue Pharma, Reckitt poured money into patient advocacy organizations, paid for continuing medical education seminars, and rewarded doctors with meals, "dinner programs," and lucrative speaking gigs.

In the early years, much of Gail Scott's job involved convincing doctors to sign up for the waiver, a process that required doctors to take a training session, take a test, and sign a form called a "notice of intent" that was then sent to the Substance Abuse and Mental Health Services Administration (SAMHSA) for approval and forwarded to the DEA.

It often took months to convince a doctor to file the notice. Most didn't want to be bothered. They didn't have time to take the eight-hour training session and "some of them were intimidated by the subject," Gail said. This is where her "clinical liaison" title came in handy. It lent the impression she had medical training and expertise, so many doctors trusted her guidance. She made the process as easy as possible for them. She directed the doctors as they took the test, read and signed the form, sent the form for them, then followed up with the agencies if there was a delay. The more doctors who had this waiver, the more they could serve the growing ranks of people in need. "We were trying to do what we saw as a public health service," she said.

To motivate Scott and the other clinical liaisons, Reckitt instituted the same incentives as Purdue Pharma. Sales reps tracked how much doctors were prescribing and encouraged them to prescribe more. The sales reps had sales goals and bonuses. They received rankings and prizes. Every year, Reckitt sent its sales reps on all-expense-paid trips to locations like Barcelona, Rome, and Hawaii for their sales meetings, where the company gave out those awards to their most successful reps.

Thanks to the work of Scott and other reps, doctors like Larry Ley did sign up. But after all these aggressive sales efforts, most of the providers were not primary-care doctors; they were doctors already providing addiction treatment services, such as at methadone programs. Even worse, because of the DEA-imposed limits, many of the doctors who were willing to prescribe Suboxone were still required to limit their rosters to 30 patients. By 2003, an estimated 4.7 million people nationwide had reported abusing prescription opioids, but only 616 doctors had obtained waivers to prescribe buprenorphine.

Rehab

With his 6-foot, 3-inch frame and ornery disposition, Larry Ley probably was not the kind of doctor Biden and the other lawmakers had in mind when they passed the legislation. "I thought he was mean at first, to be honest," recalled former patient Cameron Drury. "He kind of growls." Larry's younger brother, a dentist, joked that he had gone into dentistry because of his social skills but Larry had gone into surgery because he lacked them. "You always look up to your surgeon," Tom Ley said. "You don't have to have a big convo with the guy."

There was another reason Larry had gone into surgery, and why he was interested in prescribing Suboxone: Larry liked money. And he saw business potential in an epidemic that had created an ample customer base. Suboxone certainly had more promise than any of his previous entrepreneurial efforts, most of which had failed. Like the one time Larry invested in a children's clothing boutique in a "K-Mart town," as his brother liked to call it. Or the time a drinking buddy convinced Larry to turn over his credit card to fund an innovative way to build concrete walls. "In the middle of the night he disappeared into the hills of West Virginia," Larry recalled. "Nobody could ever find him." Or the worst of his failures, a factory that manufactured animal-blood pellets to feed fish farms. "To this day, I don't know why it didn't fly," Larry said.

In Indiana, there were two dozen providers throughout the state. Not nearly enough to meet the demand. And many were like Larry—physicians with prior disciplinary problems or even past addiction problems of their own. Larry Ley was one of the few to get his waiver, and one of the few who decided to use it.

The 30 people in Larry's group were young. Many had started off abusing drugs they'd swiped from their parents' medicine cabinet or had been prescribed pills themselves. But when the supply of pills dried up, they began abusing heroin. They fell behind their peers, dropped out of school, got kicked out of their homes, stole and got arrested, or became homeless. They were devoted to finding their next fix so as to stave off withdrawal symptoms, which start mere hours after the drugs have worn off. "Opiate withdrawal is horrendous," Larry said. "It's like the worst flu you've ever had, times ten. Every muscle of your body aches. You're having profuse vomiting, severe diarrhea. On top of it, opiate withdrawal causes profound insomnia. So, you can't sleep, you're having all kinds of GI problems, you're sweating, you're diaphoretic. It's hell." Larry watched as, with buprenorphine, his patients became functional again, almost overnight. "Some of those thirty would have been dead if it wasn't for Suboxone."

Larry met the patients weekly. He gave lessons on the science of addiction, the patients shared stories, and Larry counseled them on their lives. Katy Jo Dalton had started using heroin with a boyfriend, and after they broke up, she couldn't stop. She tried a 28-day rehab, but her insurance kicked her out after 14 days. At another program, she'd started on Suboxone, but when she finished the program, the employees didn't tell her how to get more. Within a day of returning home, she was in the thick of withdrawal. Her father, fearing she would track down heroin to relieve herself, took the day off work to watch her. Finally, after making call after call, Katy Jo reached Larry. He told her he would have room for her in two days.

After another two days of illness, Katy Jo walked into Larry's office and received her Suboxone prescription. She instantly felt better. During her next visit to Larry, he spent an hour with her and advised her to make changes in her life. Larry was like many doctors she had experienced—older, stern, kind of pompous. But she had never before met a doctor so willing to talk about addiction, including his own. Her boyfriend at the time was still using. Larry advised her to dump him, and she took the advice. Another patient might have found it patronizing or an overstep, but she felt he cared. "He was kind of like a dad figure, in a way," she said.

Meanwhile, Larry began to turn patients away. There were hardly any other physicians prescribing Suboxone in Indiana, or elsewhere in the United States, for that matter. Suboxone was supposed to revolutionize addiction treatment, destigmatize care, and place patients in the hands of medical professionals instead of the criminal justice system or a segregated program. But most doctors still viewed addicts with suspicion and wanted nothing to do with them.

Rehab

Larry, on the other hand, was uniquely positioned to treat them. He'd had his own experience with substance abuse. He'd spent time in recovery programs and therapy groups, and he wasn't afraid of people who were addicted. But the law forbade him from working with more than 30 patients at a time. His waiting list was growing. And meanwhile, there wasn't really anywhere else to send them. Across the country, the treatment options as a whole were slim—even in a wealthy Los Angeles suburb, something a white upper-middle-class mother named Wendy McEntyre knew a lot about.

CHAPTER FOUR

Wendy McEntyre

Thousand Oaks, California
2004

Wendy McEntyre learned her son Jarrod's darkest secret on a breezy day in Santa Monica, California, sitting inside a shiny red booth at a Marie Callender's restaurant, where her daughter, Jamie, had asked her to meet for lunch.

The younger of Wendy's two children, Jamie had always been the problem child, ever since she first tried meth at the age of 14. She was her mother's daughter, outspoken and headstrong, even in her fuckups. Wendy never worried about Jarrod. While Jamie's bedroom was a disaster zone, Jarrod's was always clean and tidy. Jamie totaled her car, while Jarrod liked to detail his with a Q-tip. Jamie was loud, always accidentally telling on herself. Jarrod was so shy, he'd send Jamie to ask for extra ketchup. He was a straight-A student, quiet and reserved, unless he was playing hockey.

Now Jamie was 18 and Jarrod was 20. Wendy had spent probably close to $100,000 on out-of-state residential treatment for Jamie—something she could afford to pay for out of pocket, although just barely, because of her

Rehab

high-powered job as a mortgage broker. Despite those treatment stints, and her membership in AA, Jamie still struggled.

So, it was unusual for her to invite her mother to lunch. Even more unusual that she wanted to talk to Wendy about Jarrod, the good one. Jamie looked nervous, shifting around in the squeaky vinyl seat. "You have to promise me you won't tell Grandma and Grandpa," Jamie said. Suddenly it felt to Wendy as if everyone in the restaurant had turned to stare at them.

Jamie told her mother that Jarrod was addicted to heroin.

She had discovered her brother's troubles after a disastrous trip to Palm Springs. Jamie had accompanied her NA sponsor on a business trip, only to discover the woman had relapsed and locked her out of their hotel room. Flying to the rescue, Jarrod dutifully picked up his sister and brought her back to his apartment in Los Angeles. But it was there she soon noticed heroin's tell-tale signs: Jarrod nodding off on the couch, his pupils as tiny as pinpricks; Jarrod driving his beloved car home without acknowledging the layers of paint scraped off the side. As soon as Jamie confronted him, he confessed that he was using.

Jamie hid Jarrod's car keys in her pillowcase. If her brother was going to use, she wouldn't let him drive. But one night, Jamie awoke to find Jarrod—and his keys—gone. When Jarrod snuck back in hours later, Jamie lost her composure. For most of their adolescence, she had been the one to keep their mother up at night; she'd never been on the receiving end of that worry and grief. Now, Jamie started screaming at him, punching and kicking, trying to get through to him. He was so high, he didn't even react. Then, both exhausted, the two of them cried. That was when Jamie realized she needed their mother's help.

As she once had for Jamie, Wendy made Jarrod sign a contract, stating all the efforts he would make to get sober. She gave him a folder containing a printout of AA meeting locations, bus passes, and the names and phone numbers for several sober-living homes where people in recovery could live and work while following a set of rules to stay sober.

Wendy wanted Jarrod to go to rehab, but in 2003, there were few options for a young man without health insurance. This situation was all the more frustrating because Jarrod lived only a short drive from one of the rehab meccas of the world. In nearby Malibu, ritzy private-pay programs offered pool and beachside retreats that were less restrictive than typical rehab stays—and more expensive, too. At Promises, which would later boast celebrity clientele like Britney Spears and Lindsay Lohan, treatment cost upwards of $40,000 per month. The nonprofit Betty Ford Center was also pricey, charging about $20,000 a month.

Just like for Chris in Louisiana, Suboxone was technically an option. But in the aftermath of the Drug Addiction Treatment Act, it was so scarce that neither Wendy nor Jarrod had heard of it, and many established treatment programs and 12-step groups were against it, contending it just replaced one drug with another. Jarrod tried methadone for a time, and found it worked well for him. But methadone had a stigma attached that discouraged many suburbanites like him from even trying it. Eventually a friend pressured him to stop taking methadone, and Jarrod quickly relapsed.

Wendy's sole hope was the criminal justice system. In 2000, in response to years of massive prison overcrowding, California voters had passed criminal justice reforms, allowing judges to sentence first-time or low-level drug offenders to treatment instead of jail or prison. Almost overnight, the law pumped $120 million a year into the rehab industry, stimulating astronomical growth in court-ordered treatment programs. Longstanding programs began displacing patients who voluntarily wanted treatment in favor of court-ordered clients, who had no choice but to attend, bringing state money with them. Treatment facilities and sober-living homes had begun opening up left and right.

A few months after Jamie's confession to her mom, Jarrod was busted for stealing a motorcycle. While Jarrod was incarcerated, Wendy learned he had also stolen an antique gun from his grandmother's house. Suddenly, Wendy saw an opportunity. She convinced her mother to press charges, and then pleaded with the court to order Jarrod into treatment. "Jarrod will be dead very soon without proper intervention," Wendy wrote to the judge. "I

Rehab

ask he be ordered into treatment for the maximum amount of time that you can under the provisions of Proposition 36." But when Jarrod appeared in court, the judge instead ordered him into a sober-living home, not rehab. The difference was significant: Rehabs were licensed and regulated. In an ideal program, patients transitioned out of their physical dependence on substances and started learning how to live without them. A sober-living home, on the other hand, was not subject to licensing or regulations. These were communal living arrangements—safe havens for people who wanted to avoid substances and support one another. The homes and the types of rules imposed on their residents varied, but it was basically where you went after treatment—to put those new skills to the test, alongside other sober people.

Wendy was disappointed the judge had not ordered Jarrod to rehab. Still, Safe House, in Van Nuys, was reputable; Wendy had made sure of that. The owner and founder of the program, Rick Schoonover, was well known in local recovery circles. He sat on the board of directors of the Sober Living Network—a nonprofit, voluntary accreditation agency—and he had even contributed to the training manual for sober-living home owners and managers. Membership in the voluntary network ensured the home was safe, clean, well managed, and ethical, Wendy read. The house had strict rules, with drug possession grounds for removal, as well as weekly house meetings led by managers and assignment of daily chores. Everyone was supposed to find employment and wake up by 8 a.m., and violations of house rules usually resulted in warnings, assignment of an essay, or a $5 fine. *At least Jarrod would be in a safe place, where he would not be allowed to use drugs*, Wendy thought.

Jarrod moved into Safe House, and over weekly lunches at the Van Nuys airport, Wendy watched as her son seemed to get better. He got a job at a nearby deli, and found a girlfriend, who was older and more mature. He was saving up money, and seemed happy. But about three months into his stay, Jarrod relapsed. Wendy was dismayed when the program didn't notify the judge, who might have referred Jarrod to a treatment program. Instead, the program kicked Jarrod out for three days and then let him back in. Another time, Jarrod mentioned to both his girlfriend and Wendy that he was sore because the founder, Rick, had him moving beds out of the house prior to an inspection, and back in afterward. That struck Wendy as strange. Still, by and large, Jarrod seemed to be doing well. He had not used since his last relapse.

Then, during the Thanksgiving holiday in 2004, Jarrod came home. It was the first time he'd seen his grandmother since she'd pressed charges. Wendy could tell something was bothering him. Finally, Jarrod told Wendy that one of his roommates was using. Jarrod was afraid to go back. He didn't want to be tempted.

It took all Wendy had in her not to pick up the phone and call Rick herself. Rick was Jarrod's sponsor. The two had grown close in men's groups that Rick ran. Surely, if Rick knew, he would do something. But Jarrod was an adult. He needed to do this himself. "Talk to Rick," Wendy told him.

Wendy would never learn whether or not Jarrod had followed her advice. That Wednesday, Jarrod and his girlfriend were supposed to go to the DMV so Jarrod could apply to get his driving license reinstated. When Jarrod didn't call as planned, his girlfriend started to get worried. She called the house at 8:30 a.m. No answer. She called the phone in the back room, and she called the phone in the main house. Someone there picked up and told her Jarrod wasn't there. Finally, she called again at around 4:30 p.m., and this time the police picked up.

Wendy soon received the call. Jarrod had overdosed. He was dead.

THE NEWS DIDN'T COMPUTE. Jarrod was supposed to have been in a safe place. Soon, the shock gave way to despair. Wendy could not stop sobbing and vomiting. She was grieving her son and also sick with worry about Jamie, who soon relapsed as well. "I just fucking buried your brother," Wendy screamed at her daughter, shaking her in the middle of the yard.

Wendy could hardly sleep. When she did, she had recurring nightmares about two baby birds who were flying out of a nest and crashing to the floor.

"When you lose a child, you lose all your layers of skin," Wendy told me. "I fell apart."

She was diagnosed with depression and bipolar disorder, and within months, she was curled up on the floor of a hospital's urgent care, receiving an injection to calm her down. She applied for disability coverage and she stopped working. She felt like nothing she'd done in her life, including raising her children, had worked. "I felt like such a failure," she said.

Even through her grief, though, something began to nag at her. When Jarrod died, no one at the sober-living home had bothered to call her. When Wendy tried reaching out to Rick to find out what had happened, he never called her back. And then on the day of the funeral, Rick didn't show up, didn't send a card, didn't send flowers. He had been Jarrod's sponsor. He had personally met with Jarrod at least ten times in the course of his time there. "It really bothered me," Wendy said. "I wanted answers to my questions. And so I started down a path to find those answers."

Wendy began by calling a friend of Jarrod's, who had been living in Safe House with him. Jarrod was usually a calm, even-tempered person. But his friend said the afternoon before, Jarrod had been really loud and erratic. When he asked what was up, Jarrod had told his friend to "fuck off." He was cursing. He never cursed.

On page five of the training manual he had co-written, Rick had told managers to look out for the signs of drug abuse. He even provided descriptions of all the different substances that could be misused and the physical signs someone might be using them. For example, someone who used cocaine would act "flippant," "jittery," and "grandiose," the manual said. For heroin use, "the individual will have pinned eyes, will scratch, nod, also [show] a change in behavior." Jarrod was showing these telltale signs. But nobody had drug tested him.

Jarrod's friend told Wendy that before he left the house that morning at 6:30 a.m., he had heard Jarrod snoring loudly. He pushed Jarrod, who mumbled that he was fine, so he left. But around 2 p.m., another roommate came in. Jarrod was already dead—and likely had been dead for hours.

Wendy didn't understand how that could have happened. Jarrod had been alive at 6:30 a.m. According to house rules, unless someone had received prior permission to sleep in, the house manager was supposed to walk through the building to make sure everyone was up by 8 a.m. every morning. Why hadn't that happened? A physician would later pinpoint Jarrod's time of death as between 9:30 and 11:30 a.m. If the house manager—or anyone else—had checked on him at that time, maybe he would still be alive.

Wendy assumed that Jarrod had been closely monitored at Safe House. That's how the program had sold itself to her and to the courts, and Rick was considered one of the leaders in the industry. Even still, Rick viewed the residents as primarily responsible for themselves. His house manager was another resident, a former truck driver from the county lockup, who was not paid to perform the job. She had been out running errands for the house the morning Jarrod had died. "We're not there to babysit you," Rick would later say. "It's a sober living. What really works is when you guys help each other."

As Wendy continued her investigation, she learned Safe House was part of a growing industry of sober-living homes. In this new era of addiction treatment, private corporations, nonprofits, and entrepreneurs were discovering sober-living homes could be profitable businesses. And increasingly, such homes were being populated predominantly by the newly sober, who were especially prone to relapse. Anybody could buy or rent a property, and then stick three or more people into a bedroom at $600 a month each. There were virtually no regulations or oversight. And clearly, it was a moneymaker. There were even conventions for operators of treatment and sober-living homes, where panelists offered tips on how to maximize profits. Wendy attended one such convention, where she went table to table asking the managers if anybody had died in their homes. She didn't care that nobody wanted her there.

Wendy learned that Rick Schoonover had owned or operated six sober-living facilities. When she called the Los Angeles Department of Building and Safety, she learned that he had been cited prior to Jarrod's death for housing men in unapproved structures in the backyard of two of his facilities. Wendy began taking detailed notes, which she typed up slowly in all caps. She learned that Rick's grandfather had owned one of the Safe House

Rehab

properties before him and had run an elder-care facility in the home in the 1960s. He, too, had been cited for housing patients in the backyard. Now, Wendy wondered if this was why Jarrod had been moving beds in and out of rooms: to prevent Rick from getting cited again.

Wendy made another complaint to the LA building department, but when an inspector went to the property in March 2005, he found the facility in compliance. Wendy told him he was wrong. She had the police and autopsy reports from the property, which showed that on December 1, 2004—the day Jarrod had died—the back room was again being used as living quarters. The department told her there was nothing they could do. Still, Wendy kept pushing, and she got the department to bring Rick Schoonover into court. At the appearance, he reported that he'd resolved the problems. But by 2006, the beds had returned. It seemed to Wendy that everyone was just passing the buck. The only recourse she had left was to sue.

Jarrod's girlfriend, Cynthia, introduced Wendy to Karen Gold, a fast-talking lawyer in Beverly Hills with sleek blond hair, who specialized in personal injury lawsuits but had also done pro bono work. The day of her appointment with Gold, Wendy blew in with stacks of files reeking of cigarette smoke, and she took a seat at Karen's big granite desk. Wendy rattled off facts about the treatment and sober-living home industries as if she had written them on the back of her hand. *This woman*, Karen thought, *was possibly one of the smartest people I've ever met.* "She instantly reminded me of Erin Brockovich," Karen recalled. She could see that Wendy was on to something big. But when Wendy started talking about her son, she transformed. "This is the first person I've ever met who was just insane from grief," Karen added.

The person who usually kept Wendy tethered was Dean, her husband—a stepfather even Jamie adored. But as Wendy tried to pursue Rick Schoonover in court, she experienced another loss: Dean had an asthma attack and died.

Wendy forfeited everything as a result: the lawsuit, her house, her work. She moved in with her sister, where she stationed herself inside a bedroom with her three cats and a dog. They sat around her on the bed as she ate frozen grapes and binge-watched "train wreck shows," Wendy's sister Cheryll liked to call them—television programs about people who survive harrowing life experiences, such as kidnapping, rape, or shipwrecks, and come out the other side.

The changing face of addiction—from Black and Brown to white upper class or suburban—had thrust the matter into the mainstream. Whereas earlier, people struggling with addiction were depicted on television and in movies as Black people from the inner city, now the suburban recovery narrative had become a major television trope. It was like a classic reality-show makeover—people at their worst transforming their lives—but this time with the help of a tough and sage treatment expert such as Dr. Phil, or the recovery experts on the TV series *Intervention*.

These programs reflected a monumental shift, not just in the national conversation about addiction, but also in federal policy. With then-President Barack Obama in office, healthcare reform was on the horizon. And longtime treatment researchers were lobbying his administration, making the case that incorporating treatment into healthcare reform would save taxpayers millions of dollars in healthcare costs. These savings were key to achieving bipartisan support for what would become the Affordable Care Act. And once the bill was passed, coverage of addiction treatment would be a key reason why even lawmakers in conservative states would support it. In anticipation of this influx of funding, the for-profit treatment industry was exploding, most significantly in the states of California and Florida.

Treatment was the word of the day. It seemed to be everyone's solution to the opioid epidemic. But Wendy could see that treatment was also a business. And every time she watched one of those shows, her bullshit meter rose sky high. Dr. Drew Pinsky made lofty claims about his credentials to treat the B- and C-list celebrities on *Celebrity Rehab*, but like most treatment programs, he mainly pushed some version of the 12 steps of Alcoholics Anonymous. And everything Dr. Drew did on the program seemed designed to extract maximum drama and cause his patients maximum distress. The program also paid participants to come on the show, an arrangement that had been criticized as exploitative and unethical.

Rehab

With her skepticism nagging at her, Wendy filed a Public Records Act request with the agency that regulated rehabs in California. She learned a patient had died at the program where *Celebrity Rehab* was filmed, and that the state had found several deficiencies in their program. *Surely, if Dr. Drew knew this, he would not endorse sending people there*, Wendy thought. She tried to contact the TV program to share her findings, but she never heard back.

It seemed to Wendy that the state agencies overseeing these businesses were ill-equipped for the task. To make any change at all, Wendy knew she needed to turn her attention to legislation—and forcing regulators to act.

WENDY TOLD HER SISTER she was ready to find her own place. She looked to the San Bernardino Mountains, about two hours from Los Angeles. With every curve she drove up the mountain, Wendy felt freer, less encumbered by worry and judgment, and closer to those she'd lost. She decorated her house with photographs of her son, Jarrod, and husband Dean. On the wall behind her couch, she hung a quilt decorated with Jarrod's photos and she crammed a curio case full with trophies from his hockey championships. She kept Dean's ashes in a SpongeBob SquarePants cookie jar that yelped out motion-triggered aphorisms Wendy liked to think of as messages from beyond. "Are you ready to rock!" SpongeBob shouted, from time to time. "I feel empowered!" On days when fog clung thick to the air, Wendy opened all her windows and let it roll in. She sat in her living room, closed her eyes, and imagined herself at peace, inside a cloud.

When she later saw Karen Gold, the attorney, Wendy handed her a business card. "Jarrod's Law," it read, and at the top of the card was the name of its founder, "Wendy 'Brockabitch' McEntyre."

Part Two

The Road to Recovery

CHAPTER FIVE

Chris Koon

Pineville, Louisiana
2015

Wendy McEntyre was one among many white middle-class parents who were demanding a more compassionate approach to addiction for their children. And Chris Koon soon found himself on the receiving end of this cultural shift.

It started around 9 a.m. on July 30, 2015. After a brief stint in a residential rehab—a 30-day program covered by his dad's insurance—Chris Koon had relapsed on meth. The relapse was the start of a weeklong binge that ended when he arrived at a dealer's house, a woman he didn't know. The house was crammed with other users and children running amok. Chris passed out on a black leather couch, and while he slept, a man collapsed on the porch and started convulsing. Someone called 911 to report a drug overdose, and the police searched the house. Now, they were all standing around Chris. An officer found a syringe in a black zippered bag under the couch. It was loaded, ready for use.

In his previous arrests, Chris learned to clam up and request a lawyer.

Rehab

This time, though, he quickly admitted that he had recently relapsed and told the cops the stash was his. He didn't want the mother living there with her kids to get in trouble.

A police corporal told Chris he was under arrest. The amount of meth was barely enough to fill the corner of a sugar packet. But it was enough to put Chris in the most serious trouble of his young life. The police charged him with felony possession of a controlled substance and possession of drug paraphernalia. He was going to jail.

THE LONGEST CHRIS had ever spent incarcerated was one day. Now, at the Grant Parish jail, he traded his clothes for black-and-white stripes and a pair of orange plastic sandals, and he moved into a dorm for people who were awaiting trial. The occupants slept on bunk beds in one big, open room, next to toilets that were behind short partitions not far from Chris's bed. The smells wafted easily. Chris learned that jail etiquette required him to pour water into the toilet and flush it whenever he was doing his business. If someone left the jail, he could use their sandals as a protective layer for the toilet seat.

Chris watched out for fights and for people who wanted to steal his stuff, and he tried to focus his attention on a book his dad had given him about a street kid turned assassin. The television was on constantly. In the mornings, it was *Country Music Television*. In the afternoons, *Maury* and *Jerry Springer*. Once a day, they'd go outside, where Chris kicked around "mush melons"—tennis ball–size fruits that grew in the yard. Chris was hungry from avoiding the nasty jail food, but no one dared eat the fruit. "This is Louisiana," Chris said. "Half the things grow will kill you."

One day, a guard came to collect Chris from the dorm. His attorney was there to meet with him. Chris shuffled into his sandals and followed the guard down the hall. The guard took Chris to a small room where he and the attorney his parents had hired could speak privately. Chris sat down at a glass partition with a phone connecting the two sides and with a metal drawer for passing any paperwork.

"I can get you out," the attorney said. He told Chris the prosecutor was open to sending him to rehab.

Cool, Chris thought. He had just been in rehab, the short program paid for by his dad's insurance. He could handle that. "I'm going back?"

"No. Not exactly."

The lawyer told Chris about a nonprofit program called the Cenikor Foundation, located in Baton Rouge. It was an inpatient facility, meaning Chris would have to live there for between 18 and 24 months, and it was very difficult. This was a far cry from the former corporate retreat center nestled by the lake, where Chris had previously gone. Not many people make it to the end of the program. But there were some plusses, the lawyer offered. It was co-ed and Chris could smoke cigarettes there.

"That sounds horrible," Chris said.

"Well, you can sit here if you want to," the lawyer replied.

Chris didn't quite grasp how lucky he was. For years, Louisiana had had the highest per capita incarceration rate in the world, due in large part to drug-related arrests. Louisiana's propensity for punishment meant its jails and prisons were dangerously overcrowded, which contributed to an epidemic of stabbings, murders, and inhumane conditions. The Louisiana State Penitentiary, better known as Angola, was often considered by inmates and politicians alike as the "bloodiest prison in the nation." Bucking the national trend, Louisiana lawmakers did not immediately seek to reduce incarceration rates; instead, they took on an unprecedented expansion of local jails to house more prisoners.

As elsewhere, this trend most impacted Black and Brown people in the state. In 2015, more than one in four people arrested in the United States for drug-related crimes were Black, even though rates of drug use were about equal across racial and ethnic groups. Of the 277,000 people imprisoned nationwide for drug offenses, over half were Black or Latino. And the racial disparities in Louisiana's criminal justice system were among the worst in the country, with Black defendants routinely receiving heftier sentences than others for seemingly minor crimes.

Just a few years before Chris's arrest, a 48-year-old Black man named Bernard Noble was sentenced to 13 years in prison in a nearby parish for possessing two marijuana joints. A couple hours away, in Baton Rouge, Kedric Williams, a Black father of two, was sentenced to 50 years in prison for heroin possession. After sentencing Williams, Judge Mike Erwin told reporters he wished he could have sent Williams away for life, which was the maximum sentence allowed for such crimes up until a 2001 change in the law. "When the penalty was life imprisonment, we didn't have as many heroin dealers and users on every street corner selling this poison to our citizens," Judge Erwin said, a statement not borne out by studies that found criminalization increased overdose death rates. Even efforts to remove bias from sentencing had simply magnified the bias.

Across the country, courts had begun using algorithms to assign risk scores to defendants, as a way to craft sentences based on a defendant's likelihood of rearrest. But the algorithm assigned higher scores to defendants who were Black, which only perpetuated the racial disparities. In more recent years, criminal justice reforms in the country had somewhat alleviated overcrowded prison conditions. And programs like Cenikor had become a key part of the court-reform efforts. At least half of Cenikor's 1,000 clients in any given week came from the criminal justice system. The program eagerly touted its ties to judges, giving them tours of the facilities and steak dinners served by Cenikor participants.

Judge Larry Gist had overseen one of the first drug courts in the state of Texas and was an early adopter of Cenikor. Seventy-six years old, with a round belly and a Santa-like beard, Judge Gist relied on his instincts to decide where to send defendants, and he personally liked Cenikor's tough approach. "The vast majority of folks that I deal with are basically bottom-feeders; they've been losers since the day they were born," he said. "[Cenikor] is the best thing that I've ever seen, for the right people. Last-chance people, end of the road. If you don't take advantage of this, you're never going to see sunshine again for the rest of your life." The program held annual awards banquets, during which they presented lawmakers and judges with shiny diamond-shaped trophies. Judge Gist proudly displayed his trophies on a shelf in his chambers, where he liked to host his happy hours with prosecutors and defense attorneys.

Drug courts like Judge Gist's had been widely celebrated as offering defendants an opportunity at rehabilitation—treatment instead of jail and prison. But about half of drug court participants failed, typically receiving longer prison sentences than they would have if they had just avoided drug court altogether. White defendants were far more likely to be offered the opportunity and were far more likely to succeed in drug court, while Black and poor defendants were less likely to finish, due in part to financially onerous requirements. In some places, the presence of a drug court actually increased the number of drug arrests.

In the U.S. criminal justice system, the people who fared the best were those who could afford to hire their own lawyers, like Chris. And Chris had already experienced the kind of grace and goodwill that's extended to a young white man with promise. When he turned 18, Chris had fled from the cops and later turned himself in, thinking he would be arrested. But a cop told him he had fallen in with the wrong crowd and let him go.

Sitting now in the Grant Parish jail, talking to his lawyer, Chris could see that he was being offered an opportunity. Two years in rehab sounded like punishment; he didn't want to be stuck in some strange place for two years. But he also didn't want to sit in jail. His parents were still refusing to pay his bail, and he had yet to go to trial. If he rejected this plan and was convicted, he faced five years in state prison. He could end up in Angola, one of the most feared prisons in the United States. But if he agreed to go to Cenikor and he finished the program, the judge might look more favorably on his case. Maybe the prosecutor would even consider dropping the charges.

Rehab

Two years in rehab was better than five years in state prison—Chris could see that. So, he told his attorney he would go. Back in the dorm, he started asking around and he quickly became acquainted with Cenikor's reputation.

"Man, you might just want to go to prison," one guy told him. Another guy, who claimed to be a former Green Beret, told Chris, "I'm not going to try and tell you about it and get in your head. Just, good luck."

CHAPTER SIX

April Lee

Philadelphia, Pennsylvania
2014

While Chris Koon wondered where the hell he was going, April Lee woke up flat on the floor, and wondered where she had ended up.

She squinted her eyes to survey the room. Her cheek was pressed against a matted green carpet. On the bed, there was a floral bedspread, pockmarked with cigarette burns. And a dusting of white powder lined the floor—boric acid, to kill the roaches. She remembered: The Blue Moon Hotel.

April's last memory was of her shooting dope. Then things went black, and now she realized she had probably overdosed. She didn't know what time it was—that wasn't something she usually thought to notice, except she could tell through the windows that it was night. The light was on, casting a sour glow across the cracks in the ceiling and on the itchy rent-by-the-hour sheets. April picked herself up from the floor and walked to the full-length mirror across from the bed.

It had been a long time since she'd looked at her reflection. It hadn't occurred to her to look, even when the men who picked her up on the Track

Rehab

had started calling her "Slim." In her mind, April was almond eyes and high cheekbones on dark chocolate skin. She had been all hips and thighs, and wide shoulders and long legs. She'd pretty much looked this way since she was 10 years old. Back then, she'd sneak out with some of her Grandmom's Newports and go down to the overgrown ravine by the train tracks, praying the cigarettes would stunt her growth. Now, she was 26 years old and she looked skeletal. Her collarbone jutted out. She had no thighs or breasts. Only the stretch marks from bearing her three children remained, a testament to her former life etched across her stomach.

Earlier in the day, April had been taking a break on the steps of the Blue Moon Hotel, when another girl sat down next to her and asked to bum a cigarette. She was as close to a friend as April had these days, even though—as a heroin user—she was the odd one on the Track, where almost everyone else used crack. On this day, the girl confided to April that she had AIDS.

"Do you use protection?" April asked.

With a shrug, the girl said she didn't. Then she stamped out her cigarette and answered a call from a nearby car.

April sat in silence and let sink in what the girl had just said. She had AIDS. She didn't use protection. These johns had become almost as familiar as the pack of Newports in her purse. Many of them she saw more regularly than members of her own family. The girls bounced back and forth between them. April had serviced their customers, and they had serviced hers. And of course, this girl didn't use protection. Most of the time, neither did April. It wasn't a smart thing to do, but when that sickening feeling of withdrawal starts to creep across your skin, nothing stands in the way of $100, including a condom.

April felt like throwing up. Her mother had died of AIDS in 2002, after selling sex for years to pay for her crack cocaine habit. April had been 15 and pregnant when her mother showed up at her door, a sickly version of her former self. April had tended to her mother in her final days, stolen a wheelchair from outside the emergency room to cart her around, bought her weed to ease her pain, then crawled into bed and giggled and cried with her,

April Lee

until she went to the hospital to die. Her mother had told her then that she wasn't worried about April. "You are going to survive," her mother told her. April surveyed her body in this room at the Blue Moon Hotel. *Will I?*

APRIL PACKED UP her things, left the motel, and walked down the street to a guy she knew. Even when she was this skinny and ragged, there was no shortage of men willing to take her in. She stayed at his place for a couple more days, using with him. But the stability of a roof over her head, with no immediate concern about withdrawals, allowed her time to think. That feeling she had that had started in that motel room continued to nag her. *What the fuck am I doing?*

April got out of bed, walked out of the apartment, and checked herself into detox.

She had been there before. The last time was because of her many siblings. She had been in a car with a john when an SUV screeched to a halt behind them, and they were surrounded by the entire Lee clan. April's john looked bewildered, as one of her brothers opened the door and pulled her out. She listened to her siblings as they tried to convince her to go to detox, laughing to herself when she saw a couple of them sipping on 40s. But she agreed to go.

In the past decade, Pennsylvania had made efforts to close the treatment gap, including in the state's adoption of the optional Medicaid expansion, (unlike almost two dozen other states). But the implementation had been uneven. Had April been in another part of the state, she might not have had any options at all. She stayed in a detox for a week, and from there she was supposed to go into treatment. A guy pulled up in a car to take her, and while they were en route, he began hitting on her. April asked him to take her home to pick up a couple things, and she went in the front door and right out the back. She never made it to rehab.

This time, April was serious. She wanted to stop using. On day one of detox, she started writing furiously in her journal. "Just like 12 years a slave/

Rehab

I was 12 months a slave/To Heroin my life I gave/I gave, and gave, and I just didn't care." She made it through detox.

Then detox sent her to a 28-day inpatient program inside a Victorian mansion in Chester, Pennsylvania, that looked to April like a castle. She was awed by the tall ceilings, the large windows, the spiral staircase built of dark wood. There were about 200 people in the program. They were required to turn over all their belongings, and they were not allowed phones, mouthwash, makeup, or razors. For the next month, April would be required to attend counseling and daily group sessions that were based on the 12 steps of Alcoholics Anonymous.

A couple months of that 12-step programming is what most residential programs in the country consisted of and what most insurance companies were willing to pay for. The practice had gained traction in the 1970s, when a flailing hospital chain decided to cut the cost of their inpatient treatment programs by eliminating doctors, psychiatrists, and other highly paid professionals. They replaced them with alcoholism counselors without degrees, who worked for much lower pay and evangelized the 12 steps. These cost savings proved irresistible to other treatment programs, and soon the 12 steps were the dominating rehab model.

This might have worked for the white male drinkers who often attended those early programs. For those patients, with financial resources and careers, a 28-day program with group meetings of their peers could be beneficial. But for many people struggling with drug addiction, a month-long program provided little more than a brief reprieve. These programs tended to treat drug addiction like a temporary episode in one's life. You get to rehab, you stop using, you're cured, and you leave. But without continuing support, the same problems that plague patients before entering treatment often find them again after leaving it—the same life circumstances and challenges, the same triggers. Almost 60 percent of people entering drug treatment have had at least one prior stint in similar treatment. More than one in every ten people have been to rehab six or more times.

This problem is especially acute for Black people, whom researchers have found are least likely to enter drug treatment and least likely to finish it, in large part because of the socioeconomic stressors they face in the outside world. And the longer someone remains in drug addiction, the more difficult it becomes to recover.

Especially for substances like opioids, such short-term programs can have tragic consequences. The period following rehab or incarceration is often the deadliest. Programs that last fewer than 90 days have higher rates of relapse. One study found that graduates of 28-day rehab programs were far more likely to die of an overdose in the year after treatment than those who failed to finish it. These programs proved effective at temporarily halting drug use while a patient was inside the facility, but they lowered a user's tolerance level, increasing the chance of overdose when that relapse inevitably occurred. While families pour their hopes into rehab, that a program is setting up their child for success, it actually places that child at a higher risk for death.

Looking around, April felt like she didn't belong in rehab. Though almost everyone there was Black or Brown, like her, most of the other patients had gone to jail and to prison. They had tried rehab multiple times and had spent years mired in their addiction. The longer they spent in their addiction, the more marginalized they had become and the more cut off they were from jobs and housing, and the stability that might sustain a drug-free life.

April was not like that. She had decided long ago that she would be different from her mother. This was her first time in rehab, and she expected it to be her last. She knew how to work hard. She had three kids. She had cared for them and clothed them, as she had her three youngest siblings, years ago. She wanted to be in this rehab program. She wanted to get well.

But it felt like the presumption of failure was baked into the program.

"Look around," a teacher said during one of her groups one day. They were all sitting on folding chairs, in a circle. "Only one out of 100 of y'all are going to make it."

Excuse me? April raised her hand. "That's bullshit," she said. *How good is your fucking program if only one out of 100 make it?* she thought. "It's like you're prepping people for failure."

Rehab

April understood that the teachers were trying to motivate them. She was supposed to hear this and think to herself, *Well, if only one out of 100 makes it, I'm going to be the one.* But instead, she found the talk demoralizing. *If I can be the one, then why can't everyone be the one? Why can't we all make it? Or at least more than one out of a fucking 100?*

On day five of the program, April wrote a poem in her journal.

How do I deal with this when I Just want to cry.
I don't know how to cope or Just get by
I lost so much hope, and I put it on myself.
Please God please Show me thyself.
I need you I'm falling on my knees
God pleas help.
I want to leave god please stop me.

A WEEK AND A HALF LATER, a staff member retrieved April from a group session. She walked under the spiral staircase into a group meeting room, where three of her siblings were seated on plastic chairs. At first, April was excited to see them. She wasn't allowed to use her phone, so she hadn't expected to talk with or see her family for some time. But the somber looks on their faces made her want to walk out the door. She reluctantly sat down.

They told her that two days into her stay, her older brother Chris had died in a car crash. They hadn't told her until now because they knew she would have wanted to leave rehab to attend his funeral, and if she did, she would have relapsed. So, they'd already had the funeral and the memorial service. They just wanted her to know. There was nothing she could do but stay.

April was stunned. Of all her siblings, she was the closest to Chris, with whom she shared a father. They'd never met their father, though she'd heard that Chris looked exactly like him. The last time she'd seen Chris was a year

April Lee

ago, when he offered her a place to stay. He told her, "Don't become Mommy, sitting on a table in an urn." Then she stole from him and used the money to buy dope. He was the only sibling who always welcomed her back, no matter what she did.

April took to her journal. "I just found out my brother died. My family decided to not tell me for 7 days. Because I was fresh out of detox. I blessed they did 'cause I would have left. And that needle would not have left my arm and I would be dead," April wrote. "It was a blessing, they made the right choice."

April knew she was fragile. And yet, in two weeks, when she would finish the program, she would be expected to walk out the door a new woman. Addiction researchers and policymakers were beginning to understand that this kind of quick-fix transformation simply doesn't happen. It's why Senator Biden and other policymakers had pushed for a medication that could help people stay sober. Even the DEA was pledging support for medication-assisted treatment. But in Philadelphia, and Indiana, and across the country, Suboxone doctors like Larry Ley were telling a different story. The system Biden and other lawmakers had created was not working as intended, and law enforcement officials were not as supportive as they claimed to be.

CHAPTER SEVEN

Larry Ley

Carmel, Indiana
2013

Cassy Bratcher raced up the steps to the front door of the Drug and Opiate Recovery Network (DORN), Dr. Larry Ley's fast-growing Suboxone practice in downtown Carmel, Indiana. Cassy was the face of their practice, the one who answered phones and checked in patients. It was not hard to see why. Larry's face was perpetually set in a scowl, whereas Cassy was friendly and bubbly, her fingernails always manicured. She was professional, but kind. She was the one who would deliver the bad news when a patient consistently tested positive for illicit drugs, or didn't test positive for Suboxone at all—a sign they could be selling their medication. But she also was the one who would reassure patients when they lost a job, or left a bad relationship, and the one who organized carpools for the patients traveling from hours away.

Cassy opened the door, her heels clicking quickly on the gleaming poured-concrete floor, past Dr. Ley's conference room—with its oak conference table, its walls decorated with framed pictures of the brain—and down the hallway to her desk, where she saw patients and stashed the remains of fast-food lunches and packets of Celestial Seasonings teas. She stopped when she saw Yvonne, their nurse, standing over her phone. "I don't know what's going on, but we're getting a million phone calls," Yvonne said, with a bewildered look on her face. It was only 9 a.m, and the voicemail box was blinking red.

Cassy sat down and started listening. The messages were harried and desperate—and there were dozens of them. The local drug task force and the DEA had just shut down a pain clinic in nearby Howard County, which had been accused of fueling overdose deaths across the region. That clinic was run by an elderly couple named Marilyn and Don Wagoner, who also ran a Suboxone clinic like Dr. Ley's DORN. When patients got hooked on the medications the couple was prescribing, they would simply head over to the Wagoner's Suboxone clinic for treatment.

Cassy had grown up near the clinic, one of nine siblings, and she'd seen firsthand the devastation the Wagoners had wrought. But many of the Wagoner patients had been taking Suboxone for years. Now, with the sudden shuttering of the clinic, they faced the prospect of running out of medication in a matter of days, and going into withdrawal. Cassy could hear the pain and desperation in their voicemail messages. They needed a new prescriber to take them in, and Dr. Ley was one of the only Suboxone prescribers in the area.

That wasn't exactly unusual. Although ten years had passed since Suboxone came on the market, most people who wanted Suboxone treatment had a hard time finding doctors who would prescribe it. By 2017, more than 60 percent of rural counties in the United States lacked a single Suboxone provider. Suboxone was so hard to find that in some cities, like Philadelphia, people could more easily buy the pills on the street. Some patients drove as much as four hours across state lines to get to DORN.

Doctors, nurses, and physician's assistants could prescribe OxyContin and other painkillers to as many patients as they wanted, but they were strictly limited in the amount of buprenorphine they could prescribe—to no more than 100 patients at a time. And DEA investigators could stroll in at any time, during business hours, through busy waiting rooms, past other patients, to look at patient records, and to force a doctor to answer invasive questions. These rules required financial investment and disturbed other patients. It was a hassle, and most doctors were busy enough as it was.

This was why it had taken Larry Ley so long to expand DORN. Fortunately, he'd had a little bit of help. The manufacturer of Suboxone, Reckitt Benckiser, was busy dispatching its pharmaceutical sales representatives—whom the company called clinical liaisons—to doctors' offices across the United States. Many of the reps had previously worked for Purdue Pharma, selling OxyContin. Now they were selling a treatment for the problem Purdue had partially caused.

As soon as Larry Ley decided to open a clinic, a Reckitt rep started contacting other doctors on his behalf and courting them with expensive meals. Larry himself ran ads for doctors in the local paper and wrote letters, passionate pleas to join his effort to combat the opioid epidemic. Eventually, Larry had found three other doctors to join the practice: a genial family medicine doctor, an anesthesiologist who also happened to be a golfing buddy, and a Black physician who'd made it her mission to treat underserved populations.

The doctors would work in Larry's practice part time, just one or two weekends a month. They understood they would have to submit to the DEA inspections—an intimidating prospect—but they would be paid between $200 and $450 per hour, and they felt inspired by the mission. Soon, Larry had moved DORN's headquarters onto Main Street in downtown Carmel, in a beautiful new brick building with ornate iron banisters, just down the street from a tea room. It would be the wealthy Indianapolis suburb's only Suboxone clinic. Larry later opened up satellite offices in neighboring towns and counties, where the doctors could see patients for follow-up visits. "I thought we were all on the same team, going ahead, arms wide open, come in and let's see if we can make this better," said Dr. George Agapios, the recruited family medicine doctor. "I thought we had a very good relationship with the DEA."

Rehab

THE DAY AFTER the Wagoner raid, DORN received 386 calls from former patients, and more the next. Cassy wrote down each person's name and phone number on a sheet of paper. Then she immediately called Larry.

"This is crazy," she said. "We don't have room for these people."

Cassy was the person typically responsible for ensuring the practice was following federal requirements. She had called the DEA more times than she could count. DORN randomly drug-tested its patients, checked the state prescription-monitoring database to see what other prescriptions the patients were obtaining, and operated a formal warning system for those patients who weren't following the program's rules. She was particularly worried about such things. But Larry wasn't scared of the DEA. He told Cassy to take on the Wagoner patients. Ultimately, they would take 400.

Cassy might have considered Larry's decision a violation of DEA rules—if it hadn't been for the loophole Larry had discovered. The DEA's patient limit for Suboxone applied to patients who were receiving the drug as an addiction treatment. There was no limit on prescriptions if patients were prescribed Suboxone off-label—that is, as a treatment for chronic pain. As it happened, many of his patients' addictions had started with pain problems. So, to get around that patient limit for the drug, Larry started coding patients with histories of chronic pain as pain patients, instead of as addiction-treatment patients. When a DEA investigator arrived to perform an inspection, Larry informed him of this practice and eagerly bragged. "I probably prescribe more Suboxone than any [other] physician in the state," he said.

The initial DEA investigator didn't find any violation of DEA rules during the visit, but the investigators kept coming back. At the DEA, civilian employees called "diversion investigators" are responsible for inspecting doctor's offices, making sure doctors are following the prescribing regulations for controlled substances. They are also responsible for inspecting the drug manufacturers and distributors, which were the companies driving the opioid epidemic and sending prescription opioids to pharmacies across the United States.

While Larry was building his new Suboxone practice, the DEA was failing to stanch the spread of opioid pills. The diversion investigators were vastly outnumbered. While the number of drug prescribers, manufacturers, and wholesalers had grown by about 40,000 every year of the opioid epidemic, the hiring of DEA investigators had not kept pace. By 2017, for every one diversion investigation, there were about 3,300 entities to inspect.

Then, DEA leadership made the situation even worse. Every year, the diversion investigators would receive work plans—a list of inspections and investigations they were required to complete by the end of the year. During a normal year, this list would include investigations of manufacturers and distributors—crucial tools in the fight against opioids. But with this new policy, Suboxone-prescribing doctors would also become a part of the annual work plan.

The DEA officials had always been skeptical of Suboxone. Some viewed it as just another drug, like another form of heroin. The stance mimicked the federal agency's previous response to methadone, when it was first discovered. That skepticism deepened when agents who were focused on the illegal drug trade started noticing that Suboxone was being sold on the street. Multiple studies had found that most people buying it illegally did so to self-treat their withdrawal symptoms, in part because they couldn't find legitimate prescribers, who remained scarce. Still, to DEA officials, illegal drugs were illegal drugs. Some officials felt that by legalizing the prescribing of Suboxone out of doctor's offices, Congress had simply created pill mills by another name. Publicly, the DEA supported use of Suboxone, joining other federal agencies in calling it the "gold standard" for addiction treatment. But internally, DEA leaders were very concerned about the steady growth in use of Suboxone, and it seemed they were actively working to contain its supply.

The idea of having DEA agents come to their offices and demand to see patient records was too much for some doctors. Many decided simply to avoid Suboxone all together. In Ohio, one Suboxone clinic owner abruptly shuttered his clinic's doors after a visit from the DEA. In a letter posted on the clinic door announcing closure, he wrote, "Heroin is killing people every day, and physicians are being scared out of the ability to help. This is an EPIDEMIC! Addicts need physicians, clinics, pharmacies, and everybody helping them fight to stay alive."

Even those doctors who decided to keep prescribing Suboxone found themselves sidelined by the confusing and conflicting regulations. The DEA had never explained to Suboxone prescribers how to count the number of patients who would be permitted under the law. The limit was 100 patients. But what if someone relapsed and disappeared for several weeks or months, as often happened in addiction treatment? Did that person still count as a patient? What if a doctor left a practice and the patients suddenly had no prescriber? Was it acceptable for another doctor to temporarily prescribe Suboxone to those patients until a replacement could be found? Doing so would put that doctor temporarily over the patient limit—but wasn't that better than simply kicking the patients to the curb?

These scenarios were playing out across the country in real time, but the DEA provided no clear answers, putting some doctors in the difficult position of having to choose between the law and their patients' well-being.

"I really need some help," one doctor wrote in an email to colleagues in 2014. "Our Abingdon clinic had 600 patients and 8 doctors at one time. I had 4 doctors leave for various reasons, and we have been desperately trying to recruit new ones to take the load. Meanwhile, I believe we have a legal, ethical and moral obligation to continue present care. The DEA in Roanoke feels otherwise. They have instructed us to discharge 300 patients within the next two weeks." Some of the areas most heavily impacted by the DEA's policy were those at the epicenter of the overdose epidemic—the regions most in need of expanded access to treatment. Even pharmacists were afraid, with a large number of Rite Aid, Walmart, and local pharmacies across the country refusing to fill Suboxone prescriptions due to concerns they'd run afoul of the DEA.

Some of the agency's diversion investigators were perplexed by the new edict as well. Under this new policy, inspections of Suboxone providers constituted the bulk of some investigators' caseloads, and in some other instances, their caseloads more than doubled. Agency officials complained that they didn't have enough staff on the ground, especially in places hardest hit by the opioid epidemic. Yet the DEA was devoting a good deal of its meager resources not to uncovering the doctors, pharmacists, and distributors fueling the epidemic of opioid addiction but, rather, to scrutinizing those who offered the medication designed to treat that addiction. "Why are we devoting so much time to this?" one supervisor, who oversaw the diversion investigators in three states, recalled thinking at the time. Another investigator in the middle of a probe of a major distributor was forced to pause his investigation to visit Suboxone prescribers across the state. "It made no sense," he said.

True to form, Larry welcomed the attention—perhaps even relished it. The DEA launched numerous inquiries into his large patient rolls. But Larry was incredibly open about what he was doing. He saw no shame in it. When one doctor visited DORN to consider signing on as a prescriber, Larry told him that the DEA was "pissed" at him for exceeding the 100-patient limit by using bup as a pain treatment. "But nobody's going to tell me how to run my business," Larry said. During an interview with the DEA, Larry told the diversion investigator that he was treating about 70 percent of his patients for pain—with opioid dependency as a secondary diagnosis, and about a third of his patients solely for addiction. Other doctors who worked for DORN informed the DEA that they were doing the same.

Each time the DEA questioned Larry about his practices, he would send over the DEA's own policy letter, stating that nothing prevented physicians from prescribing Suboxone off-label for pain. Each time, the DEA confirmed receipt, and closed the case—no violations found.

One day in 2014, a former Wagoner patient named Ryan Radford heard a knock at his front door. Before finding Suboxone, Ryan had spent years using the entirety of his restaurant server paycheck to buy Lortabs on the street. He bought Suboxone illegally, too, before a spot opened up at the Wagoner clinic. Thanks to that prescription, he was finally sober, back home living with his parents.

Ryan's mother opened the door, to find a DEA investigator and a drug task force detective. She started panicking. *What did Ryan do this time? Please don't arrest him.* But the investigators reassured her that's not why they were there. They wanted to ask Ryan about his experience at the Wagoner clinic.

"Had I seen anything suspicious? Could I attest to the dirty things going on?" Ryan recalled. "But I didn't have any info they didn't already know. I didn't run into any of the 'Hey, pay-me-cash-to-stay type of deals.'" Soon the conversation turned to something else. The investigators asked Ryan if he was still taking Suboxone.

"Yeah, I ended up at this place called DORN," Ryan said.

The investigators exchanged looks. There was, it seemed to Ryan, an awkward pause. "It was kind of like . . . okay . . . ," Ryan remembered thinking. They asked him a few more questions, and then Ryan showed them out. It was a brief exchange, but one Ryan would remember many years later. "You could tell by the way they reacted," he said. "They were not thinking highly of this place."

CHAPTER EIGHT

Wendy McEntyre

Skyforest, California
2014

As law enforcement was turning its attention to nascent Suboxone practices, Wendy McEntyre was trying desperately to sound the alarm about the growing for-profit treatment industry. She was trying her best to reel in her anger and grief, and to hone her image for the cameras.

That was how she found herself sitting on her sister's gray couch, playing the role of a somber, grieving mother for a major TV news program. Wendy spoke at length about Jarrod, about Safe House, and about the problems she had unearthed. "I'm not an idiot," she said. "I know Jarrod played a part in it. It took me years to come around to that acceptance. But he was paying for a second set of eyes. If they would have just followed their own rules, he would have been alive."

Then she suggested an idea. Rick Schoonover, the owner of Safe House, had a tattoo shop not that far from her. Why don't they go and talk to him? It had now been almost ten years since Jarrod's death. Wendy told the TV

Rehab

producers she wanted to dialogue with Rick and convince him to join her in her efforts to reform the industry.

It was a hot, cloudless day. Wendy and the crew parked in a strip-mall parking lot and walked across the street to the tattoo shop. She strode across confidently. Wendy was wearing a floaty top, decorated in purple and pink flowers. Her blonde hair was pinned into an elegant pile on top of her head.

She found Rick under an awning, sitting on a patio outside the shop, smoking a cigarette. He looked older, with a gray and white goatee and wire-rimmed glasses, and wore a cut-off muscle shirt that showed faded tattoos and doughy arms.

"We meet again," Wendy said smiling, her arm outstretched like a queen meeting her people. Rick smiled back and took her hand. Wendy shook it, briskly.

"Hi, I don't remember you," he said.

"You don't remember me?" Wendy sat down and handed Rick the program from Jarrod's memorial. "I just want to sit and chat with you for a minute," she said calmly.

Rick took the program and surveyed the cover, flipped it open, and looked inside. Recognition spread across his face. Wendy's voice and face remained pleasant as she began to lob the same questions at Rick as she'd wanted to ask him in person so many years ago.

"You weren't at his funeral," Wendy said.

"Yeah, 'cause he died loaded."

"You don't go to peoples' funerals who 'die loaded'?"

"Honey, I've been running sober-living houses for twenty years, and I try to stay in support of the people who are making it instead of the ones who don't make it. What can I do after that?"

Rick continued, talking over Wendy as she got more agitated. "I don't understand how you held me responsible, as the owner of a sober-living house, for your son's relapse and overdose. I never understood that."

Soon Wendy was yelling. An employee came out to escort Rick back inside. Wendy blocked the door with her body, jabbing her finger in Rick's face. She stumbled backward, and one of Rick's employees muttered: "Her son was a dope fiend."

Wendy could no longer contain her rage. She pushed the employee to the ground. Soon, people emerged from the shop, calling her crazy and threatening to call the police.

"He pushed me first," Wendy said repeatedly, before fleeing across the blacktop.

Eventually, Wendy would plead guilty to disturbing the peace and agree to take an anger management class. She was barred from contacting the employee she pushed. When the news program was aired, she was not in it.

And about a month after the confrontation, Wendy got a call. A young man was missing from a rehab in the San Bernardino Mountains, right down the street from her new home. His name was Donavan Doyle. If he was still alive, he was now 22 years old. The townspeople were assembling a search party, and the kid's parents needed support. Could Wendy help? Soon Wendy found herself immersed in another story representative of this new treatment landscape, right down the road from her own house.

JUST A FEW YEARS EARLIER, Donavan was a happy kid. He took karate twice a week, had guitar lessons, played football, and snowboarded. The Doyles were a close-knit family, going to the arcade together, the movies, jet-skiing. And so, when Donavan started using drugs and alcohol at the age of 15—like Chris Koon and April Lee—his father Shannon noticed the signs almost right away.

As a truck driver, Shannon had his own history of drug use. He started using meth to keep him awake on long hauls. Eventually, Shannon liked to say, he'd chosen his family over the drugs and recovered without treatment. Now, he felt that experience gave him insight into Donavan's challenges.

Donavan had long struggled with depression, anxiety, and ADHD. On meth, he seemed to care less about things, but he was moody, didn't keep himself clean, and slept so little that he became prone to paranoia and hallucinations. One time, Shannon tried to pass him a Pepsi and Donavan accused him of poisoning it. To pay for his drugs, Donavan sold the PlayStation, his dad's wedding ring, and the lawnmower. His parents called the police on him twice.

At his parents' urging, Donavan tried numerous treatment programs. When he was a teenager, his counselor recommended a residential program in San Jose, but when the Doyles arrived there they discovered it was a sober-living home, with none of the structure or treatment they were promised. Later, Donavan went to a program in Fresno, but it was filled with court-ordered participants, many of whom were much older than he was, and he saw that drugs were being smuggled inside. Fearful of relapse, his parents brought him home within a few weeks. His mother took him to Celebrate Recovery meetings once a week; these were self-help meetings modeled after Alcoholics Anonymous (AA), with more of a Christian focus, but Donavan didn't care for them. His greatest motivation for sobriety came shortly after his 21st birthday, when he learned that he had a son.

Donavan found out about the boy's existence after bumping into his ex-girlfriend at a convenience store. He wanted to be a part of his child's life. The child was two years old, with unkempt blond hair and a toothy grin; he had a striking resemblance to photographs of Donavan at that age.

Donavan voluntarily completed a parenting class and had his first meeting with his son at a Carl's Jr. in 2013. They met weekly after that, with his son eventually growing comfortable enough to sit on Donavan's lap. Donavan would open his juice boxes for him, go down the slide with him, and play catch with him. They spent Christmas together at McDonald's, where Donavan and his mother, Cyndi, presented the boy with a bounty from Toys "R" Us.

It was going well, until Donavan voluntarily took a drug test and it came back positive for marijuana. His ex-girlfriend told him that she didn't want the relationship to progress any further until he quit.

Donavan desperately wanted a relationship with his son. The Doyles would later find a photograph of the boy folded up inside Donavan's wallet. In the photo, the child is grinning hard, eyes squinted shut, and he's holding a big cone of soft-serve ice cream in his hand. On the back of the photo, Donavan had written the date—February 16, 2013—and a series of disjointed sentences: "The day I quit smoking determined to do what I need to do to be a good father and a better son.... Doesn't deserve to grow up without a dad... I love you, Son."

DONAVAN WANTED to go into treatment, but now that he was an adult, neither he nor his parents knew how to find a program. It was 2013, and the treatment industry—and the country—was going through a transformation. So much had even changed since 2001, when Wendy's son, Jarrod, had entered the system.

The shift started during the Bush Sr. years, when federally funded scientists began to posit that addiction was a brain disease instead of a moral deficit, a personality disorder, or a nervous condition. It continued into the turn of the twenty-first century, with the introduction of Suboxone, Reckitt Benckiser's new medical cure for opioid addiction. The industry grew again after George W. Bush signed the Mental Health Parity Act, which required certain insurance companies to begin covering mental health treatment on par with other services. And again, when Barack Obama signed the Affordable Care Act in 2010, requiring health insurance providers to cover treatment for addiction, as if it were any other disease. Prior to "Obamacare," an estimated one-third of those with private insurance lacked coverage for addiction treatment—like Wendy's son, Jarrod. Starting in January 2014, just a few months after Donavan entered treatment, providers were no longer allowed to deny coverage based on addiction being a preexisting health condition. Further, children could be covered by their parents' health insurance policies up to the age of 26. Under the law, millions of people with addiction were now entitled to treatment.

As Donavan began his search for rehab, he found a system utterly transformed. Public addiction-treatment facilities—especially those accessible to Black low-income communities, were faltering, while rehabs catering to middle- and upper-middle-class suburbanites were flourishing. Between 2002 and 2010, the number of publicly funded, nonprofit outpatient programs substantially declined. With the guaranteed windfall of insurance money—and the expectation of additional coverage from the ACA—for-profit treatment programs were now spreading across the country.

Almost overnight, treatment became a $35 billion a year industry. But there was no consensus on what treatment should look like, what services should be offered. Each state regulated their rehabs differently, and in many places, including California, almost anything could be packaged and sold as treatment, from equine therapy to vitamin infusions.

There was also no clear way to find a treatment program. While doctors were often responsible for referring patients to specialty care, addiction treatment was another beast entirely. Most for-profit rehabs employed well-worn sales tactics to recruit patients, even if their programs were not the best fit for those patients.

Looking to help Donavan's search, Cyndi Googled "drug treatment centers," dialed a 1-800 number, and quickly received a call back from a man named Shane. Shane gathered Cyndi's insurance details and assured her he would find the best program for Donavan.

Soon, he got back to her: Above It All Treatment Center, near Lake Arrowhead. "It's really nice," Cyndi recalled he said. Cyndi learned the program would last 30 days. They had doctors and therapists on staff, a music room, horses, and participants could go on hikes. "You know, he just acted like it was a resort," she said.

Shane was not a disinterested operator, a trained medical professional, or a government provider. He was paid to find patients for Above It All. In fact, Cyndi's insurer, Blue Cross Blue Shield, had its own in-network providers, with whom the company had established contracts, ensuring lower costs for both the insurer and patients. The Above It All Treatment Center was out of network, meaning that Donavan could attend, but it would cost a lot more, an average of $60,000 per month, depending on the level of care. That was more than the price of a year at Harvard University. The higher out-of-network cost would be shared with the patient via higher co-pays.

If Cyndi knew that, she might have rejected Shane's offer. But Above It All was offering to "waive" Donavan's co-pays, allowing him to enter the program for free. Maybe the company was motivated by a desire to help Donavan. Many people would simply refuse to enter treatment if they had to hand over money they couldn't afford. But the offer also had another purpose: to incentivize him to enter the program. A waived co-pay typically meant a program anticipated billing an insurance company so much for its services that it could afford not to charge a patient more. And compared to other insurance companies, Blue Cross Blue Shield was well known for high reimbursement rates. Above It All could expect to be compensated well for its services.

This was becoming standard practice in the rehab industry, even among programs with esteemed reputations—ones that had received the highest level of accreditation. But Cyndi didn't know any of this—not the full cost of the program, nor the marketing machine behind it. She trusted what Shane told her and what she saw on Above It All's website, which featured stunning photos of Lake Arrowhead, pine trees, and expansive blue skies. The website promised evidence-based care, with 24/7 medical supervision. "Each client's past history and current medication are comprehensively analyzed to create a highly individualized treatment plan," it read. Owner Kory Avarell "is truly a 100% hands on owner," the website said. "No detail is left unnoticed, especially your level of quality care."

"Dude, this is it, man," Shannon told his son. "It looks nice. I wish I would have had something like that."

On September 21, 2013, the Doyles piled into their car for the five-hour drive from Fresno to Lake Arrowhead. They stopped at an outlet mall and bought Donavan a new wallet, a belt, some Axe body spray, a warm winter coat, and a pair of Nike tennis shoes—something he could use on the daily gym visits and hikes they anticipated him taking.

Rehab

As they drove up California State Route 18—"The Rim of the World Highway"—and looked over the edge of the mountain, Cyndi felt optimistic. This was a different caliber of facility from the ones Donavan had previously tried. It was far away from any trouble he could find closer to home. "This is going to be really good for him. It's going to be great." They pulled up to a two-story cabin on a quiet street overlooking a lake, in the small town of Blue Jay. They told him that they loved him and were proud of him. Donavan said he loved them. "I am praying for this for him how much he needs change in his life," Shannon texted Cyndi, after they got back home. "And we can finally have our son back."

Donavan couldn't wait to reunite with his son. "I wouldn't rather be anywhere but with you and mommy right now," Donavan wrote to his son in a letter his parents later found. "I'd be there in a heartbeat if I could!!"

AT FIRST, DONAVAN told his parents over the phone that everything was fine. He didn't like rehab, but he wanted to get better. But his attitude progressively worsened.

Every time Donavan said he wanted to come home, Cyndi would call Kory Avarell, the rehab owner, who'd convince her that Donavan wasn't ready to leave yet. He needed to be there. Cyndi and Shannon listened to him. Donavan had gone to several treatment programs in the past and had never finished them. Cyndi was thankful for Avarell's guidance. "I appreciate everything you are doing," she texted him on October 2. "It is easy to see you really care for the people you work with. I can't thank you enough."

Cyndi assumed she was speaking with a trained professional. Kory Avarell in fact had no treatment experience or formal education. He was a devout Mormon. Beyond drinking a sip of wine when he was 17, his only experience with substance use came from a family member who'd struggled with alcoholism. He'd grown up nearby and had been a serial entrepreneur of sorts, running his own bead store and carpet-cleaning operation before joining his father's construction business. But to start a rehab, there was nothing in California law or its regulations that required a person to have special training or expertise. When the 2008 recession hit and Avarell found himself with eight brand-new, empty houses, he decided to convert them into treatment centers.

Cyndi didn't know much about the care Donavan was actually getting. But she got hints here and there. During one phone call, Donavan mentioned that he didn't like the medications they had put him on. "I told him, 'Why don't you just go and see the doctor? Go see the doctor and talk about it,'" Cyndi said. "And he's like, 'I can't just see the doctor. They're not always here, Mom. You just don't understand.'" Cyndi would ask him other questions, but he'd just get more upset and ask to leave. Still, about two weeks into his stay, it seemed like there was finally a breakthrough. Donavan met with his counselor, Rick Hughes, who convinced Donavan to stay at least one more week. "His counselor broke him, and he cried," Cyndi told Shannon.

But shortly afterward, Donavan left the facility on his own, walking 18 miles down the twisting mountain road to a Chevron station at the bottom. He called his parents and asked them to pick him up. It was two in the morning. Cyndi called and texted Kory Avarell. "I'm glad you hung up," Avarell texted Cyndi. "Don't give up now, when he calls back his only option is to come back otherwise let him know you will not answer his calls. It is hard but you need to do this. . . . Be strong!" Donavan was exhausted and had no money. When he called his parents back, Donavan agreed to return to treatment in exchange for a Gatorade. "I'll do anything right now," she remembers him telling her. "I'm so dehydrated." Avarell drove Donavan himself.

After that, Donavan was not allowed to call his parents anymore. By running away, he had lost his phone privileges.

Within the week, Avarell informed the Doyles that Donavan had stopped attending some of the group sessions. If Donavan didn't go to group sessions, Avarell said, they couldn't bill his parents' insurance—and they would have no choice but to discharge him. But Avarell told Cyndi that he had a plan,

Rehab

one he'd later claim to have successfully executed many times before: next time Donavan refused to go to group, he would tell Donavan he had to leave. And if that happened, he believed that Donavan would have no choice but to comply and come back.

Avarell told the Doyles they had to stop enabling their son. "Sometimes the family is the sicker one," he'd later say. "Because the family will continue to believe the lies." The program was trying to help Donavan reach a point of surrender and admit he needed help. To do that, Donavan needed to be allowed to hit "rock bottom." This concept, employed by many rehabs and featured in the popular television shows Wendy had binge-watched countless times, was popularized by Alcoholics Anonymous, which touts the importance of hitting rock bottom and admitting one's powerlessness, in order to begin a life of sobriety.

It is a powerful narrative device. But in practice, the possibilities are devastating and endless. Is "hitting rock bottom" losing your apartment, your job, or your kids? Is it relapsing and overdosing? While such setbacks can be turning points for some, they can also be death sentences. Hitting bottom breeds desperation, and as the bottom grows deeper and deeper, it becomes harder to find a way out.

While Donavan had entered the program feeling motivated to seek help, the approach seemed to be making him feel ashamed, and it was driving a wedge between Donavan and his parents. Donavan had trusted his parents to be there for him, and now he had nowhere to turn.

The next day, Donavan called his parents again. Following Avarell's advice, they both told Donavan they would not pick him up. He didn't respond well. On the phone with his dad, he appeared to threaten suicide, before he abruptly hung up.

"I'm sacred [sic]," Cyndi texted Avarell. "Please make sure he does not hurt himself." She felt confident that Avarell would keep a close eye on Donavan and would make sure he was safe. But the next day, Avarell called Cyndi back. He said that Donavan had taken a swing at his counselor, Rick, and walked away from the facility.

Cyndi was confused. What did you mean he "walked away"? She reminded Avarell they lived five hours away, in Fresno. They hadn't heard from their son, which was unusual. Could Avarell go out and find him? Avarell told Cyndi they couldn't. A snowstorm had descended on the mountain, enveloping the road in fog.

Cyndi and Shannon expected Donavan would make his way down the mountain and then call them, as he had before. But by the next morning, Donavan still hadn't called. They were frantic with worry. Shannon went to work at 4 a.m., like he usually did, but by mid-morning, he couldn't stand it anymore. He called Cyndi and told her he was going to go down there. He had to find their son. "I knew something was wrong," Shannon said. "I knew."

SHANNON DOYLE DROVE to the mountain, making the trek by car and by foot, up and down State Route 18. He visited the trailer park, the bus station, even the rest areas alongside the national park. Shannon called out his son's name, but the towering pine trees that had once been so striking in their beauty on the drive to Above It All Treatment Center now sheathed Shannon in a maddening silence. "Donavan, I love you. Please call dad," he wrote with a stick in the dirt, still soft from the snow and rain. All he found was a black trash bag abandoned on the side of the road, containing some of Donavan's belongings, including his MP3 player, an assortment of half-eaten fruit candies, and—most worrisome—his winter coat.

"I'm scared, Cyndi," he texted his wife.

In the months that followed, Avarell continued to suggest that Donavan was still alive and didn't want to be found. "Could he be feeling like you really did give up on him? And he just figures that he can't call anymore?" he texted Cyndi.

Cyndi repeatedly asked the Sheriff's Department to send out dogs and check the cameras at the local gas stations. But the Doyles got the sense that the department was putting few resources into finding their son. A detective

Rehab

said he was investigating, but he rarely responded to their emails, and when he did, mostly dismissed the couple's concerns. He said Donavan was considered a "voluntary missing" adult, and as such, his case was not considered as critical as a case involving someone who needed medical attention, or was a danger to themselves. "It did not meet the criteria to send our search and rescue and put them in danger," the detective would later tell the local newspaper.

Two months after Donavan's disappearance, the detective told the Doyles that he'd taken statements from Avarell and Donavan's counselor, Rick. They had said, again, that Donavan had walked away, of his own volition. "At this time I don't believe any foul play took place at the facility," the detective wrote in an email. Cyndi begged him to reconsider. "I just feel like something isn't right about what they said and what I know about how Donavan acts," she wrote to the detective. "I know he would have called me by now." The detective suggested Donavan didn't want to be found. "I just cleared a five year old runaway case from 2009," the detective wrote, as if it was a comfort. "The person was found in the east coast. There is always hope."

The Doyles didn't know what to believe, and they still clung to hope that Donavan was alive. The townspeople rallied around them, and on an early morning in May, they split off into three different groups to begin their search. They hiked up and down the highway, gingerly sidestepping the tall grasses that harbored rattlesnakes, searching through Switzer Park, and in drainage ditches. "You know, if he got a ride somewhere, he could be anywhere," one of the searchers said.

Then, a couple hours into the search, several men hoisted themselves up over the side of the mountain and walked up the road toward the group's air-conditioned trailer. None of the search party recognized them. One of the men, wearing camouflage pants and a knife holstered to his hip, pulled out his phone and showed Cyndi a photograph. It was a Nike shoe and a sweatshirt they had found down the side of the mountain. It looked like Donavan's.

Wendy invited him into the trailer and handed him a bottle of Gatorade. The man's name was Sean Bly, and he was a van driver at Above It All. He was exhausted, sweaty and rattled. That morning, he said he had received a call from a superior, telling him to begin looking for Donavan an hour before the search party commenced, and where to look: over the side of the mountain, right below the treatment center.

While Wendy and the Doyles and the other members of the search party were looking in all the wrong places, Sean and several of his colleagues were making the treacherous descent straight down from Above It All, not stopping until about a mile down, when they stumbled across the clothing Sean had captured on his phone.

What's more, Sean told them that he had been there the day Donavan disappeared. A counselor had run into the driver's room and yelled "Who wants to chase a client?" Sean quickly joined others in the pursuit outside, when someone told him they'd seen Donavan run behind the treatment program and go "over the edge," a quick steep drop onto the side of the mountain. But when Sean looked over the edge, and crisscrossed the surrounding terrain, he saw no sign of Donavan, not even tracks in the snow.

Wendy and the Doyles were shocked. Donavan hadn't just walked away. Employees had been running after him. They'd seen him go over the edge. For eight months, Cyndi and Shannon had been asking Avarell what had happened to Donavan, and here was new information that seemed to indicate that someone at Above It All might have known or suspected where Donavan was all along.

"Nobody ever said to the parents, 'Hey, we looked for him. Hey, we're concerned for his safety. He went over the edge.' That would have been a whole different ball game," one of the volunteers said.

"We could have had dogs out here," someone else interjected. "We could have had everybody out here."

"I don't know about any of that stuff," Sean said. "I really don't."

They needed answers, but first they needed Donavan. Wendy asked Sean to take the search party down the mountainside where he'd found the sneaker and sweatshirt. And that's where the search party found the remains, the final confirmation that Donavan Doyle was dead.

CHAPTER NINE
Chris Koon

2015

On a sweltering August morning, Chris Koon walked out of the Grant Parish jail. Granny and Mom were waiting for him. There was little time to embrace. It was a two-and-a-half-hour drive to Cenikor, and he had just a few hours to pack and make it there, or else the judge could revoke his bond and send him back to jail.

Granny took him home and Chris pulled on fresh clothes. He threw some tee-shirts, jeans, and flip-flops into a suitcase. Along the way, they stopped at Burger King. Chris couldn't wait for his first bite of non-jail food. The closer they got, though, the more anxious Chris felt. He knew Cenikor had to be better than jail, but what would that feel like? He knew in theory, but mentally, how quickly would this all pass? What would he miss? Would he be able to see his family? His friends? In jail, he'd gotten used to the monotony, the fights, the smells, the noise. Chris knew people there; he'd gone to the same high school as some of them. At Cenikor, he wouldn't know a soul. And what if this didn't work out, and he ended up going to prison anyway? Carrie, too, felt anxious. "Life is about hardship," Carrie later said. "You gotta

Rehab

learn to endure." If things got tough, would Chris bolt? She didn't want that kind of mistake to derail his entire life.

Chris swung his suitcase out of the car and walked up to the glass double doors. A woman buzzed them in and greeted them with a wide, unblinking smile. On the wall was a poster—"Rules of Cenikor"—with a big block of text underneath that Chris didn't have time to read. The woman ushered Chris and his mom and granny down the hallway to the intake coordinator, who would process Chris into the program.

The coordinator had been a participant himself not too long ago. Now, he was charged with guiding clients through the paperwork, visiting jails and courts, and selling the program. He was muscular, with a jowly square jaw and hair sculpted into a pompadour. Chris thought he looked sort of like a boxer dog who'd joined a boy band.

Granny and his mom stayed there with Chris while Chris learned about the program and filled out paperwork. Cenikor had been around for more than 40 years, the coordinator explained, and had one of the highest success rates in the country. The program provided weekly one-on-one counseling sessions with licensed counselors and group therapy three times per week. They'd find Chris a job and he'd be able to save money in the program. Some graduates had enough saved up to buy flat-screen televisions or new cars. It sounded really good to Carrie. She liked that the program would help Chris get established in a job and that he could save money for when he left.

Cenikor had multiple facilities in Texas and Louisiana, including detox and outpatient programs. Its facilities were licensed by regulators in both states. They had accreditation from the Commission on Accreditation of Rehabilitation Facilities (CARF), the nonprofit body that provides voluntary certification for rehab facilities. Cenikor's website touted its program as "one of the oldest and most successful substance abuse treatment centers in the nation."

The coordinator told Chris he had spent years in prison in Texas. He explained that Cenikor was going to be a hell of a ride. He knew all the games people play, and he wasn't going to let Chris just sit on his butt. He was proof positive the program worked. "We don't do time here," Chris recalled the coordinator had said. "We work on ourselves. And I'ma make sure you work on yourself." Chris wanted to get better, he really did. He wanted to be the person his mom and Granny imagined he could be. He signed the documents and said his goodbyes, then he returned to the coordinator, who began walking Chris to his room.

That's when Chris saw something he had never seen before: a man sitting in a chair, his back straight, his knees bent at a precise 90-degree angle, his elbows locked; he was looking straight ahead, unblinking and silent. They were in a big, open room that looked like a cafeteria. As they walked past him, Chris tried to make eye contact to say hello, but the man stared right through him. Then Chris spotted another man across the hall, sitting the exact same way.

What is this? Chris thought.

CHRIS MOVED INTO his room, which he would be sharing with a roommate. He unpacked his clothes, hanging them to face the right side of his closet, in a certain order, per Cenikor rules. Jackets, sweaters, long-sleeve shirts, short-sleeve shirts, pants, shorts. He placed his shoes in a row at the foot of the bed, from his work boots to his "flippity flops," as he called them. He "ranger-rolled" his underwear in the dresser and made his bed. Chris learned that another resident would come around daily to inspect his room and make sure he was adhering to Cenikor standards.

The building was sprawling, about 155,000 square feet, but Cenikor occupied only a sliver of it. When it was acquired in 2001, they found the facility dilapidated and requiring tremendous cost to repair. Participants complained of holes in the wall, malfunctioning heaters and air conditioners, rats, cockroaches, and black mold. The front desk, typically manned by a resident, was situated just inside the front door. Past the front desk was the 'Kor room—the cafeteria where residents ate their meals and took part in group meetings.

Rehab

Past the 'Kor room was the women's wing, and upstairs were the rooms for men. Residents were not allowed to be alone with a member of the opposite sex. The number of people at Cenikor was in constant flux, but during Chris's stay there were about 150 residents.

For the first 30 days, Chris learned the Cenikor way. He awoke at dawn every morning. The residents did everything in the facility, from cooking to cleaning, to holding one another accountable. If one person broke a major rule, the entire facility might be forced to wake up in the middle of the night to face punishment. Sometimes, they'd have "fire drills" at 2 a.m. If anyone stepped out of line or did something wrong during the drill, they'd have to stay awake even longer.

For the first month, he sat in a classroom and learned all the Cenikor rules. There were about 30 people in his class, most court-ordered, like him. The orientation leader handed out a thick packet that contained more than 100 rules, and day by day, they sat and recited the rules out loud, line by line. Those rules ranged from the mundane—Chris was required to shave everyday—to the minuscule. He could get in trouble for not having a pen, not wearing a belt, for an untied shoelace, for leaving a book on the table, for his shirt coming untucked. Chris was 6' 3" with a belly, so his shirt was constantly coming untucked. He quickly learned the consequences.

"Go have a seat in the verbal chair. Think about having your shirt untucked," he'd be told. To which Chris was required to reply, "Thank you." Anyone could send him to that chair, at any time. Anyone could scream at him while he was sitting in that chair, and he couldn't do anything about it. He had to sit there with his arms locked, his knees at a precise 90-degree angle, staring at the wall, not speaking, not making eye contact. Chris quickly became like one of those men he had seen when he first arrived at the facility.

There were other punishments, too. There was "mirror therapy," in which he stared at himself in a mirror and continuously shouted out what he'd done wrong. Or, there was "the dishpan," when he'd have to wear a neon green shirt and wash the dishes and scrub the baseboards, all while reciting the

Cenikor philosophy—a paragraph-long diatribe about self-change. Or, there was the "verbal haircut," in which another participant screamed at him even for just a minor rule infraction.

Chris along with every other participant was required to submit pieces of paper on which they described rule infractions they had witnessed other participants commit. These were called "pull-ups," and everyone was required to submit at least ten per week. To succeed at Cenikor, and to get enough points to graduate, Chris would have to tattle on everybody else. Anytime someone got pissed off, the participants and staff would gather in a circle and select one or two people to sit in the middle. Then they took turns confronting that person, professing their faults and errors, while the person was permitted only to say "thank you." Cenikor staff called this "The Game." Chris heard women called bitches and sluts. He saw grown men cry. Even some of the employees participated in this exercise. Many of them were former participants.

Hundreds of such programs across the country operated similarly, some with tactics even more bizarre. At a program in North Carolina, residents were forced to endure days without sleep as they sat for marathon group confessionals, deliriously relaying their life stories, their deepest secrets and sins. Behavior modification programs for troubled teens employed similar practices, with one congressional investigation comparing their methods to "the highly refined brainwashing techniques employed by the North Koreans."

For the first month, Chris lived in a state of shock. He thought constantly about leaving Cenikor. Jail, with its mush melons and *Maury Povich* on repeat, would be easier than this, he thought. His every move felt picked apart. He could get into trouble at any time. As he rounded out the 30 days of orientation, his new sobriety gave way to a well of emotions the drugs had helped him suppress. He had no drugs in his system, nothing to distract from how horrible he felt: that he was a fuck-up, that he didn't belong anywhere. And now it was the hell of being at Cenikor. He'd never felt so low. *This is like a cult*, he thought. It turned out that wasn't far from the truth.

Rehab

BEFORE CENIKOR, there was Synanon, founded in 1958, when the country was in the midst of another—albeit much smaller—opioid epidemic. Harry Anslinger, the bombastic head of the U.S. Narcotics Bureau, claimed that a shocking 60,000 Americans were addicted to drugs. His widely shared belief about addiction was that it was incurable. The only way to stop it was "to quarantine the addict and stop him from addicting others." And the best way to do that—the only way to do that, at the time—was to send an addict to a hospital ward, a jail cell, or prison.

Synanon was the first of its kind, a precursor to rehab, where addicts could live and work and hold one another accountable for slip-ups or relapses. It was founded by Chuck Dederich, a charismatic alcoholic and former oil salesman, who had become disillusioned with Alcoholics Anonymous and the way many members—in his view—lied about their slip-ups and relapses. One of its earliest homes was a run-down, three-story redbrick building in Santa Monica with dim lighting and secondhand furniture. Early meetings resembled philosophy seminars, presided over by Dederich, who weighed almost three hundred pounds, was prone to cursing, and wore only flip-flops. The fledgling group quickly gained a following, and with more people came more developed rules. Group members would hold each other accountable for relapses and bad behavior by confronting each other in regular group meetings that Dederich referred to as "The Game." Violating the group's rules invited steep punishments. After one participant arrived high on drugs in 1965, Synanon participants forced him to shave his head, wear a dress, and sling a sign around his neck; "Please help me. I tried to kill my family," it said.

The cruelty was offset by the enthusiasm of Synanon's participants and the novelty of freedom the program promised: unleashed anger and raw emotion. Those for whom it worked were united by a belief that it worked. In other words, they achieved a kind of faith and buy-in that was harder to attain if you had not truly made the choice to be there; if you were court-ordered, like Chris, for example. The diehards believed in Synanon's methods, which some likened to brainwashing. "Yeah, we brainwash 'em," an early Synanon member would later say, "because they brain is dirty."

In the counterculture era of the 1960s, Synanon quickly gained a following among celebrities and jazz musicians. Lucille Ball from *I Love Lucy*, Rod Serling from *The Twilight Zone*, and *Star Trek*'s Leonard Nimoy all came to visit. "A tunnel back into the human race," read a *Life* magazine cover story: "Where drug addicts join to salvage their lives." But institutional buy-in was also owed to Synanon's uniquely American ethos. Unlike prisons, or fledgling forms of treatment like methadone or psychotherapy, Synanon did not require any government funding. Instead, participants worked without pay in "industries," with all the proceeds from their labor going to Synanon. Rather than putting the onus on lawmakers to fund social services, Synanon placed the responsibility on addicts themselves.

This philosophy was not new. After abolishing slavery following the Civil War, the federal government had created a deliberate loophole that legalized forced labor by people convicted of a crime. This loophole forced many recently freed slaves back into involuntary servitude, and prison officials eventually began selling the practice as a form of rehabilitation. Over the decades, those officials continued to pitch the transformative power of work. "Hard honest work is usually the most potent force in the reformation and rehabilitation of the prisoner," touted one federal prison film produced in 1935. "He must learn a respectable trade or vocation, and be taught to earn his bread by the sweat of his brow." Years later, at Synanon, Dederich was reflecting this same philosophy. Anyone could be transformed into a law-abiding citizen; all it took was hard work and total sobriety, without a single dime from American taxpayers.

As it turns out, most people left Synanon, many to relapse. Studies would later find some of the practices, such as "The Game," harmful for some people, particularly those navigating histories of trauma. But the program resonated with lawmakers and with the public. Synanon soon expanded into a multimillion-dollar operation across multiple states, inspiring dozens of offshoots. And in 1967, James Lucas Austin founded Cenikor.

Rehab

At first, Austin's fledgling group existed only in the Colorado state penitentiary, where he was serving a two-year sentence for assault with a deadly weapon. But Austin was ambitious, and after he left prison, he grew the program quickly. At 6 foot 4 inches, with red hair and a wide smile, Austin cut an impressive figure with an impressive (and manufactured) background: He claimed he was a country musician who had played with Johnny Cash and been close friends with Elvis Presley. Within a year of his release, Austin was speaking at a special subcommittee hearing of Congress on what could be done about "the problem of alcoholism and narcotics." Two months after that, he was sitting at the desk of Colorado governor John Love himself, meeting with the head of prisons and parole. Austin succeeded in part because of his pitch to officials—that Cenikor could reform addicts better than any prison or government-funded program could. And the way the program survived was through that unpaid work.

Cenikor had a landscaping business and operated a gas station. Cenikor workers made and sold rabbit hutches, sawhorses, and drove 18-wheelers transporting vegetables and beef across the country. The participants who worked kept none of their pay. All the money went back to Cenikor. Austin even founded a Cenikor band—Luke Austin and Country Kingdom USA—to fuel his aspirations for country-music stardom.

By the early 1970s, Austin had expanded the program into Texas and Long Beach, California, and he had begun to treat program funds like his own bank account. The group moved its central operations into the old William Penn Hotel in downtown Houston. Participants fixed up a penthouse on the top floor for the founder and his wife, Dottie, and were required to walk Dottie's poodles, who all had painted toenails. With Cenikor's money, Austin bought himself a country western club on the south side of town, and Cenikor ran it as a night club, replete with booze.

Board member Gene Jones, a former member of the Texas legislature, started growing suspicious of Austin and his lifestyle. He recalled seeing participants drive Austin around in a limousine "He said that he had to give them a living example," Jones said. Like a prosperity preacher, Austin showcased the benefits of remaining faithful to the Cenikor way. He'd say to them, "Here I am. I've been a dope addict. I've been in the penitentiary. And here I am living a life of luxury. This is where you can be."

But even among the Cenikor diehards—the people who wanted to be there and believed in the program—evidence had started to mount that Austin cared more about the money than about the program he'd founded. The program's accountant, an unpaid participant who had joined Cenikor at the age of 16, noticed that much of the program's funds were paying for Austin's ersatz country music career, as well as his gold chains, a yacht, a plane, Cadillacs, and Lincoln Continentals. "Just living off of all of us. And we're going, 'Hmm, this is not cool. This is not kosher,'" said former participant Ken Barun, who would eventually became Cenikor's president.

All this information went to Cenikor's board members, which included the sitting mayor of Houston, who promptly referred the details to the county prosecutor and offered Austin a deal. In exchange for his resignation, Austin would be spared prosecution. But Austin was furious. "I'm going to kill you," he seethed at the accountant who had exposed him.

Six months later, in the summer of 1978, Barun was in his office when Austin and a small crew of former Cenikor participants burst in wearing black armbands and carrying mace, tear gas, and baseball bats. "That's the guy!" Austin yelled, pointing at Barun. "Get him!" At the same moment, Austin's mother led an attack on Cenikor's Colorado facility, this group wearing Halloween masks and brandishing guns, some fake, some real, none loaded. Within minutes, the Houston Cenikor participants had grabbed some two-by-fours from nearby construction and had cornered Austin and his crew. Austin was arrested and served about a week in jail before disappearing for good.

Chuck Dederich, the founder of Synanon, soon met his downfall, too. By the time of Austin's ouster, the group had transformed from celebrated rehab to "experimental society." Synanon now let in other participants who had no history of drug use, known as "squares." And Dederich began imposing more authoritarian rules on Synanon participants. He banned sugar and he required everyone to shave their heads as a sign of devotion. He dissolved marriages; children were separated and raised separately from their parents. Men were forced to undergo vasectomies. When the IRS began examining Synanon's nonprofit status, Dederich declared the organization a religion, and he dispatched his armed militia, called the "Imperial Marines," to attack his detractors. One attorney who had sued Synanon almost died after two of the Imperial Marines put a rattlesnake in his mailbox.

For the murder plot, Dederich took a plea deal that required him to give up control of Synanon. And then, like Al Capone, it was IRS accountants who took Synanon completely down. The agency stripped Synanon of its nonprofit, tax-exempt status, and suddenly the organization was on the hook for back taxes for all its donations and scenic properties, worth $55.6 million. Dederich relapsed and eventually died of heart failure in 1997.

Despite its founder's disappearance, Cenikor's downfall did not last long. Many participants had been at Cenikor for years and considered the place home. They kept it going, and soon established a lucrative new partnership with the National Football League, manufacturing safety equipment for football players.

The arrangement was good timing. As President Ronald Reagan was slashing taxes and funding for services such as treatment, his advisors were looking for examples of private industry stepping in to fill the gap. In 1983, Reagan visited Cenikor, and the program—and all other work-based rehab models—earned the firm endorsement of the president of the United States.

"I was glancing through your Cenikor booklet, and I liked the very first sentence I read: 'In all the years that Cenikor has been in business, rehabilitating lives, we have found that nothing works as well as work itself,'" Reagan declared to cheers from the crowd. "This center is self-sufficient, just like all of you will soon be." For Reagan, Cenikor served as proof that the federal government didn't need to be involved in treating drug addiction at all.

As the years passed, more programs like Cenikor began to crop up across the United States. In Georgia, one rehab owner sent his participants to work in his pecan groves and on his cotton farm. In Tennessee, rehab participants disposed of dead animals at the zoo. In California, workers labored in a Williams Sonoma warehouse and on high-rise construction sites. Many such programs could get around state licensing requirements by not providing medical services, offering only 12-step-based services, or by calling themselves "faith-based." They operated without any government oversight.

Then in 2004, Cenikor's board hired Bill Bailey. Unlike the organization's previous CEOs, Bailey hadn't gone through Cenikor. He didn't publicly tout any personal experience with addiction or treatment. He was a businessman, and like a good businessman, he began making decisions to modernize the program and grow Cenikor's profits. He hired licensed counselors, medical directors, and nurses, which allowed Cenikor to meet state licensing requirements, access new revenue streams, and bill insurance companies and Medicaid for its services. Chris Koon joined the program in this new era. By then, Cenikor had become something of a hybrid. It had the same work-based, therapeutic community program Austin had started many years earlier, but it had become professionalized. At least, that's what it was supposed to be.

UPON ARRIVING AT CENIKOR, Chris Koon had been given some documents to sign. Surrounded by his mom, Granny, and the intake coordinator, he had not spent much time reading them. A lot of it read like legalese, incomprehensible but also innocuous, like something you might see before downloading an app on your phone. He didn't quite realize that he was signing away many of his rights. Among the documents was a client agreement, stating that he would work without pay as part of his treatment. "I understand that I will receive no monetary compensation for my assigned responsibilities within the facility or with a community business partner," the agreement read. "I also understand that funds raised go directly back to the Foundation to help offset the cost of my treatment services." He also signed a document waiving his right to workers compensation benefits in case of an injury, and another acknowledging he might be terminated from the program if he was unable to work. He agreed to hand over his food stamps and any other governmental assistance he might receive, like disability payments.

More paperwork outlined some of the rules Chris would have to follow. For example, as in jail or prison, the Cenikor staff would read his personal mail and might not give it to him if it was deemed a security risk—a common protocol of rehab programs. He had to immediately hand over his suitcase, agree to searches at any time, and submit to regular urine tests. The documents outlined the three phases of the program, which lasted anywhere from two months to more than a year. And they described how residents progressed through the program based on a point system. The more points you received, the more privileges you earned, like the ability to change the channel on the television. Earn 72 points, and you could get a weekly visit from the family. Earn 216 points, and you could grow a mustache and receive uncensored telephone calls and mail. Residents earned more points the longer they stayed, and they could earn extra points the more they worked. They lost points if they broke the rules. Losing points could even set them back in the program, sometimes for months. Everyone's points were displayed and updated on a giant scoreboard.

The documents also explained Cenikor's methods. Cenikor used the "Therapeutic Community model"; this program was highly structured, using rules, hierarchy, peer pressure, and confrontation to modify participants' behavior and create long-term change. "I must adopt appropriate morals and values as promoted by the program, including development of a strong work ethic, as opposed to solely recovering from an illness," the document read. "I further understand that under no circumstances can Cenikor be under any obligation to me; that I am a beneficiary and not an employee." These also called for his signature.

Chris didn't understand most of this until day 31, when he left Orientation and reported for work. In the years following the end of the Great Recession, companies large and small had begun employing temporary workers at accelerated rates. Temp workers allowed companies to minimize their costs and maximize their profits, with as little investment in their own workforce as possible. They could fire workers at will, and they didn't have to pay benefits or workers compensation for injuries. Cenikor seized on this trend, offering its rehab patients as a temporary workforce that was cheaper and easier to control than regular temp workers. With jail or prison time hanging over their heads, Cenikor residents had little say about where, when, and how they worked.

Every night, at each Cenikor facility, a resident posted a "line-out sheet" on the wall of the 'Kor room, notifying residents where they would be dispatched the following day for work. Some worked at a mulch factory, others at an industrial laundromat, still others at a bakery or seafood store. They had also worked at Exxon and Shell oil refineries, in a sweltering Walmart warehouse, and in the cafeterias of Louisiana State University. They built scaffolding hundreds of feet high, sandblasted and painted tanks, performed electrical repairs, and lay rebars in cement in 115° heat.

Cenikor's corporate headquarters pressured their facility managers to bring in as much revenue as possible. The vocational office at each Cenikor site found the jobs for its residents, and negotiated contracts with companies for their services. The vocational office also tracked the number of hours each participant worked, knew their hourly rate, and billed the companies for the services. It was their job also to collect promptly. The more they collected, the greater the bonus the vocational director received.

At Cenikor's Baton Rouge location, the vocational director was Patrick Odom, a Cenikor graduate known for pushing punishing work schedules. Odom's second-in-command was Cody Collins, a Cenikor resident. When corporate headquarters pressured Patrick to make more money, it was Cody's job to incentivize the residents into working even more hours. To do so, he'd offer them more cigarettes.

Chris was told his work just barely covered the cost of his stay. But internal documents showed that the residents regularly made more than twice as much money as the facility's daily operating expenses. Between 2013 and 2018, Cenikor made more than $42 million from their uncompensated Cenikor

Rehab

workers. Meanwhile, the facility had lucrative contracts with the state and federal governments, received insurance and Medicaid payouts, and had residents apply for and relinquish their food stamps. In short, the residents were not just working to cover costs. They were working to make profits for Cenikor. And they were working to an extreme.

Finally, after about three months, Chris Koon had accumulated the 72 points necessary to get a visit from family. John, his dad, was coming. Chris wore his best shirt for the occasion. He tried to stay positive. He told his dad it was tough, but he could handle it. Later, on another visit, he shared some of the strange Cenikor customs he'd been learning. For example, he said, he could put anyone he wanted into time out. To demonstrate, he called over a friend.

"Go have a seat for disrespecting my dad," Chris said.

"Thank you," his friend said, and he sat down in the chair, assuming the same non-blinking, erect posture that had once creeped out Chris on his first day.

His prison-guard dad was amazed. But despite the positive spin Chris tried to give his dad, Cenikor was wearing on Chris, and on John's next visit, Chris was too exhausted to put on a front. He needed to get out of there. Could John talk to his lawyer? Is there another place the court could send him? John said he would ask.

As soon as his father left, the Cenikor staff swarmed Chris. Someone had overheard him asking his dad about leaving. *Why do you want to leave? If you leave here, you'll relapse or go to prison. Prison or death,* they said. Chris realized he was always being watched. His letters were being read, his phone calls being monitored. From that point on, Chris knew he had to be careful.

After his dad's visit, Chris tried to rise above Cenikor. He went along with the program, pretended to believe in it. All the while, he was plotting what he would do when he left the place. He fantasized about becoming a lawyer, suing Cenikor for civil rights violations. He got so good at rolling along with the Cenikor program that he got a promotion. For five months, he taught Orientation. He watched people arrive, dumbstruck, like he once had been. He watched as people sat down to learn the rules, suffered through the punishments, and adjusted to the constant monitoring. And he watched as many people left or were expelled, some facing decades in prison. Chris was one of the few people still there from his original Orientation class.

After a few months of Chris's teaching Orientation, Cenikor sent Chris back to work. And once again, Chris found himself in the center of the Cenikor churn—so exhausted he had no energy left to think, to resist Cenikor's rules, or even to participate in other aspects of the program.

At first, they sent Chris on a job where he cleaned and organized the scaffolding that came in from the chemical plants. He worked at restaurants and at Louisiana State University, cleaning up after football games. He worked at the plants, rod busting, insulating walls, power washing and sandblasting. He worked at a grain silo on the Mississippi River, and at the Shintech plastics plant, making PVC. Cenikor workers were often given the toughest jobs—the ones employers had a hard time filling. Chris had heard the bosses order up more workers, like they were hamburgers: "Give me five more Cenikors." Or, they wouldn't use his name, instead calling to him, "Hey, Cenikor."

Chris worked as much as 80 hours per week. He made up to $1,500 a week in wages. But he didn't see any of that money. His sole pay was three packs of cigarettes per week.

Chris was sober, he had a job and a roof over his head. Through it all, he had made some friends. This should have been a recipe for successful recovery. Instead, he felt expendable and trapped. The only aspect of life that was in his control was the decision to leave. But leaving rehab, he realized, could become a kind of trap, too. Even if he somehow managed to escape the prison sentence that awaited him, there was the question of where he would live and how he would support himself. And that post-rehab trap was particularly acute for those who had even fewer resources to begin with—something April Lee had learned a lot about.

CHAPTER TEN

April Lee

2014

When April Lee graduated from her 30-day rehab program, she didn't have a home. So, she went to her brother Chris's house, where his widow, Tasha, and his 13-year-old son lived. The house ached with pain, filled with the absence and reminders of her brother's death. April's brother and sister-in-law had been together since they were 13. Tasha could barely function. She was sleeping on the couch in the living room because she couldn't bear to enter their bedroom, which remained as Chris had left it, an open can of beer on his bedside table. She gave April her nephew's bedroom, a welcome amount of privacy, particularly after rehab, but it was a reminder of the children April herself was missing. April tried to ignore the sound of her sister-in-law's sobs that she heard through the bedroom wall.

The cravings began almost immediately, when April saw Chris's beer in the refrigerator. The program April had attended had prepared her for life after rehab by acquainting her with the 12 steps, so to cope with the cravings, she started attending recovery meetings. This would be her support system as she embarked on her new life in recovery. Nevertheless, April felt like she was barely holding it together. She was at a meeting one day when a guy offered her a ride home and he groped her on the way to his car. *Fuck him,* April thought. *Fuck everybody.* The next day, she called another guy she'd met in a meeting and told him she was thinking about using.

"Where are you?" he asked.

"A meeting," she said. He told her to stay there. "Raise your hand. Leaving will do no good." But soon after that, she left and relapsed on Percocet.

For two weeks, she tried to keep up the facade of sobriety, putting on nice clothes and makeup. She attended 12-step meetings and pronounced her sobriety, then trekked to Kensington to get loaded before returning to her brother's house. She quickly ran out of money, though. After she pawned Tasha's necklace, April knew she had crossed a line. She lay in bed, sobbing and writhing, the beginnings of withdrawal already settling in. Tasha was at work. She didn't know that April had relapsed. April still had time to collect herself, put on makeup, pretend like everything was fine. But she knew the facade wouldn't last. She felt like shit. Her family had already been through so much. They had lost a brother and a husband and a father.

Medicaid expansion in Pennsylvania meant that April's health insurance covered her treatment, something that was not the case in the more than a dozen states, but programs were still hard to find. Since 2002, the number of publicly funded nonprofit facilities had declined nationwide, especially in Black communities with some of the greatest need. April picked up her insurance card and called the number on the back. She needed to go back to rehab. She needed support, someone to help her get through this. She needed a place where she could live and have time to work on herself.

Studies have shown that it takes most people multiple attempts, multiple relapses, before they achieve lasting sobriety. And entering rehab quickly when someone requests it has a profound impact on their likelihood of success. People who experience delays in getting into treatment fare far worse than people who enter treatment right away. Starting on buprenorphine or methadone can dramatically increase someone's chances of success, and can also dramatically reduce the risk of overdose death. But when April called her

April Lee

insurance provider, she was told they wouldn't immediately cover another inpatient stay. April could enroll in an outpatient program, which involved attending one-on-one therapy and group counseling, but to do that, she needed income to support herself and a place to live. Putting all this on her brother's struggling widow was simply too much.

When Tasha returned home, she found a clean, empty room with a note on the bed: "I want to thank you for everything you did for me," April had written. "No matter what you're going through, know that God has you in his hands."

A FEW MONTHS BEFORE, April had been trying to turn a trick on the street when a guy walked up to her and handed her a business card. "Whenever you're ready, come give us a call," he'd told her. It was for a recovery house, unlicensed—something akin to a sober-living home, like where Wendy's son, Jarrod, had gone to live. April didn't know anything about this man, but she was desperate. She rifled through her purse for the card and called the number.

For decades, Philadelphia had been home to a robust network of recovery houses, owing in large part to a confluence of factors: large populations of heavy drug users, a large stock of vacant and dilapidated homes, and scores of homeless and uninsured residents, some of whom had been shipped in by courts from out of state. The city itself funded just 21 recovery houses, with 288 beds. As a result, the vast majority of recovery houses in the city were unlicensed and unmonitored. They survived by collecting their residents' cash assistance, fees, food stamps, and rent.

Over the years, as the number of outpatient programs in the city grew, the recovery home industry grew with it. These unlicensed recovery houses played an important role in the treatment ecosystem. Indigent patients like April needed someplace to live while they attended treatment. But since insurance did not cover housing, and patients like April did not have any money, many of these programs subsisted through other methods: by referring residents to rehab, in exchange for cash, or putting their residents to work without pay at the founders' businesses or on political campaigns.

With so many jobs and industries out of reach for people with addiction histories, owning and running a recovery house had become its own sign of success. But for the residents, these houses could become a kind of trap. As a result of not working and of turning over their government checks, the residents were unable to save money. Even if people wanted to leave, they were often barred from other forms of housing or simply couldn't afford to live anywhere else—except in a different recovery home. Some places took care to help residents avoid relapse, while others were overcrowded with mattresses or cots or sleeping bags, infested with bed bugs and marked by active drug use. Others subjected their residents to rules that ran counter to research-backed practices; for example, very few permitted residents to take medication-assisted treatment.

The new, compassionate approach to opioid addiction had expanded access to treatment for some people, but it seemed to ignore the needs of people like April Lee—people whose recovery hinged not just on treatment but also on overcoming the structural barriers that prevented them from changing their lives in the first place. While the country's welfare system failed to help people out of poverty, Medicaid barred states from using federal funds to pay for room and board, education, vocational services, or transportation—services that could actually help people stay sober. Programs that treated recovery like a meritocracy made the problem worse. All this made recovery an uphill battle for someone like April.

THE MAN SOON arrived to pick her up. He was a pastor at a Mennonite church in Kensington. The neighborhood, formerly alive with the bustle of working-class industry, had become one of the most dangerous in the city. Years of real estate redlining had forced minority populations to reside in

April Lee

neighborhoods that had been condemned by the federal government as unworthy of investment; and in the years since, the denial of opportunity had continued to reverberate, with neighborhoods such as Kensington experiencing the highest rates of poverty, poor health outcomes, high unemployment, and violent crime. As the drug trade began to dominate the local economy, Kensington had become the epicenter of the city's opioid and homelessness crises.

April stared out the car window as they drove past pawn shops, check-cashing businesses, bodegas, and fast-food restaurants. People squatted in vacant row houses and foraged through overgrown weeds and brush on the abandoned Conrail tracks to shoot up, only to be found months later, dead, anonymous, and unidentifiable. Under the shadow of the Southeastern Pennsylvania Transportation Authority (SEPTA) train tracks was the largest open-air drug market on the East Coast, attracting crowds rivaled only by tourists at the Liberty Bell. Kensington's housed residents, many working-class immigrants, were outraged by the squalor, but they were helpless to do anything about it.

Next to the church was a rundown redbrick row house, a "recovery home," with three bedrooms. A small woman who spoke mainly Spanish came out to greet April. She led April inside, to a small room with three bunk beds crammed together. She took April's detox meds and put them in a cubby hole in the dining room. She told April about their program. April was to follow strict rules at the house. She would be required to pray with the group at least three times a day. She could take her medications only at a certain time.

April was still detoxing and was often wracked with intense full body pain and diarrhea. About a week in, she was caught taking her medication before the designated time. The woman approached April and explained the punishment. She told April she needed to pray for forgiveness, for God to strengthen her resolve. She ordered April to the corner of the room, told her to face the wall, get on her knees, and pray. April kneeled in the corner for four hours. The next morning, she felt like her knees were on fire. "It gets better," her bunkmate assured her. But April had run out of faith.

Rehab

"Fuck this," she said. She walked out the door, abandoning her journal and her medication, and into the streets of Kensington. Unlike Chris Koon, April had already spent many years going without. In leaving the recovery house, she had less to lose because she never had much in the first place. She did not know where she was going. She just began to walk, her body and face soon falling into familiar rhythms. A john heeded the call and pulled over, and as April walked close, she heard gospel music blasting through the open car window. It seemed to April an especially cruel irony. Was this a message from God? And so despite herself, she laughed. "Another day in the life," she muttered, before waving the man off. Then she turned down Allegheny Avenue and receded into the forgotten ranks of Kensington's homeless population.

CHAPTER ELEVEN

Larry Ley

2013

On August 19, 2013, the Madison County deputy coroner opened her email browser and hit Compose. She typed: *To: Aaron K. Dietz, Subject: Drug Task Force.*

It was 6:31 p.m., past normal business hours, but the coroner was tired of waiting. She had information the Carmel Police Department needed to see. About a month earlier, the deputy had arrived at a single-story pale brick house on Loral Drive to retrieve the body of a local pipefitter. For days, the man had been vomiting, and blood streaked his urine and stool. But he refused to go to the doctor or to the hospital. He soon passed away. By the time the coroner arrived, his body was already cold and stiff. The man's brother blamed one person: Dr. Larry Ley.

"He has been on suboxone for six years and he just goes to Dr. Larry Ley's office, pays $120, and gets a prescription written for him without even seeing the doctor," the deputy coroner wrote. Meanwhile, the man had continued to drink and use drugs. The account reminded the deputy coroner of the pill mills she'd heard and read about; they were of great concern in Anderson,

Rehab

Indiana, and were all over the news. Just a few months ago, the drug task force had raided the Wagoner clinic. She had seen firsthand how the pills had ravaged her hometown, where she still lived and worked, making about $3,000 a year as a part-time coroner.

"I'm so tired of going on death calls of young kids who overdose on these pills," the coroner wrote to Major Dietz, the head of the local drug task force. "I know you guys are working hard on cracking down on drug mills. . . . If someone could look into this guy, I'd greatly appreciate, as well as this family!"

The information the coroner provided looked damning. Dr. Larry Ley seemed to be pushing dangerous drugs for a profit. His patient had allegedly continued to abuse alcohol and drugs during the time he was a DORN patient. But the coroner's email was also riddled with factual errors. She seemed unaware that Suboxone was a treatment for addiction and not the cause of it. She wrote, for example, that Suboxone was a "short-term drug." But Suboxone was intended to be taken long term. She'd written that the man's mother had once picked up his prescription. But that wasn't against the law.

In fact, by the time of the man's death, he was no longer a patient at DORN. A toxicology test would show he had neither drugs nor alcohol in his system. Eventually, his cause of death would be declared gastrointestinal bleeding—a rare complication of Crohn's disease, an illness for which he was not taking medication, and chronic alcohol abuse. His death had nothing to do with Suboxone, or any other drug. Nonetheless, the coroner had sent the email, and it was now in the custody of the Drug Task Force. Major Dietz forwarded it to Carmel police detective sergeant Marc Klein, who promptly contacted the DEA.

THE DEA'S Gary Whisenand was assigned the lead on the case. Athletic and muscular, Whisenand looked the part of a law enforcement officer. He'd trained at Quantico and regularly worked criminal investigations. But as a diversion investigator, he lacked arrest authority and needed the manpower of local law enforcement. Aaron Dietz, the head of the task force at the Carmel Police Department, and Kokomo detective Tonda Cockrell, the lead investigator on the Wagoner case, joined the team. They didn't have to look far to find information that seemed incriminating.

A quick search of Indiana's prescription-monitoring database showed that Larry Ley was writing thousands of prescriptions every year. The DEA had previously investigated Ley's practice of issuing Suboxone prescriptions for pain, and deemed the practice lawful. But now Whisenand again raised concerns, asking in his notes whether Ley and his fellow DORN doctors had any experience or training in pain management.

Patients told Cockrell that they would line up down the street for their prescriptions. A sheriff's deputy who had been hired to provide security at DORN said that after working there one time, he felt it was "'sketchy,' and did not go back," Whisenand wrote. Patients, too, complained about having to pay in cash. Other patients were disturbed by Ley's own sordid past, complained that he smoked cigarettes, and alleged he was on hard drugs himself. "There is nothing different from him and the drug dealers on the corner," one former patient said. "Might as well buy heroin," said another. Patients complained about having to wait hours to see a doctor, with the experience feeling transactional and often informal, devoid of typical medical care, such as the taking of their weight, height, and blood pressure.

Some of DORN's business practices were the result of the scarcity Reckitt Benckiser and lawmakers had imposed. Few primary-care doctors and treatment programs prescribed Suboxone, so there was a dire need for prescribers like Ley. They offered quick and easy access to the medication without requiring patients to jump through hoops, like prior insurance authorizations, or the extra services and tests that rehabs and methadone programs often required. Research had found that doing away with some of these requirements actually increased treatment retention.

But since there was so much demand for Suboxone, some of these doctors—like Ley—also seized upon the opportunity to turn a profit. They could charge exorbitant prices, cut corners on support staff and services, and require patients to pay with cash. Indeed, some of Ley's earlier patients had begun to notice a shift. Whereas Ley had previously seen patients every day, sometimes for an hour at a time, now DORN seemed overrun with patients, and they rarely saw Ley at all. "I think when he started doing it, I did feel like he cared," said Katy Jo Dalton, one of his first patients. "And then it went cash-only, and he followed the money and numbers." The cash-pay practices made some sense, since few private insurance or Medicaid plans covered Suboxone treatment, and the administrative burden of billing insurance companies for visits could be costly and complicated. Many psychiatrists did not accept insurance, for this same reason. But the segregated cash-only practices—some charging much more than DORN, up to $400 per month—made treatment unaffordable for many people who needed it. And it did little to convince other doctors—and law enforcement—that prescribing the medication was an above-board affair.

This problem had some solutions, though. The FDA could re-examine the company's orphan drug status that was driving up prices; it was based, after all, on a fiction. Congress could have taken steps to loosen the restrictions on methadone programs or permit willing pharmacies and mobile vans to dispense methadone, which would have created more routes to treatment medications in places where it was hard to find. But Congress did not intervene in these ways.

With doctors now allowed to treat 100 patients—thanks to a law signed by President George Bush in 2006—those who were already prescribing high quantities of Suboxone began increasing their patient loads. Their clinics began to flourish as stand-alone businesses, fueling the perception of Suboxone clinics as "pill mills." Lawmakers had wanted to integrate addiction treatment into medicine so as to avoid creating siloed, stigmatized programs akin to methadone clinics. But in effect that is exactly what they had done. And now these structural problems—endemic to Suboxone prescribers—drew the DEA straight to Larry Ley's door.

Larry Ley

WITHIN A FEW MONTHS of receiving the coroner's email, Whisenand had seven undercover agents visiting DORN's offices on a regular basis. The hundreds of hours of their undercover footage were revealing in some respects. They showed that some of DORN's offices were overwhelmed with patients, some lined up outside the door, and many patients complaining. Larry rarely physically examined patients. Even worse, investigators uncovered evidence that on some occasions, Larry had pre-signed prescriptions, which was against the law.

But much of the footage and intel gathered undermined the team's underlying premise: that DORN was merely a pill mill, and not helping people at all. Larry routinely referred patients to outside doctors and counseling. Several of the undercover agents were asked to provide urine samples. Larry Ley questioned each person about their drug use, what they took and how much. He took notes with a pencil as each person described their histories of pain and addiction problems. Then Ley launched into his two-hour-long seminar on addiction. "Our goal is to help you get better. But it does take work on your part," he said to a roomful of patients during one visit; he was wearing jeans, a red sweater, and wire-rimmed glasses perched on top of his bald head. He told everyone about his own history of addiction. He wanted their experience to feel different from a typical doctor's office experience, he said. "My feeling is, I come waltzing in here with a white coat on and a stethoscope around my neck; it's just kind of a barrier," he told them.

During one visit, an undercover agent, seemingly impatient, tried to hurry the doctor along by interrupting his educational diatribe with questions about the medication. "I'm not trying to cut you off," Ley told him. "We'll talk about it in just a minute. I want to make sure you've got the disease concept, the genetics, the environment down first. It's so important you have that." Ley explained he had materials for them to read, that he would go over expectations in the program, and then he'd go into detail about the medication. The agent begrudgingly accepted.

Rehab

The videos showed Larry Ley loved to hear himself talk. He was gruff, with a smoker's rasp. For some people, especially his suburban patients, Ley's manner and even the presence of other lower-income patients did not inspire confidence. "I'm not racist, but..." one former patient told the DEA. "These are true drug addicts. It looks like they came off the streets of downtown." But the information Larry Ley offered patients was scientifically accurate and valuable. He urged them to find a recovery group like AA, which could help them sustain their sobriety. He advised them not to combine their Suboxone with other medications, like benzodiazepines, which increased overdose risks. "If you combine Suboxone with an opiate or benzo, there's a lot of deaths," Ley said during one visit. In fact, unlike at Above It All Treatment Center, Ley said he would not prescribe them.

As the agents progressed in the program, Cassy Bratcher started to flag some of their drug test results. During one visit, Cassy gingerly approached an agent to inform him that he couldn't continue in the program. His previous two urine screens showed that he didn't have any buprenorphine in his system, she said.

"It doesn't make any sense," the undercover agent replied. "I took it this morning."

Cassy told the agent she would check the sample again and would speak with the doctor. In the background, the agent's video showed a warm if somewhat chaotic office, where patients and nurses were discussing everything from a new fitness app someone had downloaded, to another patient's sleep troubles, for which a nurse suggested melatonin, an herbal remedy. Cassy came back with a two-week prescription, enough to help the agent—going by his undercover name, Dave—get by until he could find another provider to help him.

"We won't let you come back here without bup in your system," Cassy said, apologetically. "If you're taking it that way, and it's showing up with no bup in your system, something else is going on. And what ends up happening in that situation, 90 percent of the time, those patients are selling their medicine. And that's what we cannot take the risk of. I mean, everyone in this program is at risk of it. I'm so sorry. Take care of yourself, okay, Dave?"

Larry Ley

At another appointment in Carmel, as an undercover DEA agent waited to meet with Cassy, he struck up a conversation with a woman named Marie in the waiting room, who was leaning against the wall in a hooded sweatshirt, her hair piled into a messy bun.

"How long you been in?" he asked her.

"A year," she said, turning toward him.

"Yeah, it's going alright?" the agent asked.

"Oh yeah," she said enthusiastically. "My first-year anniversary just came up two weeks ago." Marie retrieved a cellphone from the purse resting in the crook of her arm and pulled up an old photo of herself, taken at a time before her treatment days. "That's my difference," she said, with pride.

"Cool," he said.

The woman knew the agent was new to the clinic. She pointed to an older man in the waiting room and laughed. "Just stay committed," she told him, "like this guy."

"Thank god I don't have any more addictions other than cigarettes," the older man said.

"Ugh, it's a horrible thing to try to fight, that's for sure," Marie said, sympathizing.

The older man told the undercover agent and Marie that he started taking pain pills when he was recovering from heart surgery. "When I woke up, 'Here, take this. Take this,'" he said. "They runned my life for a long time."

"That's how I was. I got cancer when I was seventeen and got it for years, and that's where I was," Marie said, turning back to Holbrook. "Dr. Ley and everybody here, they're amazing. When you first start, it's every two weeks. Once you start lowering dosages, it's once a month. If you ever have, like, you know, 'I'm having a major panic attack, I just need someone to talk to,' I'll call them here and talk to them, and they'll talk me through it, or you call your addiction specialist and talk to them. It's not just the everyday clinic. They actually care here."

Cassy called the agent into her office, and he sat down to go through his

Rehab

intake paperwork and pay the $300 intake fee. From behind her desk, Cassy heard a woman's voice out in the hallway.

"Is that Marie out there?" Cassy asked, with a huge smile. "I haven't seen you in forever!"

"Wait until you see me!" Marie called out from the waiting room, her voice beaming.

In the report the agent later filed, he made no mention of Marie.

CHAPTER TWELVE

Wendy McEntyre

2014

While law enforcement had set their sights on pill mills and nascent Suboxone practices, the burgeoning treatment industry, now worth $35 billion annually, was escaping scrutiny from almost everyone except the townspeople of Skyforest, California, population 221, and their newest resident, Wendy McEntyre. Just a few months earlier, the remains of a patient named Donavan Doyle had been found on the side of the mountain, right below the rehab center he had attended, called Above It All.

Wendy and the Doyles still had many unanswered questions about Donavan's disappearance and death. Since meeting the Doyles, Wendy had focused on nothing else. She and Cyndi had become best friends, talking on the phone almost nightly, with Wendy reporting what she'd learned. And after months of investigating, Wendy felt certain that Above It All was hiding something. It was just hard to know what—and the employees at the treatment center, which included some of the owner's children, had been ordered not to talk. "We recently have had a few employees contacted by a woman named 'Wendy' from an 805 area code," wrote Kyle Avarell, the owner's son, in an email to staff. "If you do receive a phone call please DO NOT continue any conversation with this woman."

But the email seemed to have done nothing more than alert people to Wendy's presence. On Labor Day, three months after the group had found Donavan, Wendy and the Doyles returned once again to the scene of Donavan's death. Wendy wore a bright floral purple dress for the occasion, delighting in the fact that anybody from Above It All could simply look down the street and see them standing there, on the mountainside on Kuffel Canyon Road. And soon, employees arrived to talk.

These conversations finally gave the Doyles clarity on their son's final days. Among their visitors was Chris O'Keefe, a house manager who had seen Donavan the day before he disappeared. Heavily tattooed and stocky, wearing a backward-facing baseball cap, O'Keefe's eyes were rimmed red with tears. He was grieving the loss of his first child—a stillborn—and when he saw the Doyles standing on Kuffel Canyon Road, he realized that he finally understood their pain. He sat down on a log to tell them what he knew.

Donavan had been a difficult patient from the start, Chris explained. When he arrived and received detox meds, he became lethargic, couldn't wake up for breakfast, and couldn't attend groups. Some staff thought he had received too much medication or was psychotic. "It seemed to have gotten worse the longer he stayed here," Chris told Wendy. About a week into his stay, Donavan started wetting the bed, and the other residents started teasing him mercilessly. Chris called his boss and asked if they could move Donavan to a smaller facility, where he could be in a closer-knit group, or transfer him to a different rehab all together. This procedure was laid out in Above It All's own policies and was required by state law: if the program couldn't meet a patient's needs, the operator had a duty to refer or transfer him to another program with adequate services. In this case, that might have included a program with more intensive psychiatric care, or perhaps a call to Donavan's parents to allow them to find a more suitable program. But nothing happened.

Finally, the night before Donavan disappeared, something even more disturbing happened. Chris—who was not qualified or legally allowed to provide medical care—had given Donavan his medication at 9 p.m. Chris was talking with the other house manager at about 11:30 p.m., and was about to leave for the night, when they heard a loud crash upstairs. Donavan was the only person up there, he recalled; they had moved him into his own room because of the teasing. The two of them raced upstairs to find Donavan on the floor inside his closet, rocking back and forth. The closet rod lay on the floor behind him.

This was the same day Donavan had suggested to his dad that he might attempt suicide. And it was the same day that Cyndi had informed Kory Avarell about her son's suicide threat, asking him to keep a close watch over Donavan. Chris had no knowledge of these conversations. But it looked to him like Donavan might have just tried to kill himself. "Are you okay, Donavan?" Chris asked, repeating his name, over and over. Donavan stared right through him, as if he weren't even there.

Chris immediately called his supervisor and told her he wanted to call 911. She denied his request and told Chris to "stabilize him," he recalled. "What the fuck do you mean 'stabilize him'? I'm a house manager. Are you kidding me?" Chris stayed past his shift, and the two house managers helped Donavan to detox. They figured the detox nurse, who was required to check patients regularly, could keep an eye on him. That was the last time Chris saw Donavan alive. The next morning he disappeared.

Chris didn't know that Cyndi had texted Avarell earlier that day, telling him that Donavan was suicidal. "Please make sure he does not hurt himself," she had texted him. Not only had Avarell not ensured Donavan's safety, he also had allowed staff to leave Donavan in a room by himself, and then the program had denied him needed medical care.

AIA's own policies required employees to call 911 in the event of a suicide threat or attempt. If Donavan was trying to commit suicide, he was a danger to himself—the legal threshold for a 5150—a 72-hour psychiatric hold. But Chris's supervisor told him not to call 911. Above It All typically did so sparingly; Avarell believed many patients, including Donavan, acted out for attention, not out of real suicidal intent. "That's something the clients do a lot in order to leave," he'd later explain. "This was a call for help."

Regardless, Avarell would later say he knew nothing about this event until after Donavan had already gone missing. Chris had not entered information about it into Donavan's client file, another violation of the program's own policies, although Chris likely didn't know that because he had never received training—an additional violation of state regulations.

Then, in a meeting the next morning, Avarell again brought up Donavan's poor group attendance. He told Donavan's counselor, Rick, that Donavan should be discharged if he did not attend group. And if that happened again today, he told Rick to tell Donavan that he would have to leave.

Typically, a discharged client would receive a ride down the mountain, or a phone call, Avarell said. But that's not what happened in Donavan's case, according to Rick's notes in Donavan's file: That morning, Donavan, still in detox after his possible suicide attempt, told Rick that he "was sick and did not feel like attending" group, Rick wrote. Rick spoke to him and Donavan agreed to get ready. But when the driver arrived, Donavan refused to go, and Rick followed Avarell's orders and told Donavan that he had to leave. He didn't offer Donavan a ride, or a call to his parents. Donavan packed his belongings in a black trash bag and stalked out of the facility, swearing at Rick and grabbing for the counselor's cellphone, before attempting to punch him. Then he walked off. Soon after, Rick called Avarell, who told him not to call the police. (Avarell said he did not recall saying this.)

To Wendy, the takeaway from all of this new information was clear. Donavan had been medicated to a possible point of impairment. His concerns and preferences had been ignored, and his parents seemed to have been turned against him. When he appeared to be psychotic, and potentially suicidal, multiple AIA employees had failed to call 911. Then, the next morning, Above It All had kicked Donavan out without so much as an advance call to his parents. The program's own policies required authorities to be called if a client was in danger. As fog and snow began to obscure the road and hours passed with no sign of Donavan, no one from the facility had called 911. After all this, Wendy felt certain: Had Donavan Doyle not come to rehab at Above It All Treatment Center, he might still be alive.

Cyndi was convinced Kory Avarell had concealed what had happened to avoid being held accountable for these failures. The thought that she could have prevented her son's death haunted her. After returning home, she couldn't stop thinking about it. "I am left to wonder for the rest of my life what really happened. I am a different person than I was before all of this. It has changed me in so many ways," Cyndi texted Wendy one night, later that month. "I guess I just want you to understand why it hurts so bad to think the county can get away with what they did to me and are still doing by not investigating AIA for what they did to my son."

WENDY HAD STARTED out her investigation with the intent of finding out what had happened to Donavan. She might have stopped there. But it turned out what had occurred at Above It All seemed to be occurring at rehabs across the state, even the country. For several years, Wendy had operated a hotline for parents whose children were stuck in exploitative rehabs or sober-living homes. She advertised the hotline on her website and calls went straight to both her landline and her cellphone, 24 hours a day, seven days a week. Now, as Wendy continued investigating Above It All, she became deluged with calls.

The problem, as Wendy saw it, was that prior to the Affordable Care Act, there was little incentive for businesses to expand into treatment. It was a niche industry, largely occupied by nonprofits like Cenikor or organizations that had government contracts. But now treatment—much like the U.S. healthcare system as a whole—had become a profitable business enterprise. And unlike many other forms of medical treatment, there were no real standards or even a proven addiction cure. Most insurance companies paid for a maximum of 30 days, an arbitrary limit that contributed to high relapse rates. The industry just folded the high failure rate into its business model. "There

Rehab

is no such thing as too many trips to rehab," one rehab advertised. Many patients returned repeatedly to Above It All. "We did everything we could to make it so that they felt better. But you can't do that in 30 days," Avarell said. "It's just a cycler, you keep going over and over and over to treatment."

This was a perfect breeding ground for fraud, something that insurance companies were notoriously bad at reeling in. Despite being one of the richest nations in the world, the United States has the poorest health outcomes of any developed nation, along with the highest healthcare costs. One major reason for this is fraud. An estimated 10 percent of the $4.9 trillion spent each year on healthcare is considered fraudulent.

Insurers are uniquely poised to identify and reel in such fraud by analyzing claims and other nonpublic data. This would be particularly useful in the rehab mecca of California, which also happens to be one of the largest private insurance markets in the country. But insurers have little incentive to deal with those problems. Rising healthcare costs simply mean larger profits, and reeling in fraud costs money, which hurts their bottom line. In America's uniquely profit-driven healthcare system, unethical business practices thrive.

Wendy heard just about every scam and unethical practice that pervaded the rehab industry. For example, urine drug testing was so common and lucrative that it had become known as "liquid gold." Wendy met a mom whose son had received 42 urine tests over 88 days during his rehab stay. Soon after leaving the rehab, he died of an overdose and she received a bill for $202,860. Rehabs routinely overcharged insurance companies or performed unnecessary services. In a single year, one rehab went from billing less than $50,000 a month to more than $13 million a month, thanks in part to frequent drug testing and other unnecessary services.

When patients called Wendy's hotline with complaints about overmedicating and abuse at one particular rehab, Wendy helped extricate them from the facility, working in one instance with Michael Lohan—father of actress Lindsay Lohan—to arrange a flight for someone trying to get back home. Lohan had become something of an influencer in recovery circles since appearing on *Celebrity Rehab*. And he'd gained a reputation for helping families and patients navigate the obtuse and overwhelming treatment system.

Some years later, though, police arrested Michael Lohan on charges of selling multiple patients to one Florida rehab for close to $30,000. This practice, illegal in some states, was called "body brokering," and many of the rehabs Wendy was investigating were engaged in it. Even high-profile members of the Addiction Treatment Advocacy Coalition, a nonprofit group that represents the for-profit treatment industry (including Above It All), relied on "marketing companies" to fill beds. Treatment programs paid hefty fees for patients—from $7,500 for a client who stayed for several levels of care, up to $12,000 for a patient with especially good insurance. To find clients, marketing companies relied on body brokers, some of whom trawled AA meetings or poached patients from other rehabs, offering money or drugs. In some places in Southern California, it was so easy to get paid to attend rehab that many patients gave up on recovery and simply used rehab to fund their drug use. Others entered rehab with the intent of getting help, but found themselves kicked to the curb, like Donavan, after their insurance money ran out. In coastal cities like Costa Mesa, young people from all over the country populated homeless encampments, caught in a relentless cycle of rehab and relapse.

Regulators were ill-equipped for this rehab revolution. Despite the nearly 2,000 licensed rehabs in the state, the department employed only 16 inspectors, who worked out of the department's office in Sacramento, the capital city in northern California, near the opposite end of the state. Meanwhile, in just three years, complaints about rehabs had doubled. And deaths at rehabs were occurring at a rate of one every two weeks, not counting the many deaths that occurred off-site, at hospitals, or on the job, or in unregulated sober-living homes.

Someone who dutifully submitted a complaint, as Wendy now did incessantly, could expect to be sorely disappointed. It often took months for the department to send an investigator out on a complaint, if at all. Investigations were cursory, leading the department to declare many violations "unsubstantiated." And when the complaints were substantiated, the providers were given the opportunity to submit a "corrective action plan" and thus incurred few consequences. Despite everything she was uncovering, Wendy found that most of her complaints did nothing to deter rehabs from exploiting patients for profit. And then there was Above It All. Even after Donavan's death, the problems at the program seemed to Wendy so severe that she felt certain that someone else was would soon get hurt.

CHAPTER THIRTEEN
Chris Koon

2015

John Koon was starting to get worried. Chris was only six months in, but it seemed to John like his son was losing his grasp. Chris was sipping the Kool-Aid, accepting Cenikor's rules, and lately, instead of talking about his plans for the future, he was complaining about not getting enough cigarettes as compensation for his work.

John didn't feel like his son needed brainwashing to get better. He just needed support to become the best version of himself. But now that Chris was in there, he had to stay. Leaving would piss off the judge—and if Chris thought Cenikor was bad, wait until he saw an actual prison.

This week, Chris had worked 80 hours, partially to get away from the facility. And yet, he hadn't received extra cigarettes. Those stupid cigarettes made him feel slightly less miserable. And he was supposed to get more of them if he worked longer hours. He'd earned them. That was the rule. The rules at Cenikor could not be broken.

When his dad came to visit, this was all Chris wanted to talk about. There were so many stupid small rules Chris was required to follow at Cenikor.

Rehab

He was getting into trouble constantly, and yet here was this rule *they* were required to follow and *they* weren't doing it. He couldn't stand the injustice of it. The double standards and special treatment some people received. His family—his mother, his stepfather, as well as Granny—told Chris: "It's better than jail." Or, "at least it's not prison." Granny believed strongly in rehab over incarceration. "The alternative is far worse, Christopher," she'd say. "What do you gain in prison? Nothing. There's no purpose, there's no goodness that comes from putting some young people in prison with hardened criminals."

John noticed how isolated Chris seemed. How the structure and surveillance was breaking him. It reminded John of the prison where he worked. "We have several [prisoners] that have lost their minds through isolation," John said. "They don't come out the same." And with all his talk of rules and cigarettes, Chris seemed to have lost his way. John felt Chris had a strong mind. He was kind and always wanted what was best for people. John didn't want his son believing that he couldn't trust his own thoughts, that he couldn't figure out what was best for himself. Chris could still decide his own future. "The only way you can defeat the game that's in front of you is if you know the game," John said. "But they can't know that you know."

One day, John was at a store when he spotted a book near the register. It was a slim hardback with a dark brown cover that featured an illustration of a brain, encircled and radiating like a sun out of a man's skull. *Mind Games* was the title. It was one of these gag-gift, impulse purchases you might put on a coffee table or in a bathroom. John had a lot of those. But he opened it and one of the chapters in the book caught his eye—and now he thought about Chris.

On one of his next visits to Cenikor, John brought the book with him. Sitting next to them was another resident, who was there to monitor their conversation and make sure Chris didn't say something he wasn't supposed to say. John took out the book and silently slid it across the table. "There's some good stuff in there," he said to Chris, with a wink and a nod. Chris nodded back and accepted the gift, tucking it in the waistband of his pants.

After his dad left, Chris went to his room and opened the book to the folded page. "Mind Control Techniques," page 97, and read: "We are all vulnerable to manipulation, and there are a myriad of ways of controlling the mind. This list will help you to recognize where in your life you might be most susceptible to having your thoughts controlled by another person or organization."

Interesting, Chris thought. He continued reading.

Sleep deprivation. Creating disorientation and vulnerability by overemphasis on mental and physical activity while withholding adequate rest and sleep.

Strict rules. Often simple and benign, they are uncompromising and sometimes illogical, the repeated acceptance of which reinforces obedience and discourages individual reasoning.

Fear. Stressing of frightening consequences, including punishment and loss of salvation for the slightest transgression.

As Chris read, he began to connect the dots. These techniques resembled his experiences at Cenikor.

Sleep deprivation. Chris often worked 80 hours per week in the program. There was hardly enough time to eat, or wash, or sleep before his next shift. He never knew when the entire house would be awoken in the middle of the night for a "fire drill"; when they'd remain awake for hours, as the Cenikor staff counted off the residents and assessed everyone's behavior. During the drill, if even one person wasn't fully dressed, or stepped out of line, or broke another small rule, the staff would punish the entire group.

Strict rules. There were so many strict rules, just like this book said. They were uncompromising and illogical, and in Chris's view, just plain stupid. And the punishments for violating those rules were substantial.

Chris recalled how, when he entered the program, he was required to memorize and recite Cenikor's handbook—a lengthy list of rules, from the diet-oriented (no coffee allowed) to the obtuse (always carry a pen).

Rehab

Fear. Every week, they were required to report to staff anyone who broke a rule. And every week, each person was required to sit in the middle of a group circle while other patients screamed at them.

The words on the page shifted and clicked into place. His dad wasn't just warning him about mind control, Chris realized. He was also warning him about Cenikor. Cenikor was brainwashing him. The program was manipulating him. And he was falling for it.

When Chris had entered the facility, he was told to expect three group-counseling sessions and one one-on-one session with a licensed counselor per week. The program had begun enrolling participants in Medicaid, which required those patients to receive a certain amount of counseling per week. But unlike nursing homes and hospitals, and other facilities that received federal healthcare funds, the rehab industry was subject to little oversight. Just as in California, there was little in place in Louisiana or Texas to ensure that its rehab programs were actually providing what they were required to provide.

Chris quickly found there was no time for the counseling Cenikor had promised. At one point, there was just one full-time counselor for nearly 140 people. Cenikor seemed to have trouble hanging on to the counselors. Not only was the pay paltry—typically, between $11 and $15 an hour—but also the residents worked so much that they had no time for counseling. Many times, Chris would come home from work so exhausted he simply went up to his room, forgoing even his dinner. He didn't have the energy to talk to another human being, let alone a counselor.

One counselor, Melanie Cefalu, had managed to see Chris a couple times by tracking him down when he was already in bed. "How are you doing?" she'd pop her head into his room and ask. "Fine," Chris would reply, and she would mark that down as an hourlong session.

Melanie never imagined she would end up working for Cenikor. She had learned about their program years before, when she worked at another rehab nearby. One day, a fire alarm sounded at Cenikor and everyone exited the building. Outside, she could see men wearing pig masks. Melanie smacked her boss's arm repeatedly, trying to get her attention. "What is this?" she asked. Her boss replied, "All I can tell you is never go to work for that place." Melanie later met a friend at AA who had been court-ordered to Cenikor. She told Melanie she'd been forced to stay up all night, scrubbing the floors with a toothbrush. "I thought they needed to burn the place down," Melanie said.

Like most of the counselors who came through Cenikor, Melanie didn't have a degree or any formal training to treat addiction. Most counselors were not even technically counselors; rather, they were "counselors in training," meaning they had not yet accumulated enough experience to qualify for a license. After a nearly 30-year addiction to alcohol and pain pills, Melanie's main qualification for the job was her own recovery, spurred on by her Christian faith. She was struggling to find a full-time counseling job and had started cleaning houses to make ends meet. She called an old colleague, Peggy Billeaudeau, to catch up. It turned out Peggy was now at Cenikor and was looking to hire.

Melanie recoiled. She told Peggy what she'd heard about the Cenikor program. But Peggy told Melanie that Cenikor had changed. She said that the state had come in and forced a stop to the use of pig masks, which she explained had been a punishment imposed on residents who took second helpings at meals. And they weren't supposed to be making participants scrub the floors with a toothbrush, either.

"You'll love it here," Peggy reassured her.

"Let me pray on it," Melanie said.

Melanie decided to take the job. She didn't really have any other options. But as it turned out, neither did Peggy. She was miserable working at Cenikor.

Peggy may have been clinical director—typically a position of authority in a treatment program—but she routinely found herself sidelined by the program director, by Cenikor's corporate headquarters in Texas, and even by lower-level administrators like Patrick Odom, the graduate turned vocational director charged with putting the residents to work. She didn't have enough counselors, which is why she had been so desperate to hire Melanie.

In a previous job, Melanie had about 14 people in her caseload, which was more than enough in her view. At Cenikor, she had 50 people. It was physically and mathematically impossible to do the job. "There's not enough hours in the week to do what y'all are asking me to do," she told Peggy. And there didn't seem to be enough time for the residents, either. If they got home from work in time to go to counseling, most opted instead to eat a meal or take a bath. Work took priority over everything else. Sometimes people told her they'd go to a group session, and then Melanie watched as other residents signed their names to make it appear as though they'd been there. Counselors pretended not to notice. Falsifying the counseling records seemed to be the Cenikor way.

Tara Dixon saw this happening and felt increasingly infuriated and demoralized. The assistant to the Baton Rouge facility director, Tara was also working on her master's degree in social work and was on her way to becoming a licensed counselor. Because she needed intern hours for her degree, and because Cenikor was short-staffed, the director agreed to let Tara see residents on top of her administrative work. Short, with a round face and big eyes, Tara was used to being underestimated. Some people had warned her about Cenikor, but most counseling internships were unpaid, and she needed the wages.

But treatment at Cenikor didn't resemble anything she was learning at school. "In order to see change, you have to build trust and rapport first," Tara said. Tara didn't have enough time with residents to cement trusting relationships. She'd learned, too, that changing a person's behavior and perspective takes time. "Change out of fear isn't long-term change," she said. But fear seemed to be the basic premise of the Cenikor program.

Tara was especially alarmed at the ethical violations that occurred in the "family meetings," also known as "games," when residents would scream at the person in the middle of the circle. "It was supposed to teach the person in the chair, in the hot seat, to be humble and accept they have flaws, and all of this," Tara explained. "But nothing was really off the table. You could bring up things from their past, you could cuss at them; you know, you could completely degrade their character. And for me, from a psychological standpoint, it was very alarming."

Tara and the other counselors were encouraged to join in and to yell at the participants when they saw them sitting in the verbal chair or breaking a rule. Everyone was supposed to participate. Some counselors did. Tara couldn't bring herself to do it.

But the worst part was the work. Tara fielded phone calls for her boss and overheard every argument he had with Cenikor corporate. She listened as the director was reamed out for the facility's poor financial performance. He faced increasing pressure to make more money, and as a result, Tara saw the center ramp up the residents' already packed work schedules to unsustainable levels. She couldn't stand seeing the residents worked to the bone, too exhausted to spend any time on the issues that had brought them to Cenikor in the first place. The staff routinely canceled doctor's appointments, mental health appointments, and psychiatric care so that the participants could go to work instead. Many people who needed medication weren't getting it, either.

The exhausting, unhealthy conditions at Cenikor rendered many of its residents extremely vulnerable. Tara saw some of the employees, who were almost all graduates of the program, sexually harass the residents or start sexual and romantic relationships with them. She also saw patients who relapsed with the drugs they easily found at their job sites. It made Tara feel physically ill.

Melanie Cefalu saw the program differently than Tara. She tried to do what she could. It was certainly better than nothing, right? And speaking out was doing nobody any good. Ten-minute check-ins in a client's bedroom were not counseling sessions, but they were better than nothing at all. She could tell a lot about how a patient was doing just by looking into their eyes. Marking that check-in as a one-hour session just ensured that she—a good person—kept her job.

IN ADDITION TO Chris, another of Melanie's patients was Justin Marshall. Unlike most of her clients, Justin had not been court-ordered there.

Rehab

He was about to finish three years in prison for prescription fraud when he realized he would be better off going to rehab than going home. "Nothing there waiting for me except for drugs," he'd said. A prison case worker told him that the only place that would take him—someone without money or insurance—was Cenikor.

Justin went straight from prison to Cenikor. Unlike Chris, though, he bought into the rules immediately. Cenikor, he understood, was a behavior-modification program. He did need to change his behavior, and maybe Cenikor would help. He started working a $17 an hour job. He accepted the fact that he wouldn't get paid, except in cigarettes. He had been at Cenikor about a year when Chris arrived, and he had a court date coming up. He expected Cenikor to drive him to court, like the program did when he went to his job. But there were no available vans and drivers because everyone was working, and the staff would not allow Justin to use the wages he'd earned from the program to take a taxi or a bus. The only person Justin knew in Baton Rouge was his ex-girlfriend, but he knew she was still using and he didn't want to be around her. He told Cenikor staff that he was terrified he would relapse. Justin's fear was legitimate. Melanie and Tara and Peggy had seen a lot of people relapse at Cenikor. Some bosses had even called Melanie to retrieve workers when they were too high to work.

This was happening at other Cenikor facilities, too. People would come home from work, testing positive for all sorts of stuff. At the Houston Rodeo and after the Louisiana State University games, Cenikor workers downed leftover beer they found in plastic cups and they swallowed unidentifiable pills littered on the ground. After the hurricanes that swept through the region, Cenikor residents cleaned up peoples' homes, trawling through the fetid waters, where they found prescription medications that had fallen from people's medicine cabinets. Also treacherous were the manufacturing assembly-line jobs—the fastest, most dangerous jobs—with which many of the Cenikor participants had previous experience. The dull repetitive motion and the long hours meant some workers routinely used meth to stay awake and opioids to relieve the pain. "A vast majority of Americans that work over a certain number of hours a week are medicated or on some sort of substance," said Cody Collins, the vocational manager. "That's just the cold hard truth."

At Cenikor, none of the administrators seemed concerned that Justin was worried about relapsing. After all, these temptations were everywhere. In recovery, he had to learn to deal with them. That was the Cenikor way. With no alternative except receiving a contempt-of-court charge and jail, Justin accepted a ride to court from his ex-girlfriend, then came back with heroin and overdosed in his room. An ambulance took him to the hospital, where he spent several days recovering. When the hospital discharged him, Justin arrived back at Cenikor to find the doors locked. No one would let him back in, not even to retrieve his belongings. He spent the night on the street.

Melanie Cefalu called his mom to let her know. "It killed me," Melanie said. "You think your child is safe in treatment, you can rest." What happened to Justin bothered Melanie. And then she started mulling over the repercussions. If someone overdosed and died at Cenikor, the state would come in and investigate. "And if that happened, we were all gonna lose our licenses." She told her boss they needed to start searching the residents when they came back to the facility.

Melanie was sure the state would come in to investigate. And they had, many times before. But most of the time, Cenikor violated state regulations without any consequences. In Louisiana, rehab programs were required by law to provide at least one counselor for every 20 patients, already a large caseload by professional standards. In 2008, after consistently violating this legal requirement, Cenikor CEO Bill Bailey wrote a letter asking the state to grant an exemption and allow them one counselor for every 30 patients. The state immediately granted his request. And yet, four years later, Cenikor was violating even its own carve-out regulation. One counselor on the staff had 72 patients in her caseload—more than triple the number permitted by the original regulations. In response, Cenikor wrote to the state that they were hiring more counselors—the same response they had provided in previous years. Case dismissed.

Amid these chronic violations, the board of Cenikor—a collection of prestigious business leaders, a district attorney, and a state senator—rewarded CEO Bailey with hefty raises. In 2017, when Chris was at Cenikor, Bailey earned his highest compensation yet: $488,950.

NO CORPORATE EXECUTIVE or government official was going to stop the problems at Cenikor, so one day, Tara Dixon decided to do something about it herself. She marched into the business manager's office and requested all the time sheets for the previous six weeks. The manager handed her a thick stack of binders containing hundreds of handwritten notes. With the same rigor as she applied to her studies, Tara went through them all, entering the information into a spreadsheet and highlighting the names of those who had worked more than 40 hours each week. Most participants, Tara saw, were working between 60 and 70 hours per week.

There were even some participants who'd worked over 100 hours a week. That meant they would have had no break at all. Tara signed into the center's therapy database, where they kept track of each person's case notes and assessments, treatment plans, and attendance, and she typed in each person's name. Tara noted how many counseling and group sessions each resident had attended. Most of them went two to three months without seeing a single counselor. It was clear: her patients were spending the vast majority of their time working. The evidence was unassailable.

Tara shared what she'd learned with Peggy Billeaudeau, and Peggy offered to present Tara's findings at the Wednesday manager's meeting, where she'd see the director and other program managers. Almost everyone but Peggy was a former Cenikor graduate. Typically, a lowly counselor like Tara Dixon wouldn't be allowed to attend. But since Tara was the director's assistant, she was also there.

Peggy pulled out Tara's spreadsheet, which showed that the vast majority of participants were not getting the counseling Cenikor itself claimed to offer. Cenikor administrators launched into all their best arguments: The time sheets aren't always correct, or the work is a financial necessity. Don't you want to keep the facility open? they asked. And they pointed out that the participants *want* to work.

"Well, if he asked to shoot up, you wouldn't let him," Tara pointed out. "So why are you—if he's asking to do this other harmful behavior, working seventy hours per week—why are you letting him do that?" Her question went unanswered.

Tara left the meeting feeling dejected. But there was some reason for hope. The poor conditions in the facility had led so many clients to flee that the house count had recently dropped to 110 people. That was enough to get the attention of headquarters. Tara learned that Cenikor's vice president was planning a visit. He was a Cenikor graduate and a former facility director, but he also had a background in social work. Surely, he would understand the counselors' perspective.

On the day of his visit, the VP called all the employees to an all-staff meeting in the 'Kor room. The goal of his visit, he said, was to address the facility's poor performance. *Here we go*, Tara thought. *Rip 'em a new one*. But her hope quickly withered.

The executive told everyone that he had been addicted to drugs and alcohol, and that "psychology didn't do me shit," as Tara recalled. He was a Cenikor diehard, as if founder James Luke Austin himself were in the room. If the Baton Rouge facility wasn't working, it was because the counselors refused to get with the program. "Forget what you've learned," he told Tara and the other counselors. "If you can't do what we're doing, get out."

Peggy Billeaudeau was aghast. One of her constant frustrations with her boss was that he seemed to view former graduates of the program with no training or a high school diploma as better authorities on the treatment and counseling needs of her patients. The Cenikor way was one way. But each person is different. Each person has different needs. Peggy knew how to address that. She began listing her credentials. She wanted to remind them all that she was educated, she knew what she was doing. "So, you're telling me my master's degree means nothing?" she asked.

Rehab

"I don't give a shit about your master's degree," the executive replied.

Tara realized that Cenikor was never going to change. She finished out her internship hours and left. Peggy soon did, too. She put in her two-week notice, then just stopped showing up.

ONE NIGHT, Chris was given an unusual assignment: an overnight shift at the spice factory where Cenikor residents often worked. Chris had worked there during the day a few times. The smells and spices in the air—an acrid combination of nutmeg and chili powder and sweat—scorched his throat and eyes. That night, instead of working the assembly line, though, he'd be helping a few other workers build a support for a crane that would be used to hoist up sacks of spices.

Chris had never seen anything like it. A forklift dangled a 20-foot beam overhead while Chris and another worker scrambled beneath it to guide it into place. Chris estimated the beam weighed at least three hundred pounds. And then the guy at the other end of the beam suddenly let go. The beam shifted and knocked into Chris's shoulder. He heard a loud pop, felt a numbing sensation, and then suddenly his arm felt like it was on fire. Chris fell to the floor, grasping his shoulder and cursing. The other worker rushed over to ask if he was okay. The boss stood back. Eventually, though, he came over and told him, "Look, man, calm down. I don't want you to go into shock . . . just calm down." Another worker said they could finish the job without him. Chris overheard a manager nearby say something he wasn't meant to hear: "Man, that boy got hurt. Thank god he's from Cenikor."

Eventually, Chris got up and sat on the side. He told everyone he was okay, but he refused to keep working the shift. He was surprised when they left him alone. He watched the remainder of the work in silence. The next day, Chris awoke with a throbbing arm and another assignment on the work sheet. He couldn't believe it. He went to the vocational office to find Patrick

Odom. He had to go to the hospital. Something wasn't right. To his relief, Patrick agreed.

At the hospital, Chris told the doctor that the pain felt like a mean little man in his shoulder, just stabbing him constantly. The doctor reviewed X-rays to rule out other causes of pain, like bone spurs, and told Chris he had probably torn his rotator cuff, a common injury in manual labor and construction jobs. The doctor recommended Chris come back for an MRI to confirm the diagnosis, and to determine the best option for treatment. At minimum, Chris would need physical therapy. If it was really bad, he might even need surgery. Regardless of the cause, the doctor told Chris he needed to rest his arm.

Back at Cenikor, Chris tracked down Patrick and and told him he needed to go back for an MRI. Patrick barely acknowledged the hospital paperwork. "You're a strong guy, Chris. You can handle this," Chris recalled he said.

Chris felt like a fly whose wing had been pulled off. "Man, I don't think I could go to work right now," he said.

"The work is not optional," Patrick replied. If Chris wanted to stay at Cenikor, he needed to work. "If you're not helping us, then we can't help you," he explained. If Chris wanted an MRI, he could get it where he came from. Chris, like many of the residents at Cenikor, had come from jail. He was already halfway done with the program. If he left now, he'd probably end up in state prison.

Chris knew so many people at Cenikor who had gotten hurt. There were a lot of small injuries, like chemical burns and cuts and scrapes. And there were even worse ones. Like Chris's friend Scott; in his first two months at Cenikor, he broke his cheekbone in several places after he fell off a scaffold. Or Cory, who was working the overnight shift at a plant without adequate lighting and damned near sawed off his index finger. And there was a guy who crushed his hand in an industrial press, another guy who fell off a scaffold at a chemical plant and shattered his knee. Two different people had broken their backs on the job—one who was trimming a tree without wearing a safety harness and another who was repairing an electrical wire without any training.

Chris didn't know it, but in 1995, one guy had even died in the program. Larry Hart had been sentenced to Cenikor for a DUI. He was stacking office chairs onto storage racks at an office-supply warehouse when he stepped onto a scaffold, lost his balance, and plummeted to the concrete floor. After a lengthy investigation, the federal Occupational Safety and Health Administration (OSHA) had found that neither the company involved nor Cenikor had provided Larry with safety training and personal protective equipment, nor had they installed guardrails that might have prevented Larry's fall. Still, the agency let Cenikor off with a warning: "Cenikor officials should take a more active role in providing quality training," the letter said.

But more than 20 years later, Chris and several of his friends had been hurt because of similar unsafe conditions in the workplace. "It's like a fucking drop in the ocean. Who doesn't get hurt?" Chris said. Of course, his shoulder hurt. It really, really hurt. But he was used to hurting, so he didn't get an MRI. For several days, he did chores around the facility. Then he went back to work.

CHRIS CONTINUED TO work while the pain in his arm persisted. He found that if he didn't lift his arm up over his head, he could keep the worst pain at bay. But it was bad during hard work days, when he woke up in the morning, or couldn't sleep at night. Chris was about 15 months into his time, one of the very few people from his original group to make it this far. There was some comfort in being one of the lone survivors, but with it came some fear as to how long he could possibly last. What would happen to him if he didn't make it to the end? People who considered leaving Cenikor faced threats from staffers. They might relapse, they might end up homeless, or penniless, or back in prison. It didn't seem like a day went by that someone didn't mention another person who had overdosed and died.

Chris Koon

Throughout his life, Chris had struggled with pilonidal cysts, or small sacs of skin that become infected, usually at the top of the buttocks, just above the sacrum. Sometimes they went away on their own, but until they healed, even the touch of a sheet or his underwear could cause Chris sharp jolts of pain. One day, Patrick sent Chris out to one of his least favorite jobs, at a construction company called Coastal Bridge, a prolific contractor for the state of Louisiana that often won highway and bridge projects by submitting the lowest bid. It did so by skimping on other costs—for example, by pocketing the money intended to pay for an employee's health insurance or almost $1 million in payments for a police security detail.

When Cenikor sent workers to Coastal Bridge, the company frequently worked them for over 14-hour days, in the sweltering Louisiana heat. One day, Chris was bent over, shoveling gravel, when a cyst burst. He had suspected it was infected, and when he went to the bathroom, he realized it was. But Cenikor refused to send a van. He'd have to wait until his regularly scheduled van pick-up came, seven hours later. Chris kept working as his wound oozed. He never got to see a doctor.

The longer Chris stayed at Cenikor, the more acutely aware he became of how little his life mattered to the program. It wore on him. One night at work in January 2017, his ankle—the one that had been shattered in a three-wheeler accident when he was a teenager—started hurting. When a coworker offered him a Lortab, Chris took it. When he was back at Cenikor, he attempted to fake his urine test, but the facility director caught it and set Chris back a month. It was Chris's second relapse since he'd arrived. Cenikor sent a letter to Judge Warren Willet.

Judge Willet, Christopher Koon was recently placed on the Program Managers wall for suspicion of using. He was caught using fake urine by the Facility Director. . . . Chris Admitted to using Opiates (Lortab). This is Chris' second relapse here, all times he has attempted to falsify the test using fake urine. Please advise what you would like done, he is separated from our client base at the moment. Thank you.

Rehab

A month later, Chris developed another cyst. This one felt even more painful than before. When he talked to his mom, she didn't understand why he hadn't gone to see a doctor. "Tell them to take you to the doctor, Christopher," Carrie said.

"Mama, you don't understand," he said. "If you miss work, it's a problem."

Carrie didn't understand. Chris lived at Cenikor. He didn't have a choice. That made Cenikor responsible for his safety and health. She pushed Chris harder. He had to insist on going to the doctor. When he finally made it to the hospital, Chris learned he had MRSA, a highly contagious staph infection.

A program manager at Cenikor told Chris he'd have to leave. He could come back in a month, once the MRSA cleared up. But Carrie felt that something wasn't quite right. As a nurse herself, she didn't understand why Chris had to leave because of the infection. With the proper precautions, no one else would catch it. All this time, she'd been dismissing Chris's complaints. But maybe there was something to them after all.

When she arrived to pick Chris up, she hit the Record button on her phone. "So you're discharging him for a medical reason?" she asked.

"Yes, ma'am," said the female program manager. She called Chris a "gentle giant." "He's welcome to come back once it's resolved."

A day later, Chris's attorney showed him another letter that the judge received from Cenikor written by a different program manager just a few days before Chris's departure:

> I would like to know where we stand on the termination of this client.", Chris K. should not be permitted to remain in this program. Chris K., in my opinion, [is] "Non-responsive" to treatment. He left his room a mess this morning, was found to be sitting in the kitchen office reading a book while in behavior management. He has relapsed repetitively, his standards are terrible, he is consistently late to the floor and today has made the decision to not honor his assessment. I would like an update as to the status of his legal action to remove Chris K. from this program.

Chris Koon

Chris was on the verge of beginning the reentry phase of Cenikor's program, when he might have been able to begin earning a wage and pay Cenikor monthly rent to live there. It's when he might have been able to begin saving money to leave and plan his next steps. And now, just as he was about to attain some independence, just as he was about to stop forfeiting all his wages to Cenikor, he was being expelled.

Despite what they'd told Carrie, the letter showed Cenikor had had no intention of letting Chris return to the program. Judge Willet had several letters from Cenikor staffers, all badmouthing Chris's performance in the program. Now, one and a half years after beginning at Cenikor, Chris would return to Judge Willet's courtroom for sentencing. He was back where he'd started: facing five years in prison.

CHAPTER FOURTEEN

April Lee

2014

At first, April Lee viewed herself as above the people living on the street. Kensington was just where April got her dope. She'd find the dope man, go to the corner store, and buy a cherry-filled honey bun. Then she'd hurry over and plop down in a sunny patch of grass in an empty lot across from the towering Roman Catholic community center. She portioned out the bun throughout the day, eating a little before she shot up, licking and savoring the sticky syrup from her fingers, then saving the rest for after she awoke. One day, she threw the plastic wrapper on the ground, and a man who was sleeping there asked her what she was doing. "Excuse me, this is my home," he said. "I sleep here." Suddenly, April got it. What was home, anyway? It was better not to remember. This was her life. This was home now.

She began squatting in abandoned row houses, which were plentiful in the neighborhood. She found used furniture on the street and moved it inside. She shared her drugs and collected people. Many of the users were young—in their early 20s. At 26, April was usually the oldest, and sometimes they called her "Mom." She took "bird baths" at the McDonald's at Second

Rehab

and Lehigh, and sometimes at the drop-in center for women. At the drop-in center, she would also pick up toiletries and clothing, like a pencil skirt and a button-down shirt that made her feel "high class." Indeed, as April began working beneath the gigantic shadow of the El, she found men picking her up who seemed to belong to another world entirely. One man claimed to be a judge, another a lawyer. The clientele gave her a feeling of status. She looked with disdain at some of the people crowding the streets who wore the same clothes day in, day out, who slept in filth and seemed like they hadn't washed themselves for months. At least she wasn't like them. She took care of herself. She was proud when a guy picked her up and remarked on how good she smelled.

In Kensington, turning tricks came with considerable risk. For one, the police regularly patrolled the area to stack up arrests. More than 77 percent of the 1,420 prostitution-related arrests that year were of sex workers, with many repeat arrests, including April. The job was physically dangerous, too. Only a few years earlier, the police had been pursuing the "Kensington Strangler," a serial killer who targeted prostitutes by picking them up, taking them to secluded spaces, and strangling them. The police initially arrested the wrong man, sowing further distrust among Kensington residents, before finding the actual culprit. By the time April entered Kensington, the strangler had finally been arrested, but other predators were known to prowl the Track.

One time, a john had just paid April $20 for a blowjob when he pulled out a gun and told her he was a cop. He demanded she give him the money back, but she refused and jumped out of the car, intent on delivering her hard-won pay to the dope man. Another time, she was with a john on the top floor of an abandoned house when someone downstairs knocked over a candle. As flames licked the foot of the stairs, April's john got up to flee, but April refused to let him leave until he paid her the money he owed. He did, just in time for them both to make it out alive.

Once scared of needles, April became excellent at finding a vein. Soon, all the old timers who'd blown out every vein began lining up, calling her "Doc." April plunked herself onto a ragged love seat outside a corner store

April Lee

near the Conrail tracks and took people first come, first serve. Sometimes a line formed against the side of the bodega.

April felt like she was following a GPS navigator that had accidentally been programmed to the wrong destination. This was not where she wanted to end up, but she could not figure out how to chart another path. She couldn't go to rehab. Aside from her participation in the drug economy, she had no reliable income. She had no home. She had nowhere else to go, no one else who was in a position to help her. *This shit ain't normal*, April thought, when something crazy happened. But the longer this went on, the more her sense of what was normal shifted.

The only time the old semblance of normal returned was when she thought of her kids. From time to time, she brought bread, meat, and cheese to her sister's house, where her oldest son, Derrick, was living, to make him a sandwich. Derrick seethed as the adults in the room rolled their eyes at his mother, who didn't seem to notice their contempt—probably because she was loaded. She wasn't allowed to use any of their food, including the condiments. So, she made Derrick sandwiches without mayonnaise.

IN NOVEMBER, April awoke to find herself dusted with snow. A flattened cardboard box that had so far protected her from the mud underneath had become soggy. She looked down at her feet, and once again she recalled her mother. Her feet were cracked and bleeding.

She was tired, and it began to show. "Aren't you guys tired of this shit?" she asked one day, a needle sticking out of her arm. They were all squatting for the night inside another decrepit row house. A fellow squatter looked up at her, shaking his head. "April, get the hell out of my house."

Down the block was Prevention Point, a prominent nonprofit located in an old church in the heart of Kensington that had originally started as an underground needle exchange in 1991, during the height of the AIDS crisis. At the time, possessing a syringe was illegal in the state of Pennsylvania.

Rehab

State officials threatened to arrest the group, but after heavy activist lobbying, Philadelphia's mayor legalized the possession of syringes in the city, beginning the organization's ascent. By the time April had landed in Kensington, Prevention Point had been credited with preventing more than 10,000 HIV infections from injection drug use. Although it was unlicensed, unmonitored, and partially underground—needle exchanges remained illegal in most of Pennsylvania—Prevention Point had grown into a behemoth of city-funded services, clean drug use supplies, homeless shelters, and case management. It was the first line of help and support for many of the drug users in Kensington. April began picking up used needles and taking them to Prevention Point to exchange for new ones. An employee trained her on how to use naloxone, an overdose-reversal drug that, at the time, was administered via needle.

Fentanyl, a synthetic opioid that is 50 times more potent than heroin, was beginning to overtake the drug supply, causing escalating rates of overdose deaths. April sold the works—three for a dollar—to support her own habit, and as she encountered people overdosing, she tried to bring them back to life. April liked to go to a particular row house to shoot up. It was a shell of a house, with part of the roof missing and with only joists and beams in many places instead of floors. The walls were black and gray, smudged with feces. Empty bottles and dirty syringes littered the surfaces. April was making her way down the treacherous stairs when she spotted a man on the floor.

He stuck out. He was young and white. He had weight on him. His clothes looked not only clean but also expensive. "Fucking fresh," April noted. On his feet were a pair of gleaming white and blue Nikes. April knelt down and started shaking him. When he didn't wake up, she shot him up with naloxone, but he was no longer breathing. He was gone. April leaned back and took in the scene. A young man with all the privileges of this world, laying dead in the filth of this house. She wondered who he was, how he had arrived at this place. Before she could check for ID, another man searched his pockets for cash. Finding none, he took his shoes and left. April sat there awhile longer. This was the fourth person she had tried to save but had been too late to help. Then she too walked out the door.

April Lee

ONE DAY, April was nodding out with a white girl she knew when the girl became unconscious and began to gurgle—the telltale sign of overdose. April shot her up with naloxone, then called 911. April rode with her to Temple University's Episcopal Campus hospital.

The spires of the castle-like complex, more than a century old, towered above April as she followed the girl, who was barely conscious, through the sliding doors, metal detectors, past a garbage bin full of liquor bottles and confiscated paraphernalia, and into the waiting room of the emergency department. The teaching hospital sat in the epicenter of the city's epidemic with security guards stationed at every door. Between the low-income immigrants who lived in Kensington and the homeless drug users who crowded the streets, the hospital was overwhelmed with demand for its services. One time, April saw someone leaving the hospital in the dead of winter, in the middle of the night, wearing nothing on her feet but slippers.

For emergency rooms all over the country—particularly those serving low-income communities—this scene had become the standard state of affairs. Overcrowding became a concern in the medical community in the 1980s, when federal law mandated that hospitals and ambulance services provide care to anyone needing emergency treatment, regardless of citizenship, legal status, or ability to pay. Ever since, amid declining rates of primary care, emergency rooms had become one of the main sources of medical care, particularly for low-income and uninsured patients, who were three times more likely to use ERs than insured patients. Those crowded emergency rooms also led to astronomical wait times, to ambulances being turned away, and to burnt-out providers. A survey by the American Hospital Association found the problem was especially bad at urban and teaching hospitals, with more than 50 percent of hospitals reporting their ERs at or over capacity.

This situation made the emergency room at Episcopal one of the only sources of medical care or help for people in crisis, especially unhoused people struggling with addiction, like April. At any given time, there could be up to 100 patients admitted to the hospital suffering from complications of drug use—overdoses, abscesses, sepsis. But the hospital was ill-equipped for the task.

Like most hospitals and even most treatment programs, Episcopal at the time responded to addicted patients by providing a short-term taper—methadone in decreasing amounts, for just three days. This might be enough to temporarily ease some withdrawal symptoms, but it did little to relieve other symptoms of addiction that could linger for months. And it did nothing to address a patient's underlying addiction. "It's absolute nonsense. You can't fix someone's dependence on a substance in three days, no matter what it is," said Dr. Joseph D'Orazio, who would later join Episcopal. "That's like snake oil. That's what Dr. Oz sells. Not treatment."

Most patients never stuck around long enough to receive the three-day detox, opting instead to leave the hospital. Others would awake from the overdose, or even an amputation, and abruptly leave, knowing the only solution to their agony was another fix. Nearly 4.5 percent of patients who came to Episcopal after a nonfatal overdose died within the year—a rate of death far higher than for any other medical emergency, such as chest pain. And most of the patients who died were young, in their 20s and 30s, in contrast to the patients who died from other medical conditions such as diabetes or heart attack.

In 2015, a study at Yale New Haven Hospital found that emergency-room patients who were given buprenorphine were twice as likely to be in addiction treatment a month later than patients who received a pamphlet with phone numbers for treatment programs. Buprenorphine by this point had been available to patients in the United States for nearly 15 years, and yet Episcopal, and most other emergency rooms and hospitals across the country, didn't even have it on the premises. But even at those that did, Black patients were half as likely as white people to receive the treatment after an overdose.

April waited at the hospital for hours, standing alongside the girl, who was placed on a cot in the crowded hallway of the emergency department. Still, April recalled, hardly anyone came to check on her or to tend to her—no

April Lee

nurses, no medical technicians. Finally, the girl woke up, and an employee came and asked if she was alright. After April's friend nodded, the employee cleared her to leave.

"You're not going to offer anything? Detox or anything? No counseling? She almost died," April remembered asking. "They're, like, 'No, this happens all the time.'"

As they left the hospital, the girl scurried away—likely to quell her withdrawal symptoms. April barely registered her departure. She felt numb. Even in this brief reprieve from street life—in the aftermath of someone almost dying—there was no one willing to help them. The only relief came from drugs.

April returned to the Track. She had been arrested twice in Kensington, both times related to prostitution. The last time around, she had failed to show up for her court appearance. She knew there was a warrant out for her arrest. She'd learned to recognize the vice squad and their tactics. This time, when she spotted an undercover officer, she would not flee. Instead, she got into his car. He was a Black man who looked to be in his 50s. She had never seen him before, but he pretended to be a regular, yelling out the window at another woman who was walking the Track, as if to prove he knew her. April went through the motions. She told him her price, took his money, and anticipated that other police officers would open the passenger side door and pull her out. April was so tired. She needed to stop herself from using. She needed to get away from all this. And the only option she saw was a jail cell. When the officers swarmed the car, April put up her wrists and went willingly.

THE CELL WAS FRIGID, but April felt hot as she detoxed, catching glimpses of her cell mate between feverish bouts of vomiting and shitting on the jailhouse floor. Still, April didn't want to leave. She knew that if she left, she would relapse.

So she told her family not to bail her out. She insisted they leave her

Rehab

there. Within about three weeks, a nonprofit group that provided financial aid to low-level offenders posted her bail. Suddenly, April learned she would be leaving jail in two days. She panicked. She needed a plan for how to stay clean when she returned to the streets.

"Listen. I'm telling you," she begged the jail's social worker. "One of three things is going to happen if I go back on the streets. I'm going to end up back here. I'm going to abscond because I'm not going to show up for probation. Or I'm going to die. Put me somewhere."

April might have hoped to enter one of the select programs that contracted directly with the courts and the city of Philadelphia. These formal recovery homes provided housing, structure, and sobriety while the residents attended intensive outpatient treatment. But these programs, monitored and inspected by the city, were few and far between.

When the program started in 1995, the city funded five homes. Since then, the number of city-funded homes had grown to 21, making up a grand total of 288 beds—far fewer than the thousands of beds needed to serve Philadelphia's sprawling population of homeless people in need of treatment. Overdose deaths alone totaled more than 720 in 2015.

Consequently, most people who needed recovery housing went the informal route. Some 200 recovery homes existed in the city, serving about 4,000 people across Kensington, Frankford, and North Philadelphia, which were the low-income neighborhoods in the city that had some of the highest rates of poverty, overdoses, and gun violence. The vast majority of those places were not licensed or regulated, allowing their operators—in the worst cases—to cram in as many people as possible, with little concern for squalor, bed bugs, or active drug use. Many homes accepted kickbacks from treatment programs for sending them their residents, or they farmed out the residents for labor, including work on political campaigns, attending rallies, hanging posters, or working the polls. Nonetheless, these homes—like the one April had been forced to kneel and pray in—were often the only option for people leaving jail and without a home to go to.

The jail's social worker told April about one recovery program. The

April Lee

Christian lady who runs it, she said, comes up to the jail every so often. Maybe she has a spot. So, April and the social worker called the program together. The next day, a guard retrieved April from her cell. They walked into a holding area, where April and several others retrieved the scant belongings they had carried into the jail and waited to be released. It had been raining when April was arrested, so her clothes and book bag were soaked. Now, everything stank of mildew and body odor. Her white puffy jacket was stained gray. She changed back into her jeans, and she was surprised to find she had trouble zipping them up. After months of living on the street, subsisting on one honey bun a day, those few days while incarcerated had gifted her some extra pounds.

April rifled through her book bag and found another surprise buried at the bottom: a bag of dope. She averted her eyes, checked the bag, and looked away again. How the hell was that still there? How the hell did the guards not find it? The police who arrested her? Someone from her cell block, whom she knew from Kensington, came over to ask her what was up.

"I got a bag of dope," April said through gritted teeth.

"April, knock the fuck off."

April couldn't believe it. She needed to get rid of that bag of dope. She cradled the backpack in her arms and ran to the toilet, quickly flushing it all down. April breathed a sigh of relief. The immediate temptation was gone. All she needed to do now was make it to this recovery house.

Another woman getting discharged told April she could give her a ride to the train. She and three other women got into the car and rolled down the windows. Soon, April regained a sense of calm, as the cold wind blew through the window and swept the odor away from her nose.

Then one of her companions in the car pulled out weed and a crack pipe. *What the fuck?*, April thought, as the women began passing it around. She was practically bouncing around in her seat. *Let me the fuck out of here. Let me out now.*

The woman pulled over at Kensington and Allegheny, April's old stomping grounds, and let April out. April put her blinders on. Around here, she was

Rehab

known as "Mom," or "Doc," because she was especially gifted at finding even the most blown-out veins. She was only a side glance away from throwing away those few days of sobriety. The stakes were high; overdose is the leading cause of death among recently released prisoners, and studies have shown that the risk of a fatal overdose goes up dramatically after a stint of incarceration.

April ran into the SEPTA train station and got on the train. Then she realized she was going in the wrong direction. She got off at the Somerset stop, in the heart of Kensington, and started hauling ass.

"Hey, Doc!" someone yelled. "Where the fuck you been at?"

April ducked her head down. "Nowhere!" she screamed. "I'm getting on this train!" She went down the stairs and back up onto the platform, this time headed in the right direction. April took a train and then a bus to Germantown, getting off outside a convenience store. The sky had begun to darken. It was freezing cold, and April could not feel her big toe. The snow had developed a top layer of ice that crunched under April's feet as she walked. She walked past a Chinese restaurant, a donut shop, a beat-up mailbox, and up half a block. She stopped at a brick building with a square stucco storefront. There were two frosted windows in the front, formed in the shape of crosses, and a movie-style marquis that confirmed her arrival at the program.

She knocked. There was no answer. April began pounding on the door. Still, no one came. *No*, April said to herself, *I'm not fucking leaving.*

She looked around. There was a fire escape that had not been cleared, still covered in snow and ice, on the side of the house. She began climbing the rusted metal steps, finally ascending to a door at the top, where she banged again. No answer.

April went back downstairs and surveyed the street. Next door was a beige Victorian building that seemed connected to this one. She could see lights on through the windows. She squeezed through the locked metal gate and knocked on the front door. When no one answered, she climbed the fire escape on the right side of the building. This time, a woman appeared at the window. She was short, with dark hair.

"Please," April yelled through the window. "I'm supposed to be here."

April Lee

The woman gestured for April to meet her downstairs. April made the treacherous descent back down the fire escape. The woman was waiting for her at the front door. She told her that the building was closed. Come back tomorrow, she said.

April burst into tears. She told the woman the whole story. How she'd just been released. How she'd found dope in her bag. How she'd flushed it down the toilet. How she'd hitched a ride in a car in which everyone was smoking crack. How she'd taken the wrong train, back to Kensington, where she was sure she'd relapse and die of a heroin overdose, just like her uncle had. Or maybe of AIDS, like her mom. The lady stared in silence as April unburdened herself, snot dripping down her nose, the numbness in her toe creeping up her leg. "I can't guarantee I'll make it back tomorrow," April said. "I ain't going to make it back."

CHAPTER FIFTEEN

Larry Ley

2014

While April Lee begged for her life on the snowy doorstep of a sober-living home, local authorities and the federal government were closing in on Dr. Larry Ley.

In June 2014, seven months into the investigation, the team decided it was time to bring Dr. Ley's case to the U.S. Attorney. Federal charges made the most sense, since the investigation was led by the DEA and it spanned several towns and two counties, which otherwise would require filing in two separate courts. They set up a meeting with the Department of Justice prosecutor who had approved Gary Whisenand's request to use undercover officers. The meeting did not go well. The federal prosecutor thought the officers hadn't unearthed enough to make the case. He said he would pass.

Major Aaron Dietz of the Carmel Police Department—and the head of the local task force—decided to try again. He told Dennis Wichern, the head of the DEA's regional unit, that he had a relationship with another federal prosecutor, had spent time with him over the years at annual Christmas luncheons. That prosecutor, Joe Hogsett, had told Dietz to call him if he ever

Rehab

needed anything. Dietz decided now was the time to call and "plea or beg for assistance on this case," he'd later write. "If this case doesn't fit in the federal courts, I have no idea one that would."

Dietz called and set up another meeting with Hogsett and his second-in-command, the longtime chief of the drug and violent crimes unit. This, too, went poorly. The case was not prosecutable, they said. The investigators needed more.

Josh Minkler offered suggestions. Have you had an undercover try to buy a prescription from Ley outside of the office? They could try calling him and arranging a meeting at a McDonald's to deliver a prescription, "like a dope deal," or have an undercover officer hired as an employee and unearth damning information that way. Dietz made it clear he didn't want to hear what Minkler had to say.

Minkler felt the officers had "treated me like I was a first-year deputy prosecutor assigned to screening misdemeanors, rather than the First Assistant U.S. Attorney who had also prosecuted all sorts of drug cases in federal court (including several docs) for the last 20 years," Minkler later wrote, scolding Wichern for his team's conduct. "[T]o treat me like that in front of Joe—who happens to be the United States Attorney—was embarrassing for me." Nonetheless, Hogsett offered to have someone on staff give the case another look. Wichern sent Minkler a lengthy summary of the case, all the details that would be in a probable-cause affidavit to authorize Ley's arrest. Minkler said he would share it with his prosecutor Matt Brookman, the lead drug-enforcement task force attorney. "I trust you when you say this is a worthy case, and that is why I will send it to Matt and ask him to take a hard look," Minkler wrote to Wichern on June 25.

About a week later, Brookman emailed Wichern his verdict. "After a careful review, my analysis is exactly the same as that which [the U.S. attorneys] provided to your agents and investigators," Brookman wrote. The case was not strong enough.

Fortunately, Dietz still had the backing of Hamilton County. A local prosecutor was willing and ready to file the case. And since the DEA was the lead agency involved, all of Ley's and DORN's seized assets would go straight to law enforcement.

AS THE DEA prepared the case, Dr. Larry Ley and the men investigating him had an unlikely convergence in a local news article published July 8, 2014, on the news website *The Carmel Current*. The story centered mainly on an interview with Major Aaron Dietz, who painted a picture of Carmel's seedy underbelly and reflected law enforcement's long-held beliefs about addiction treatment. Dietz explained that anyone—young, old, professional, criminal—could develop a heroin addiction. It spared no one. And it had arrived in Carmel. "Heroin is not new. It's just new here," Dietz said. "Until we change demand, we won't eliminate the problem."

To curtail demand, the task force was focused on surveilling and arresting drug users, Dietz explained, repeating talking points on addiction that were now almost 100 years old, such as the idea that addiction was incurable, and that incarceration was the only way to stop its spread. Since February, Dietz said, they had identified 100 people who were criminal drug abusers. And they had recently arrested seven drug users for theft—arrests he promised would impact the rate of other crimes. Dietz claimed that each of their seven arrestees had admitted to committing "more than 100 crimes apiece in the previous 30 days."

Dietz said he wished his investigators could arrest more drug dealers, but that undercover officers needed money to purchase drugs to seal the deal for arrests, and his task force just did not have the funding to do that. "We're really working on a slim budget," he said, not mentioning the resources the task force was pouring into undercover operations at DORN.

As for how to deal with drug users? Rehabilitation doesn't work, Dietz said. The real solution to the opioid epidemic, he offered, is to restore law-enforcement funding and allow police to adopt the punitive approach utilized during the crack-cocaine epidemic. Mandatory minimum sentences work, he said. "Incarceration does affect in a positive way our crime," Dietz concluded.

Rehab

To evaluate Dietz's claims, the journalist for the piece turned to Larry Ley, the only Suboxone provider in town, and thus the authority on opioid addiction treatment in Carmel. Dr. Ley told him that the city was "in the midst of a horrendous epidemic." But with proper treatment, "families and lives can be restored," the *Carmel Current* piece read. "A phrase he said he often hears is, 'What a miracle,' or 'We had Christmas for the first time in four years.'" The problem, Ley explained, is that most people—including doctors—do not believe addiction can be treated. "The public doesn't buy into the disease model [of addiction]," Larry said. "The answer isn't arresting and sending them to jail. It's treatment."

And then, in typical Larry Ley fashion, he gave himself as much credit as he could. "I've put more dealers out of business than any cop has," he said.

The article soon reached Major Aaron Dietz. A few hours after it came out, he dashed off an email. "You might like this article in the *Carmel Current*," he wrote to the local prosecutor and Wichern.

"Holy Schneikies!" the prosecutor replied.

The team had been officially investigating Larry Ley and DORN for eight months. Their names had intermingled on confidential investigative reports, but they never had appeared publicly. Dietz was particularly amused by Larry's assertion that he'd eradicated more dealers "than any cop has."

"He's right!" Dietz wrote. "He took the dealers business by becoming the Pablo Escobar of opiates!!!" It was almost as if the doctor were taunting them, challenging them to prove him wrong.

AS THE SUN began to rise, about two weeks after the article appeared, the team swarmed their targets. More than 70 agents, investigators, and officers from more than a dozen different departments fanned out across Hamilton and Howard counties, carrying a 60-page-long briefing document, replete with photographs of all DORN employees and information about their cars, homes, schedules, and families.

Larry Ley

In Noblesville, officers screeched to a halt in front of a DORN facility, pushing Larry Ley against the trunk of a police cruiser and handcuffing him while patients gaped at them from outside the front doors. In Fishers, Dr. George Agapios, his wife, and children awoke to banging on their front door. In Carmel, Ley's second-in-command, Andrew Dollard, was en route to the clinic when officers pulled him over at gunpoint. Office manager Cassy Bratcher answered the door in her pajamas and watched in shock as officers searched her home. They even arrested Joe Mackey, Cassy's brother, who worked four hours a month as the parking lot attendant. They took in everyone on staff, except for the police officers who'd provided security.

"I don't understand," Dr. Luella Bangura said at her kitchen table, an officer and agent standing over her as she stared blankly at a document they wanted her to sign, forfeiting her right to prescribe controlled substances. The doctor was still dressed in her slippers and pajamas.

"Let me explain something to you," an agent told her. "By not cooperating, by not voluntarily signing your DEA registration, by not cooperating, your chances diminish significantly after your arrest."

"I am cooperating," she said. It had not quite gotten through her head that she was going to jail. "This all a misunderstanding." It was a refrain that would be echoed throughout the day by Andrew Dollard and George Agapios and Cassy, as they, too, encountered law enforcement for the first time in their lives.

THE SUN WAS high in the sky by the time Dietz, Wichern, and other officials filed into the council chambers at Carmel City Hall, a grand colonial-style building with mint-colored walls, an ornate blue-and-rose–patterned carpet, and a gleaming brass chandelier. The officials, wearing grim expressions suitable for the occasion, sat side by side in plush red chairs behind a wood-paneled dais. Dietz sat in the middle, beneath the official Carmel seal, with the motto "A Partnership for Tomorrow." A half dozen mic stands littered the table.

Dietz launched the press conference that would become a showcase for law enforcement and journalists' ignorance about addiction. He framed their case as a win in the nationwide battle against opioids. "Opiate drugs are a problem in our communities. According to the Centers for Disease Control, more people die from prescription drugs than car accidents in the United States," Dietz explained. He read off the names of all 11 people arrested and their charges, identifying Larry Ley as the ringleader. "We make no distinction between Dr. Ley and any other drug dealer," he said. Then he opened the floor to questions.

"Do you expect more arrests?"

"Yes, there's a possibility more people could be arrested."

"Give us a sense of these people who were buying these drugs and how he cultivated this clientele and how much they were paying for this Suboxone," another reporter asked.

"I'll take this one," Wichern said, peering over his wire-rimmed glasses. "Hundreds of patients. The standard fee every month was $120 to $160, and word would get out that the DORN clinic was an easy provider for Suboxone."

"Is this going to be affecting the drug trade here?"

"I'll take that," Dietz said, offering an answer that reflected common police perceptions of Suboxone treatment. "This type of ruse of a clinic perpetuates the problem because people are still addicted to a drug. This is not fixing the problem . . . Opiate drugs and prescription meds [are] a gateway to heroin. That's why we have heroin . . . people get addicted to the opiate drug prescriptions and then go to cheaper, readily available heroin."

A reporter wanted to know why the case had been filed locally, rather than at the federal level. Wichern sidestepped the question, making no mention of the fact that federal prosecutors had declined to take the case. It took skilled attorneys to take on such a challenging case, he explained, implying his team had deliberately chosen local prosecutors. He pointed to the Howard County prosecutors sitting beside him. "To my right are two accomplished and skilled attorneys who were the lead people in the prosecution of Dr. Wagoner."

"Should people feel comfortable that we have rid the scourge of Suboxone in the community?" another reporter asked. It was the last question and the most powerful one during a press conference littered with factual errors and misunderstandings about opioid addiction treatment.

"I would classify [Dr. Ley] as the ringleader for our area. Our state. He's really significant," Diez said. "I would classify him as the Pablo Escobar of Suboxone prescriptions of Indiana, if you will. One of a kind that we've seen."

Without acknowledging the treatment shortage, Dietz said DORN's former patients could look up other providers for help. Then he brought the media event to a close.

THAT NIGHT, EVERY TV station in Indiana seemed to carry the news of the DORN raids and arrests. "This was a thorough investigation, involving 27 undercover visits" reported Derrik Thomas, a 35-year veteran of Indianapolis's ABC news program *RTV6*, standing outside DORN's office door in Carmel. His report, echoing the press conference, portrayed Suboxone as no different from OxyContin or heroin, and DORN as no different from pill mills, which were fueling the epidemic. "Patients would come to the doctor's office and obtain Suboxone without a physical examination," he said, implying Larry Ley had sold and distributed the medication himself. "Suboxone was selling for $120 per visit."

Outside DORN's office, Derrick Thomas stopped a man who'd climbed up the back staircase for his appointment, only to find the doors closed. The man, David Hayes, avoided the camera, barely looking up from behind his gray trucker cap, and told Thomas he had been a patient of Ley's for four years.

"Are you upset he got arrested?" Thomas asked.

Rehab

"Well, I didn't know anything was going on," Hayes said, ending his sentence with a question mark, as if he were still confused about what had occurred. "I'm upset that I'm going to be without medication."

In his report, Thomas continued, "the dilemma Hayes faces haunts investigators," cutting back to Dietz at the press conference: "These people are still addicted to a drug and this is what's happening. This is not fixing the problem."

The DORN patients who arrived later that morning were turned away, and they watched as agents streamed in and out of the offices, lugging out computers, hard drives, and stacks of confidential patient files. As the news spread across the region, Ley's patients realized they were being cut off, and they began to panic.

At home in Kokomo, former Wagoner and then DORN patient Ryan Radford watched the news in shock. Sure, DORN had had some problems, but he had no idea anything illegal was going on. He had picked up a paper copy of his prescription from DORN not too long ago and hadn't immediately taken it to the pharmacy; now he realized it was null and void. No one would fill it now. Soon he'd run out of medication, and not long after that the withdrawal symptoms would start setting in. What if he didn't find another prescriber? Frantic, he and his parents looked up the names of doctors and began calling.

Since Larry Ley had started DORN, more doctors had joined the cause. But there was still a national shortage of Suboxone prescribers, worsened by federal regulations that imposed patient limits. DORN had been one of the few Suboxone prescribers in Ryan's area. As he and other DORN patients called around, they found most doctors in the surrounding counties had already met their quotas. Others were hesitant to take on anyone associated with Dr. Larry Ley.

"It's not the type of medication you can just stop taking and be a functioning person," said DORN patient Sean Hays, who found out about DORN's closure when his boyfriend saw the news on TV. "I was freaking out obviously because it's a huge part of my life. My heart, my stomach, I'm, like, oh my god," he said.

Ultimately, Sean could not find another doctor willing to take him. He ended up switching to a methadone clinic in Indianapolis, which required him to wake at 4 a.m. every morning and drive an hour and 15 minutes each way to get his daily dose. The program cost $20 a day, or $600 a month—more than three times the cost of Larry's program, on top of the cost of gas to get there. "I felt like I was working just to have treatment because it is the only thing that has ever worked for me," he said. "I had to do what I had to do."

Across the country, drug overdoses had been steadily rising for more than a decade. But paramedics on the ground in Indiana said the closure of Larry's clinics drove people to the illicit market. In the weeks and months following the raid, overdose deaths climbed. In just six months in Kokomo, 25 people died from overdoses, surpassing the entirety of the previous year, when 20 people had died. And the year wasn't over yet. "If the 2015 trend continues, it'll be one of the worst years in county history for overdoses," an editorial in the local newspaper said.

Around the same time, former DORN patient Aaron Courtney fell asleep while driving a newspaper delivery truck and collided with an oncoming semi, crushing Aaron inside. His official cause of death was attributed to the crash, but his girlfriend knew the real cause: he'd had a relapse.

Eventually, every DORN employee met bail and was released from jail, some at great expense. Dr. Ron Vierk posted $175,000 bail. Dr. George Agapios posted $400,000. But Larry Ley remained in jail. The court had set his bail at $1 million, and with his bank accounts seized by law enforcement, he couldn't afford the bail. Sheriff's deputies had processed him into the general jail population, where he found himself next to a man in the thick of withdrawal.

Here was someone who needed help. But not a single jail in the state allowed opioid addiction treatment. Even someone taking Suboxone or

Rehab

methadone was not allowed to take their medications. This was a potential violation of the Americans with Disabilities Act, and a common problem in jails and prisons across the country. There would be no treatment for him.

Larry settled into his bunk and squeezed his eyes shut. Inside his head, his arrest played on repeat, punctured only by the pain that shot up and down his back, and the sound of his cell mate shivering, moaning, and vomiting into the toilet.

CHAPTER SIXTEEN

Wendy McEntyre

2015

Like the investigators who'd gone after Larry Ley, Wendy McEntyre refused to let Above It All go. She sat outside program facilities and conducted surveillance constantly. She called and emailed state regulators incessantly, forwarding surveillance photographs, videos, and recorded interviews. At one point she shared a Dropbox link that regulators were unable to open. In two months, she called the office more than 25 times. "Korey [sic] Avarell is scurrying like a rat on the mountain," she wrote to one deputy director, then followed up a couple days later with photographs of Cyndi and Shannon Doyle crying at Donavan's memorial. "Your silence disturbs me greatly," she wrote, when she didn't get a response. "I have gotten NOWHERE!!!!!!!!!!!!" she later added.

These emails contained solid leads and good information, including recorded interviews, and names and phone numbers of witnesses, but Wendy was prone to paragraphs-long rants and exaggerated, typo-filled claims. Karen Gold feared Wendy was being ignored. Her desperation was as much about the state's inaction as it was about Above It All's misconduct. But the bureaucrats she was emailing had little power to enact systemic change. "When she first started on this, I think I got 100 emails from her every week. She was attacking everything—DHCS, regulations. She came across as a raving lunatic," Karen later told me.

Then Wendy struck on something that seemed to get regulators' attention.

Under state law, rehab programs like Above It All were not allowed to dispense medications or provide medical care. So programs contracted outside doctors to prescribe medications, and treatment clients were supposed to administer the medications to themselves. But at Above It All Treatment Center, employees like the van driver—many of whom lacked medical qualifications—routinely doled out drugs to their participants.

She'd first heard about it from Chris O'Keefe, the house manager who had found Donavan on the floor of his room after what appeared to be a suicide attempt. When he had started at AIA in 2010, Chris said that he immediately began dispensing medications and controlled substances. And to Chris, it seemed like the program was overmedicating patients to the point of impairment. "It was like switching seats on the *Titanic*," he said. "I mean, I'm not a doctor, but I could not figure it out." He did have one guess. The medical services that AIA provided allowed them to bill insurance companies for a higher level of care. "There's more money the more meds they take."

The program's website touted Above It All's "individualized" treatment plans. But several nurses and medical assistants told Wendy that each detox client usually received the same medications. When a client left early, as they often did, the program was required by law to dispose of their medications. Instead, they often saved and reused them.

"We don't destroy meds," said Diana Veles, a medical assistant and mother of four who decided to contact Wendy after one of her patients had died. She believed the patient had been overmedicated with drugs that weren't prescribed to her. "We have an extra set of boxes that have extra meds. So, let's say a client comes in and he doesn't have medication or can't afford it, what we do is we grab from whatever we have left over," she said. "Sometimes I would sit there, and I would just look at everybody and just say 'Really?—that is, should we really be giving these people medication?'"

"Really," Wendy said, trying to mute her anger. "So, you had concerns yourself?"

Diana continued. "Their answers to me were 'You're just a medical assistant and this is what the doctor's prescribing.'" The dismissal was all the more upsetting to Diana because of her personal experience. Her own husband had struggled with drug use, and she herself had struggled with her mental health, following childhood abuse. She wanted patients to get the help she had never received. She thought in a place like AIA, patients would be able to get better. Instead, like Donavan, she saw many of them getting worse.

This system of detoxification was somewhat unique to California. Detoxing from drugs posed serious health risks, ranging from dehydration to death. That's why many states required detox services to be provided in a medical setting, such as a hospital. In California, on the other hand, a program operator like Above It All could rent a two-bedroom house, move in some bunk beds, and open for business.

When the state eventually came to conduct an investigation of AIA, Diana saw how easily the program evaded accountability. "Before the State turned the corner, everybody already knew—everybody was getting that message over the phone. 'The State's turning, the State's in the parking lot, the State is about to hit your door.'" Diana sat in the office as an investigator asked questions, but no one ever asked her anything and so she hadn't shared what she knew. Now, in the aftermath of her patient's death, she felt like she had to do something.

Soon other employees began coming forward. It seemed to Wendy like Above It All was cleaning house. Numerous people complained they had been fired for reasons that felt manufactured, and they weren't always getting paid for all their hours worked. Call center employees; nurses; and van driver Sean Bly. They all were now willing to talk, and in exchange, Wendy helped shepherd them through the process of filing wrongful termination cases or complaints with the state. She tallied her discoveries on a gigantic whiteboard and filled binders and notebooks with handwritten notes. She made herself available for phone calls any time of day or night. "I was really swarming them like I was a fly and they were the shit," Wendy told me. Karen Gold, the attorney who had helped Wendy with her son's case, was now preparing a wrongful-death lawsuit for the Doyles and she was relying on Wendy—in her obsessive pursuit of justice—to find witnesses to testify. "You never want to cross her if you're a bad guy," Karen said.

After almost every interview, Wendy forwarded her findings to the Department of Health Care Services. She felt confident she could get Above It All Treatment Center shut down. "I want you to know that because of what you shared with me, all authorities are about to open up a can of whoop ass," Wendy told one of her sources, a former nursing assistant. "Hell is going to rain down on Kory."

By January of 2015, it seemed as though Wendy's efforts had finally paid off. During multiple days of inspections, the State discovered that Above It All employees were saving old prescriptions; storing various unlabeled medications in plastic baggies, envelopes, and a toolbox; and using and refilling bottles of medications that had been prescribed to former patients, by just crossing out their names. The agency cited Above It All Treatment Center for these problems, but just a month later, the problems still remained. "Provider is exposing residents to harm that could lead to temporary or permanent physical or mental injury, or even death," a division chief wrote. The department delivered a letter revoking Avarell's two residential licenses, requiring him to cease operations immediately.

But Kory Avarell didn't shut down his rehab. Instead, he claimed the facilities were sober-living homes, and he continued to fill them with patients. A sober-living home was where Wendy's son, Jarrod, had died. They were unregulated and increasingly owned by treatment operators who exerted total control over their patients' lives. And according to regulators, it was completely legal. This claim allowed Avarell to sidestep completely the licensure and state oversight.

Wendy McEntyre

A month later, Avarell filed a complaint in Superior Court, seeking to lift the suspension order and arguing that patients' lives were at risk if they couldn't get into treatment. "I don't want to get dramatic," AIA's attorney said. "But what happens if one of these kids who can't get treatment, you know, goes out and robs a 7-Eleven and gets shot?"

The judge ruled against AIA, keeping the suspension order in place. "When I look at the irreparable harm at issue, it's hard to imagine any more significant risk posed by a facility that handles drug rehabilitation, than the mismanagement of prescription medication," she said in court.

But soon, Avarell dropped the legal fight. His son had applied for new licenses, including for at least one location that the department had previously ordered closed. About one month later, the program was featured on the A&E show *Intervention*. "So what has your treatment been like up at Above It All Treatment Center?" host Ken Seeley asked Samantha, the "full-blown drug addict," they'd sent to AIA. "Really inspiring," she said. "I had an amazing counselor and therapist and other staff."

By July, Kyle Avarell, Kory's son, was boasting to a news reporter that they had 18 facilities on the mountain and their biggest victory yet: Above It All had retained what is considered one of the highest standards of approval, the certification from CARF, the Commission on Accreditation of Rehabilitation Facilities. The accreditation was proof of Above It All's quality, even better than licensing, because "CARF accreditations are written by clinicians and state standards are written by politicians and bureaucrats," Kyle Avarell told the reporter at the time. The same accreditation, viewed by many state agencies as unimpeachable, had also been bestowed on Cenikor.

Wendy was apoplectic. Despite the problems she'd uncovered, and despite the fact that the department had revoked two of Above It All's licenses, the program was more successful than ever. "As a result of the coverage AIA got from the show *Intervention*, they are now busting at the seams. Several new patients A DAY!!!," Wendy wrote to supporters. Money was pouring in.

Wendy believed it was only a matter of time before someone else died. Soon, she would be proven right.

Rehab

BY THE TIME James Dugas arrived at Above It All Treatment Center in December 2015, the 25-year-old from Massachusetts had spent years churning through the new U.S. treatment system.

James had attended two different programs operated by American Addiction Centers, the country's first publicly traded treatment chain, in the same year the company was charged with murder for a patient death. He then went to a rehab in California, then to one in Las Vegas, to another in Florida, and then back to California again. Each treatment program was similar to the last. Each provided a combination of 12-step programming, group therapy, and medication. Each required James to start over, with a new treatment staff, new counselors, and a therapist if he was lucky. And once the program was over—when the insurance funds stopped flowing—that was the end of treatment. James had to find a job and a place to live, or return home to face the same environment and triggers, without the support from which he'd benefited in rehab. These programs all treated recovery and complete abstinence like something that could be achieved in a matter of weeks. It was a practice fueled by insurance companies that paid for short bursts of treatment, rather than ongoing support. And instead of motivating James, these short-lived attempts made him feel like a failure.

Before he went to AIA, James had decided he didn't want to do another rehab. He wanted to try being sober on his own. But when he left rehab early and tried to enter a sober-living home, he was told he would not be allowed inside. There was nowhere for James to go. He had no job, no money, no way to pay for housing. So, one of the house managers recommended he go to another rehab—Above It All. After using again and gaining admission, James called his parents to let them know he was safe.

The first step in AIA's residential program was detox, for which the program could charge insurance companies especially hefty fees—up to $3,200 per day. The program would pick up patients and take them to urgent care on their way up the mountain, where a doctor could take their vitals and make sure they were medically stable enough to enter the program. Employees would fill out new-patient forms and send them to a separate contracted doctor—Dr. Robert Treuherz—who would either clear the patient for admission or determine, based on the patient's medical condition or history, that the patient needed a higher level of care. Once a patient was admitted, a member of AIA's medical staff would conduct a more detailed medical examination, and would send their treatment recommendations to the doctor, who would either order the requested medication or authorize AIA nurses in writing to send in the prescription on his behalf.

That's how it was supposed to work. But that's not always what happened.

On December 10, 2015, Dr. Treuherz received an email with preliminary information about James, who would arrive later that day. Under this arrangement, this email was supposed to contain certain key pieces of information that would allow the doctor to assess whether James should be admitted to Above It All. The email said that James was healthy, with a history of GHB, meth, benzodiazepine, and opioid use. At 2:10 p.m., Dr. Treuherz submitted his approval.

Then, the AIA staff did another assessment, this one much more detailed. A nurse noted that James had had two recent seizures, a strokelike event just a few months prior, showed hypertensive symptoms, and had asthma. Under the arrangement with Dr. Treuherz, AIA staff should have shared these details with the doctor for his review. But the staff never sent Dr. Treuherz the assessment. If they had, Dr. Treuherz would later say, he would not have approved James for admission. And the staff failed to disclose to Dr. Treuherz another key piece of information: Although James had claimed he was addicted to opioids, he had tested positive only for THC and meth.

The next day, an AIA nurse used Dr. Treuherz's prescriber ID—without the doctor's knowledge, he would later say—to order several medications for James, including Suboxone, gabapentin, hydroxyzine, Zoloft, and propranolol. Despite the order missing Dr. Treuherz's signature, the pharmacy filled it.

Suboxone is a treatment for opioid addiction. It is not a treatment for meth addiction. For someone who has been using opioids, Suboxone eases

Rehab

withdrawal symptoms without producing a high. But for people who have no opioid tolerance, like James, it has a sedating effect, and when combined with gabapentin and hydroxyzine, can bring on respiratory depression that can easily cause a fatal overdose. Soon after receiving this potentially deadly cocktail, James vomited, then started to have trouble breathing. Records showed no indication that AIA called a doctor. Then an employee gave James more medication.

Under state requirements, AIA was required to perform face-to-face checks on new detox patients every 30 minutes. The staff performed only 12 physical checks. At about 3:40 a.m., almost three hours after someone had last checked his vitals, James was found unresponsive and not breathing. He was then airlifted to a hospital, where he was pronounced dead.

Over the phone, all the way across the country in Massachusetts, James's parents were asked to make the difficult decision to take their son off life support. "So, it was a day from hell," his mother said.

Soon, the bills would start rolling in. For less than three days of treatment, AIA made more than $10,000.

THIS IS WHAT Wendy had been warning would happen. She wouldn't learn about Dr. Treuherz for months. But she had spoken with medical assistants and nurses, including one who claimed she had been fired after she refused to send a medication order to a pharmacy without doctor authorization. Though Wendy did not yet know it, something similar had happened with a previous AIA patient who had died. A nurse had used the prescriber ID of Dr. Harinder Grewal to order her prescriptions, without the doctor's authorization or examination. Dr. Grewal had discovered that AIA had used her name as the prescribing doctor a half dozen times before, and had even spoken with Kory Avarell and his son Kyle about it. "It was very, very upsetting," she'd later say in a deposition. "I don't want my name involved in patients that I have never seen," she told Kyle Avarell. "And Kyle promised that he would look into it and take care of it." That was in 2014. And here was James, having died after the same AIA procedures, in late 2015.

A day after James's death, Wendy sent an email to a detective at the sheriff's office and to the Department of Health Care Services. It was in all caps: "URGENT URGENT . . . ANOTHER DEATH AT ABOVE IT ALL"

Above It All reported the death, as required by law, and the DHCS dispatched an investigator. On March 1, 2016, the DHCS notified the Avarells that the investigator had found three deficiencies. The program had not checked James frequently enough in accordance with its own detox policy, the staff had not recorded the medications James was taking, and the staff was not adequately documenting the detox client checks. The investigator had interviewed five clients who gave the program rave reviews. There was no mention of the unauthorized prescription—potential fraud—or the fact that the medications James was given were inappropriate and potentially lethal. Avarell submitted a "corrective action plan," including tweaks to the program's manual. The DHCS then approved the changes and closed the case.

WENDY CONTINUED HER investigation. With the sheriff's office and the DHCS taking no action against Above It All, she had begun funneling her efforts toward helping the families of Donavan and James, and other patients, to collect evidence for filing wrongful-death lawsuits. She introduced each of the parents to Karen Gold, whom she referred to as "the blonde assassin." She was excited about Gold's subpoena power, about bringing Kory Avarell in for a deposition, and about forcing him to answer questions concerning all that she'd found out.

By 2016, the problems in the for-profit rehab industry had grown so immense that some insurers began denying claims. But the Addiction Treatment Advocacy Coalition fought back. After one insurer, HealthNet, stopped payments, the group filed a complaint with the California Department of

Rehab

Insurance in the form of a letter signed by 118 rehab operators, including Avarell and Above It All. The rehabs claimed that HealthNet had singled out for audit almost the entirety of the state's for-profit treatment industry, a violation of the federal Mental Health Parity and Addiction Equity Act of 2008. The insurer had also stopped paying some facilities outright, while for others, the company was now paying "pennies on the dollar." As a result, some facilities were in danger of closing, which in turn would endanger the lives of people desperate for treatment, the group claimed. The DHCS ultimately sided with the treatment companies and ordered HealthNet to resume payments.

The more convinced she was that Avarell was escaping accountability, the more enraged Wendy became. "It's on like Donkey Kong," she'd say, again and again. She sat outside AIA facilities and took videos of the vans coming and going. She posted incessantly on Facebook.

Karen Gold, the attorney with whom Wendy had become close, told Wendy to be careful, to not give anyone ammunition to discredit her. "People can ruin you online without even trying," she said. She added, "Guess who wanted her to look crazy? Above It All. She's not crazy. She was never crazy."

As Wendy continued her investigation, the Avarells decided to fight back. Just three months after James's death, Kyle Avarell filed a restraining order against her. She took Avarell's petition as affirmation of her efforts, and it riled her up. "If they want a battle, they're going to end in scorched earth with me," she said. "Forget lemonade. If life gives me lemons, they're going right in the fucking freezer until they get hard as rock, and then I pull them out and throw them at your throat. I don't like lemonade, I never did."

Wendy relished the chance to defend herself and confront Avarell in court. To have a captive audience in a judge who would finally have to listen to the evidence she had amassed on all of AIA's misdeeds. She began assembling her exhibits, her hundreds of 911 calls and the DHCS inspections and interview transcripts. She stuffed it all into a leather briefcase, and put on a gold skirt suit and a pair of four-inch-high heels. They made her feel powerful—over six feet tall. But when Wendy appeared in court for the restraining order and she tried to unveil the contents of her briefcase, Judge Michael Sachs told her that it was irrelevant.

"I just wanted to advise you again that this case has nothing to do with the deaths that have occurred there," he reminded her. "It has nothing to do with billing practices. It has nothing do with being licensed or not being licensed. It has nothing to do with the number of homes in the community."

Soon, the Avarells were on the stand, painting a picture of Wendy as unhinged and dangerous—a grieving mother who was now projecting her pain and blame onto an innocent family. "I believe her to be a sick person," Kyle Avarell said. "I think that she is not stable because I've never seen anybody act the way she does against someone who's trying to help people and run a business."

"I know what you've done to my family so far with slander, and I don't know what you're capable of. I really don't," said Kelly Washburn, AIA's executive director of marketing and Avarell's daughter. "I am truly fearful for my life and my family's."

"I'm fearful of your passion as a mom who lost a son and that you lost focus, and it's affecting my family. That's what I'm fearful of," said Avarell's ex-wife.

Wendy's tactics were suddenly on full display. Even after the restraining-order petition had been filed, she had called Kyle to accuse them of running an illegal detox facility. She had sent out mass emails calling Avarell a murderer. She had reached out to people the Avarells knew in the industry, and in many of these interactions, Avarell said that Wendy claimed she worked for the Department of Health Care Services. Wendy denied this, saying she had claimed to be a member of the department's advisory board, which was not exactly true; her position with the board was long defunct.

The clinching moment, however, came when it was revealed that Wendy had left a voicemail for Kelly, in which Wendy had said, "I'm coming for you." Wendy explained that she had meant it as a legal threat—the argument was over a former client, from whom AIA was trying to collect money—but Wendy conceded that it was inappropriate and said she had misspoken. She tried to plead with the judge to "end this right now." She promised to stop contacting Avarell and his family. Judge Sachs politely declined. "I'm not going to dismiss the case," he said.

Before Judge Sachs issued his ruling, Wendy gave her closing argument: a passionate defense of her investigation of Above It All and what was driving her efforts. This hearing, Wendy noted, was happening the day after Mother's Day—a day she had spent on the phone with other mothers who had lost a child in rehab. She took a breath and tried to calm her shaking hands. She remembered how she'd felt after losing Jarrod. Everyone had looked at her as if it was her fault—or Jarrod's fault—that he had died. "I'm not crazy as was testified to earlier. I don't have a vendetta," she said. "My goal is to try to keep people safe. That's what I do. My advocacy is all about keeping people safe."

She continued, "I believe that the fear that they're speaking about is not fear for their safety. It's fear for their money going bye-bye. That's what—they're fearful of me.... Sometimes I get angry. It makes me mad when people get hurt. It makes me mad when the state doesn't do what they're supposed to do. It makes me mad, and it's on me. And it's three years—three years of trying to illustrate to the district attorneys, to the county, to the state that something needs to be done."

Ultimately, Judge Sachs told Wendy she could picket and investigate Above It All, and she could contact current and former employees. But he would grant the restraining order—to an extent. Wendy must stay three feet away from Above It All's administrative office, he said, and she must stop contacting the Avarells.

"I applaud you for what you are doing," Judge Sachs said. He had overseen drug court for three years, and he had seen this problem firsthand. "There is a need for somebody like yourself to be their voice. But again, you have to exercise that voice in a reasonable way and not an illegal manner."

Wendy was required to stay three feet away from AIA's main office in the Lake Arrowhead village complex. Three feet was about the width of a poodle skirt. So, Wendy bought one, and then she brought her granddaughter along to conduct surveillance in the parking lot.

Wendy McEntyre

DESPITE ALL THE legal scrutiny, Wendy was convinced that Above It All was continuing its unethical practices. But over the next year, she started to fall apart. She still answered her phone at all hours of day and night, making herself middle-of-the-night snacks with the toaster and coffee pot she kept beside her bed. But the state's inaction and her mounting legal problems were beginning to weigh on her.

Even though the restraining order allowed Wendy to legally continue her surveillance and investigation of AIA, program staffers had started calling the police whenever they spotted her parked car outside the program houses, and the officers who responded didn't seem to understand the restraining order's minimal scope. The Avarells had also filed a libel lawsuit against her.

Despite her relish for courtroom drama, Wendy wasn't prepared for all this. She had gone on disability after the death of her son, so she couldn't legally work full time and she couldn't afford to hire an attorney to represent her. She had decided to represent herself, but she was floundering, and her investigations were suffering. Meanwhile, AIA continued operating. And then, another patient died.

Matthew Maniace was just 20 years old, short and slight, with spiky red hair and striking blue eyes. At home on Long Island, he volunteered with his mother at an animal shelter. But when he moved to Florida for treatment, he was quickly submerged in a subculture that was difficult to escape. He told his mom, Lynn, that life was good, but the sporadic photographs he sent—like stacks of cash from his job, he said, finding patients for rehab—disturbed her. Then Matthew stopped responding to her messages and left for California.

When he was admitted to AIA on February 23, Matthew was sober. His urine test at intake showed no illicit substances in his body—no heroin, no THC, no meth—which meant he should have been deemed ineligible for AIA's detox services. But his treatment records indicate he never saw a doctor. Then, on February 24, an AIA nurse used a doctor's prescription pad to order heavy detox medications, including Suboxone, Klonopin, and Robaxin, followed

Rehab

by gabapentin. Even though the order had not been placed by a doctor, and did not bear his signature, the pharmacy filled the prescriptions, and a nurse gave Matthew the medications.

Just like James Dugas before him, Matthew received a strong cocktail. Especially for someone without drugs in his system, the combination could easily cause sedation and intoxication—or worse. The U.S. Food and Drug Administration warns that combining buprenorphine and benzodiazepines can cause difficulty breathing, coma, and fatal overdose. The Suboxone label also warns that combining the medications can lead to respiratory depression and death. Suboxone alone, if provided to someone without opioid tolerance, can cause overdose death in quantities as small as two milligrams, and gabapentin and Robaxin are known to increase the effects of Suboxone.

Despite having no drugs in his system on arrival, the AIA staff gave Matthew more than 30 milligrams of Suboxone in one 24-hour period, along with several doses of Klonopin, Robaxin, and gabapentin. Most patients who take Suboxone receive a maximum dose of 16 milligrams a day—half the dose Matthew received. The result was consistent with someone who had taken intoxicating substances after a period of sobriety. He "had a hard time standing," Matthew's roommate would later say. He told a sheriff's deputy that Matthew's medications were "causing him to act strange" and that his breathing was raspy, shallow, and labored. Another roommate told deputies that he believed Matthew was "overmedicated."

Matthew himself reported feeling horrible. When the nurse brought out another round of medications later that night, he refused them—another act that should have prompted a call to the doctor. When Matthew's mother later hired a medical expert to review the documents, the doctor wrote that the combination and amount of drugs Matthew was given "are particularly dangerous when used together without appropriate monitoring."

Under state law, Above It All was required to check Matthew every 30 minutes. An hour passed and no one came. Another hour passed before a nurse found Matthew under a sheet, unconscious and with foam coming out of his mouth and nostrils. It took more than 30 minutes for AIA to call 911. When paramedics arrived, they declared Matthew dead.

IT WOULD TAKE almost a year for the DHCS to complete their investigation into Matthew's death.

In February 2018, his mother, Lynn, finally received the results. The investigator found that Above It All had falsified medical records. In one case, therapy session notes stated that Matthew was making good progress, but at the logged time, Matthew had yet to even enter the program. The investigator also found that a house manager responsible for checking patients every 30 minutes had pre-signed his checks without visiting him.

These were extraordinary problems, proof that AIA had failed to monitor Lynn's son, but it seemed like the investigator had not examined anything else—how his roommates thought he was overmedicated, or the fact that AIA staff had potentially obtained the drugs fraudulently. Also, the fact that nurses had given Matthew powerful narcotics when he had no drugs in his system. On top of all this was the fact that AIA seemed to be providing medical care—dispensing potentially dangerous medications—which it wasn't allowed to do under state law. Instead, the investigator found what amounted to paperwork violations and had given AIA two Class B deficiencies—in other words, a slap on the wrist. Kory Avarell would be allowed to submit a corrective action plan and retain his license.

Lynn, a nurse herself, was a fastidious documenter. She expected more. She called the investigator immediately. "This is all bullshit," she wrote in her notes following the conversation. "She didn't do her job and let those monsters get away with killing another innocent person." The investigator told Lynn that her hands were tied. She had requested the sheriff's report, but had never received it. So, she had never seen the interview with Matthew's roommates, and had never interviewed the doctor who allegedly authorized the prescriptions. "I told her it was very obvious that AIA didn't do their jobs and neither did she. I told her I hoped she never gets another good night's sleep the rest of her life for letting them get away with killing another person. I told her I couldn't believe she didn't look into any of the things that really mattered, and she said that as far as she is concerned, her report stands as it is." Lynn called the investigator's supervisor, who repeated what she had said: "The report stands."

But Lynn didn't leave it at that. On March 1, she called the chief of compliance. She emailed the DHCS attorney and all the unit supervisors. She called and called, until someone called her back. The next month, she emailed again. "Plain and simple, she botched the investigation and did not do justice for my son. As a result of this incomplete DHCS report, all that Mr. Avarell got was a slap on the hands for the death of my son. My son's life was worth a lot more than that. I don't know how any of you can live with yourselves for allowing this to continue. How many more lives have to be lost before you finally step up and do the right thing?"

Soon after, a DHCS supervisor called Lynn to tell her they were reopening the case, and that a new investigator would be in touch. But two months later, Lynn had heard from no one. It wasn't until December 31, 2018, that Lynn received a copy of the department's new report. When the investigators arrived, Avarell had simply told them he was relinquishing his license. His son Kyle was already running a new state-licensed rehab—charging patients up to $75,000 per week.

Part Three

Relapse and Recovery

CHAPTER SEVENTEEN

Chris Koon

2017

Chris Koon returned home and re-entered the courtroom of Judge Warren Willet. After almost two years, he felt like he was right back where he had started. But there was one thing that had changed. Chris did not want to go back to Cenikor. He did not want to go back to drug use. He just wanted to move on with his life. He was grateful to be back at home with his dad. He had finally found some motivation to do something different.

Judge Willet did not like that Chris had failed out of Cenikor. But the state of Louisiana was also experiencing massive prison overcrowding, and this was Chris's first conviction. The judge decided to use his discretion. Chris would serve three years of supervised probation. He'd have to pay more than $4,000 in court fines and supervision costs, pay for random drug testing, get a job, abide by an 11 p.m. curfew, and stay out of bars, casinos, and restaurants that serve alcohol. If he violated these rules, he could go to prison, and he'd have to serve hard time.

Chris agreed. He had wasted almost two years at Cenikor. It was time to begin a new life.

Rehab

CHRIS MOVED BACK in with his dad and his dad's girlfriend. It was a small, two-bedroom house, crammed full with his dad's collections—books stacked on sagging bookshelves, plastic bins of Warhammer toys, and psychedelic art. Chris tried to figure out what to do with his life. There were the two paths his former high school classmates had taken. One faction continued to use. The other group had moved on from their partying days, had gotten married, had kids, started careers, or at least had jobs that paid the bills. Chris felt woefully behind.

At first, he had grand aspirations of going to law school. He fantasized about suing Cenikor for civil rights violations. His father had gotten his bachelor's degree, and had even gone back a second time for his nursing degree while working full time at the prison. But Chris realized that higher education was an unrealistic goal for him. There was no way he could afford a bachelor's degree program, let alone law school. Instead, he enrolled in welding school.

Pretty much everyone there was about ten years younger than he was, but Chris tried not to dwell on that. There was something calming about watching that white hot pick. "It's just you and that little spark in front of you that you have to keep going just right," Chris said. "Just calms me down." Once in a while, Chris would go outside to take a break for a cigarette and get a Dr Pepper from the vending machine, and he'd glance over at the knuckleheads getting high at the house on the far end of the parking lot. He was thankful to be where he was.

Carrie and John and Granny saw a new maturity in Chris. Maybe Cenikor did some good after all, they thought. Chris felt Cenikor had no part in his growing up. But he acknowledged that the place had helped him in some respects. For instance, it made him understand that he never wanted to be there again—not in Cenikor, nor in a job that treated him as expendable, that cared so little for his life—not that he would always have control over that, of course. He was able to step away for a substantial period of time, gain perspective, reimagine his future, and bond with other people trying to do the same. Now that he was out of Cenikor, he relied on some of those friendships for support. He needed to talk to people who understood what it was like to resume regular life, to assimilate into a society that judged and discriminated against him, to be around people who had never shared his life experiences, including those experiences of surviving a place like Cenikor. He was tempted to tell people he had been in prison these last two years, because it was easier than explaining the truth.

Sometimes it felt like the past was trying to claw him back. Like the time a girl from high school posted his mug shot on Facebook. "I'm so glad you're doing good," she wrote. But Chris saw right through that. *Bitch, you must still be on meth or something, posting a mug shot for everybody and their mom to see,* he thought. It was humiliating. Chris reported her on Facebook three times before it was taken down. Or there was the time he ran into an old high school buddy at Walmart, and he tried to convince Chris to help him lift an $80 knife set. Chris cut all those old friends out of his life.

Then he got another cyst, and this time he needed surgery. Afterward, he was in so much pain that the doctor prescribed him Percocet. Chris began taking the pills, believing he could handle it. He even gave them to his dad to hold on to, to make sure he didn't take too many of them. But soon Chris couldn't stop thinking about them. He would be lying in bed, trying to go to sleep, thinking about those pills. *Oh, Dad's asleep, them pain pills, I know they're probably in his lunchbox. Man, I'd like another pain pill. That would be awesome. Eat like six of them things right quick.* He couldn't stop thinking about it, no matter how hard he tried. *Nah. This is the road to hell right here.* He realized he couldn't handle those pills anymore. He needed more help. For the first time, he went to his parents and asked for it.

AS CHRIS TRIED to reset his life, I was working with my colleague Amy Julia Harris on an investigation into Cenikor. In April 2019, we published the first of several stories on the program. Suddenly, companies began canceling their contracts with Cenikor, cutting ties with the program. Several lawyers tracked down former participants and filed lawsuits.

Inside Cenikor, the participants reached out to us. They said that Cenikor was telling them to be quiet, not to talk to anyone, that it would be fine. Eventually, investigators from the state regulatory agency came to the Cenikor facility and spent about two days looking through documents. Then they left. No serious violations were found.

Investigators from the Louisiana attorney general's office also came in. The focus of their investigation was possible Medicaid fraud. After interviewing dozens of former participants and employees, a senior official said a successful prosecution seemed unlikely. Most participants wanted to talk to them about the unpaid labor—something the agency seemed to have no interest in prosecuting. They closed the case.

Meanwhile, Cenikor's CEO, Bill Bailey, kept getting raises. In 2018, he received his highest salary yet: $521,449. And the organization continued to expand and collect government contracts. In 2019, the program received more than $7 million in federal grant funding, including from the U.S. Department of Health and Human Services and from SAMHSA (Substance Abuse and Mental Health Services Administration). The state of Texas gave Cenikor more than $2 million for treatment services.

In Texas, our reporting and Cenikor's expansion did not go unnoticed. State regulators began to ramp up their enforcement efforts, pelting Cenikor with repeated inspections and fines. Their investigations confirmed much of our earlier reporting. In the state, programs licensed as therapeutic communities were required to provide at least six hours of treatment services per week, including four hours of counseling and two hours of educational and therapeutic group sessions. But investigators found that clients rarely got the required services. They uncovered one participant who hadn't attended a single group session in almost two years while at the facility. Other clients had histories of depression, PTSD, and psychosis, but Cenikor provided no mental health plans or referrals to needed services.

The investigators also found that Cenikor participants were poorly treated on the job. In Fort Worth alone, 100 clients were injured between 2016 and 2019. In Deer Park, there were at least 30 injuries in just two years, according to state records; also, Cenikor staff routinely sexually harassed the clients. In Corpus Christi, 16 clients banded together to file a complaint about their AA instructor, who kept making degrading comments about women. "Please help," their report read. The facility provided no response.

Cenikor was plagued with other serious problems, most of which had never been documented or reported to the state authorities, as required by law. Clients routinely brought drugs into the facility. Clients reported being sexually assaulted by other clients. In several instances, Cenikor staff refused to provide investigators with the documentation they needed to perform their inspections, including grievance reports, incident reports, and lists of residents who were working more than 48 hours per week. In Amarillo, an inspector asked for copies of the vocational contracts, but minutes after beginning her review, an employee took the records away and refused to give them back.

Ultimately, regulators would find the program was exploiting residents for financial gain. They would uncover overdoses, filthy and unsafe facilities, and relationships between staff and clients. Finally, it looked like Cenikor would be held accountable. In a period of just two years, Cenikor in Texas was fined more than $1.4 million by state regulators. In the end, however, the agency agreed to a settlement. Cenikor refused to admit to any wrongdoing, but in exchange for a portion of the fines, the state would drop the matter and Cenikor could continue to operate. Cenikor ultimately paid $125,160.

Amid all this, Cenikor made a familiar announcement: It was "transitioning" its long-term residential treatment programs. Moving forward, they would be sober-living homes.

"I'M STRUGGLING," Chris told his mother. "I'm afraid I'm going to fail. I think I need to be on Suboxone." A few years ago, Chris might have been unable to find someone. But now there was a cash-only Suboxone doctor like Dr. Larry Ley just a few towns away. The doctor had his own history with alcoholism, and he saw a lot of patients with opioid addiction. Chris thought he was cool.

At first, Carrie was not supportive. She felt Suboxone was a crutch. "You're gonna be forever battling," she told Chris. "You've got to face the battle." But then she realized that response was kind of selfish. "I'd rather see you on that and maintain and move forward with your life, than to not get on that and fall back into where you were," she said. Carrie agreed to help pay for Suboxone treatment, and Chris started seeing the doctor.

The medication kept Chris from using drugs, and helped him break the habit while he set about learning to live a life without drugs. In that sense, the medication shared a purpose with Cenikor and other long-term programs. At Cenikor, in theory, Chris was supposed to have abstained from drugs while he worked on himself and engaged in the long-term process of change. But the problem with many residential programs—aside from the profit motives and exploitation—was that they inevitably ended. And once clients were back out in the real world, once they were beyond the confines of the culture and the community of rehab, they faced the same challenges as they always had. The longer someone stays on a medication like Suboxone, the more effective it is at helping them sustain sobriety. Like Chris, most people need some assistance and support as they navigate those challenges. Life is hard enough, without the constant fear of relapse or overdose or failure.

Most rehabs promise change in one or two months. Cenikor had promised Chris change within two years. Now that he was out of Cenikor, Chris began a process of change that had no deadline. The process of growing, from birth through childhood, through adolescence, through young adulthood is a slow one. And it is gradual. So was Chris's change from someone who used drugs, who felt called to the social connections they granted him, to someone who could delay instant gratification, who could handle failure, who could tuck away the disappointments he could not control. Many people have found this kind of support in 12-step groups, but Chris didn't want to hang on to

Chris Koon

the identity of addict. He just wanted to move on. With his family's help, he found that he could.

Eventually, Chris reconnected with a girl he'd known since he was 15 years old. They got serious, he proposed, and the woman—Paige—and her two daughters moved in with Chris and John. John was doing everything he could to support his son. He worked constantly, and he didn't charge Chris rent or utilities. He collected all of Chris's medical bills from Cenikor in a sneaker box, and helped Chris pay them off when he could. John was not rich, but he had the financial resources to give Chris the time and space to find something that made him feel valued.

Paige's girls started calling Chris "Daddy." He relished it. He bought them Easter dresses, and let them adopt a couple of kittens. He started eating healthier, eliciting jokes from his dad when he brought home a gigantic tub of alfalfa sprouts that was too big to fit into the refrigerator. This was the family Chris had always wanted. He graduated from welding school and started applying for jobs. He found a job he liked, but he was rejected after they discovered he was taking Suboxone. Eventually, though, he ended up at a company outside of Austin. He hasn't taken a drug recreationally for eight years.

CHAPTER EIGHTEEN

April Lee

2016

As April Lee began a life of sobriety, she had much less than Chris to aid her. Instead of family, financial support, a lawyer, an education, or a job, she had the recovery house—actually, two houses crammed with 18 women, two to three women to a room. The house April was in was small, with three bedrooms located down a long dim hallway and a living room with overstuffed brown couches, green plastic plants, and mauve flowers. Every morning, at 6 a.m., the women gathered in the dining room to read the Bible.

The women were responsible for doing the chores, mainly cooking and cleaning. The program used their food stamps to purchase food for the house. April loved to cook; she would make the women mac and cheese, fried chicken, beef stew. All the women had plastic tubs for their personal snacks. April kept hers stocked with Tootsie Rolls, Zebra Cakes, and Charleston Chews—her sweet-tooth replacements for drugs.

For the first six months, April barely slept two hours a night. The withdrawal symptoms were still with her, at first physical and then mental. As the fog cleared, as she oriented herself to this new reality, her anxieties came to

Rehab

the surface. "You wake up and you're, like: this is not my life," April recalled. When she couldn't sleep, she would come out of the bedroom and crouch in the dark narrow hallway and write in her journal. "You don't deserve to be here smiling. You shouldn't be laughing. You shouldn't get your children back," she wrote. Other times, she sat outside on the fire escape, smoked cigarettes, and sobbed. It felt to her like it'd almost be easier to use—to give up before she disappointed herself or someone else. She wrote unaddressed letters to her children and put them in the blue mailbox on the street, knowing they wouldn't be delivered. She wanted to talk to her kids, but felt guilty about her absence. In one letter, she wrote:

Hey Son,

How you doing my child? I love you so much. Happy B-lated Birthday I'm so sorry from the bottom of my heart that I wasnt there to spend it with you. I have a lot of making up to do not just your birthday, and I really want to apologize for everything for now thats all I can do.

April leaned on her roommate for support. She had been there for almost a year. She confided in April about being a survivor of child sexual abuse, and she poked fun at April's inspirational Post-It notes, which April put everywhere—the closet, the walls, the dresser. They said: "You got this." "You're beautiful." The two would argue about April's breasts, which were long gone and had become, as April put it in her skinny state, "flabs of skin" on her chest. "Watch. My titties gon' come back," April told her.

"April, keep fucking dreaming," her roommate would reply.

Everyday, April's roommate would sing a gospel song by Yolanda Adams so mournfully that April would cry. "Prepare my mind, prepare my heart," she sang. "For whatever comes, I'm gon' be ready." It felt like a song for her life, for this moment she was in. And then one day, April came back to the room and her friend was gone. She hadn't left a note or said goodbye. She'd just relapsed and left.

April Lee

The recovery home was like this. It provided the women with the necessities, but it also segregated them from outside life. In some ways, April felt held back from ascending. Unlike Chris Koon, April couldn't lean on her family, and although the house afforded her some level of freedom, it was also highly prescriptive, as if she couldn't be trusted to make her own decisions.

The founder of the home was Christian and didn't like April exploring Islam. When April, who had a fluid sexual orientation, had sex with another woman in the house, she was brought into a group meeting where she was confronted, then punished. They took her phone away, and she was barred from attending outside 12-step meetings for a week. As April started getting more involved in recovery outside of the house, and attended more meetings, the founder told her she was out of line, that she wasn't ready. Studies have shown that this dynamic of control and surveillance is especially common in programs that serve low-income people of color.

April couldn't wait to leave, and she finally did—ten months later. But it was difficult to find housing, so she ended up back at the recovery house, working without pay as a house monitor in exchange for a room. She was still early into recovery, and she felt stressed by the intensity of the job. On top of that, she wasn't getting a paycheck, so she couldn't save up money to leave. It was the same loop that thousands of recovery-home residents had found themselves stuck in. "Don't really know how to feel right now," she wrote in her journal. "The lady I work for— for free, mind you—wont me to watch over women witch mean I have to stay in every night." She felt physically trapped. She couldn't even leave the house, because her job entailed monitoring the women. "I wanted to snap this morning," April wrote. "Miss my children so much."

APRIL GOT HER babies back, slowly. She began with her oldest, 12-year-old Derrick in March of 2016. When he returned, he carried all his belongings in a plastic bag. A year later, her 5-year-old arrived, and finally, two years later, her middle child.

Now it was 2021, and April and her kids were finally together under the same roof again. They were learning how to be a family. Derrick realized he couldn't be the boss of his younger brother anymore, because after so many years apart, the kid didn't really know him. April was struggling under the weight of her new responsibilities, occupying a financially precarious position, with housing more expensive than ever. She had found a job at a law firm, providing support to women whose children were in the foster-care system. Gone were the days of tricking at the Blue Moon Hotel, but April still wasn't making as much as she needed, and because her income wasn't below the poverty line anymore, she was ineligible for assistance. She was living in debt, struggling to balance the financial needs of the household and the emotional needs of her extended family. And April's younger sister was living with them, too, with her baby.

April's youngest would soon be suspended for smoking a cigarette in a stairwell at her school. A few months after that, April was outside the grocery store with her daughter when someone in the parking lot fired a barrage of bullets from a nearby car. April threw her body over her daughter, shaking. Her daughter barely flinched. Soon Derrick would share that his girlfriend was pregnant. At 19, he was going to become a father. By this time, he and his girlfriend lived in April's basement, and he worked part time as a security guard at Burlington Coat Factory.

In some respects, April had benefited from the city's treatment system. She stayed at a recovery home while she attended an outpatient program, and she participated in 12-step meetings and Recovery Idol, a talent competition intended to celebrate people in recovery. Through that competition, she found an outlet for her poetry. Some of the same poems she had composed in the depths of her addiction now drew applause from audiences. She started getting involved and tried to make use of her tribulations. Some of these opportunities would not have been possible without the city's funding. But at the same time, April saw how she was in many ways the exception. Treatment

April Lee

was still inaccessible for most people, and changing one's life was an uphill battle that came with obstacles the vast majority of people couldn't overcome.

By 2021, April Lee had her own home. She had earned her GED, she was taking college courses online, she had a job, and she had her kids back. And yet many days she felt she was teetering on the edge, one crisis or unpaid bill away from making a terrible mistake. If she was this close to self-destruction, she knew many others fared far worse.

That year, April took me back with her to Kensington, where she had started bringing fresh food and water to people living on the street. She chain-smoked Newport cigarettes as she steered her car toward the intersection of Allegheny and Kensington and coasted to a stop in front of a sign that said "NO STOPPING HERE." Outside, in the shadow of the teal-colored steel beams of the SEPTA train track, the sidewalk was littered with people; the stairs and street were covered with orange plastic syringe caps and liquor bottles, with old suitcases and Amazon boxes and shopping carts overloaded with piles of discarded clothes. Someone blasted rap music. Another couple clutched each other, swaying slowly to music that wasn't there. Usually some of the mess was sheathed by row upon row of tents. Today there were no tents—the city had cleared out those encampments a few days before.

April parked the car and walked around to the trunk. She was wearing her Kensington shoes—black Pumas with a red stripe—and a red tee-shirt and black jeans. It was an outfit that seemed to say: *I have my shit together, but you can talk to me.* She had spent almost all of Monday morning boiling hundreds of turkey and pork hot dogs, then placing each one inside a bun that she wrapped in individual foil, all the while warding off the advances of her daughter, who never can resist a snack. Now, the hot dogs sat on large aluminum platters, alongside cases of bottled water and hygiene bags with masks, toothbrushes, and fentanyl test strips—April's version of harm reduction.

April popped open the trunk and immediately people turned and gathered. "How you doing?" she asked the folks surging forward. "Pork or turkey?"

Rehab

A young woman approached the car, glancing from side to side. She had long braids dotted with the colors of the rainbow. She was wearing a rainbow backpack. She was slim and her skin was a clear caramel brown. "Stand back," she said sternly, almost paranoid, to the other people waiting in line. She put her hands out to clear space. Then, she approached April and leaned in to whisper into her ear. She said that her mother had lived with April at the recovery house. The woman had been clean briefly, then she relapsed and went back, she said. Now she was using again. April stood back for a moment to survey the young woman's appearance, and then gave her a hug. The girl explained that she had started using, too. First, she'd taken pills, and she had just switched to heroin. This was her second week in Kensington, and she was having trouble sleeping. April wrote down her phone number on a slip of paper and passed it to her. "Call me," she said, before the woman disappeared into the crowd. When she was ready for treatment, April would help her.

April had helped many people into treatment. But it remained difficult for people to access the services quickly, when they needed it—an issue that plagued Black users, who were more likely to use substances other than opioids. The fastest way to get into treatment is to go into a detox program. But those programs prioritized alcohol or opioid users, not people using crack or meth. "God forbid if you're homeless and you're looking for rehab and you smoke crack. You gotta wait days, you gotta make all these phone calls, just to try to get into rehab," April said. Whereas, "if alcohol or opiates is your issue, you go to detox, you have a bed, a roof over your head. You have people working with you over five to seven days to find a rehab." The city had assessment centers, where someone could walk in to get help finding treatment. But the process often took hours or days, amid agonizing withdrawal symptoms, only for many people to be told there were no treatment beds available at all. "Try again tomorrow," they were often told, and released back onto the street.

As a result, April had found herself in the uncomfortable position of suggesting people use in order to get into detox. "You gotta use something—pick a beer, pick a perc—in order to get into treatment," April said. She felt similar discomfort about the city's recovery-home industry. "We know that there's kickbacks," she said. "But it serves its purpose. At the end of the day, it's still housing hundreds of people." In the absence of better alternatives, she would take what she could get. For April, all this was one more sign that, despite all the talk of helping drug users, the structural racism that plagued her mother's generation persisted.

For a long time during the opioid epidemic, white people had the highest rates of overdose deaths. But as the epidemic continued, the death tolls in Black and Native American communities began to rise at a disproportionate rate. One of the reasons for this imbalance was the introduction of fentanyl into the drug supply, including in substances other than opioids, like cocaine and meth, in order to produce a more potent high.

The pandemic, too, hit Black Philadelphians harder. Lack of jobs and financial opportunities meant that rates of unemployment and gun violence had escalated. More businesses in Black neighborhoods, unable to access small business loans, had closed. Also, with Black neighborhoods having fewer green spaces, there were fewer community outlets for escape, fewer ways to destress and balance one's mental health. And then there was April's lifeline and so many others, her 12-step community of people trying to live without substances amid so much pain. Those meetings had mostly moved online, and they were just not the same. Drugs and alcohol were so effective at numbing pain. April could will herself through it, day by day. But for how long? What if the pain never stopped? People she used to see in meetings began dropping, left and right.

Even after the pandemic petered out, the number of overdoses continued to rise and the racial disparities widened even more. In 2022, overdose deaths in Philadelphia increased for a fourth year in a row, with many of the 1,413 deaths concentrated in Kensington, reflecting more than a 20 percent increase in overdose deaths among Black residents. In 2023, for the first time in five years, the city saw slightly fewer deaths.

But as April has seen the drug epidemic shift back into communities of color, she has also seen how concerns about treatment access have receded, replaced by concerns about public safety and crime. In Philadelphia, this has meant police crackdowns and the defunding of harm-reduction services, including the needle exchange program that had once been so vital to April's survival. Among Black Philadelphians, such measures are likely to make the epidemic worse. Punishment can help people tap into motivation. The very concrete value of substances begins to erode when their use leads to consequences. Indeed, many people credit an arrest—or a loss of a child, relationship, or money—as a turning point that led them to sobriety. Incentives and motivation for recovery matter, but when treatment is imposed through the criminal justice system, Black people tend to fare worse than white people. In fact, studies show that they fare better when treatment is attached to employment and education—when sobriety is rewarded with hope and better, more positive alternatives, instead of punishment.

While the federal government and communities across the country vow a return to the policies of the earlier drug war, officials have also doubled down on medication as the answer, repeatedly calling for expanded access to buprenorphine. But this expansion, as it unfolded during the opioid epidemic, disproportionately benefited white people, who continue to have greater access to it than other ethnic groups.

The longer someone stays on buprenorphine, the more effective it is. But rates of long-term use are low across all ethnic groups, and the rate of Black and Brown patients who stay on the medication for at least 180 days—the minimum recommended duration—is far lower than for white patients. This gap is rarely acknowledged at the national level, even as officials have continued to point to medication as the answer.

After Purdue Pharma declared bankruptcy in 2019, the U.S. Justice Department appointed a committee to advise on the use of the settlement funds. The committee members all seemed to agree that more treatment was needed. But what about other needs that are crucial to sobriety, such as recovery support, housing, and employment assistance? Ryan Hampton, an activist and recovery advocate on the committee, said most members rejected any proposals that didn't involve treatment. "Every time anything other than treatment was brought up, there was resistance to trying it," he said.

Ryan Hampton was homeless when he started his recovery with a 28-day treatment stint, but when he looked back on it, he felt that what would have helped him more was starting on medication-assisted treatment (MAT), plus housing, food stamps, Medicaid coverage, job assistance, counseling, and peer coaching. "The industrial treatment complex in this country is just bullshit," he said, pointing to the for-profit programs Wendy had made it her mission to investigate. "The bigger problem with the 28-day model is that it leaves the majority of Americans behind."

Those people left behind were the people April saw in Kensington. It wasn't just treatment that they needed; they also needed access to the most basic human needs. Kindness. Friends. Housing. Jobs. Food. Addiction had devastated their lives, but it was the punishment imposed on them for their addictions that had pushed many of them further to the margins. Having a criminal record barred people from voting or obtaining licenses to work in certain professions. Parents who were reported to child protective services were placed on state registries that showed up on background checks, making them ineligible for basic entry-level jobs, like caregiving or childcare. Without any savings or ability to obtain credit, finding housing was close to impossible. Falling behind on paying court fines or fees or for drug tests, people lost their driver's licenses, further impacting their ability to find jobs. Meanwhile, positive drug screens could render someone ineligible for government assistance.

"How do we address all those barriers?" asked Dr. John Kelly, a professor of addiction medicine at Harvard Medical School and a consultant to the Biden administration. "How hard is that, for somebody with a lack of resources, to be able to address their substance use disorder when they have all these other crises going on in their lives?" In addiction-research circles, someone's financial and housing stability, social supports, and community are considered "recovery capital"—the combination of internal and external resources that people draw on to successfully recover from addiction. The more recovery capital a person accrues, the greater their chance of success.

But access to recovery capital is unequal. The same structural barriers that create inequality along race and gender lines also impact someone's chances of successful recovery. In Dr. Kelly's view, this is the missing piece in U.S. drug policy that the government has consistently failed to address. People lack the ability and opportunity to change their circumstances. Treatment most benefits white people who have some semblance of means, like Chris Koon. It most helps people who have access to recovery capital.

Soon, April ran out of hot dogs. We got back into the car to head home. On the way there, April noticed a man lying flat on the ground, in the middle of a Taco Bell drive-through lane. His eyes were moving, but he otherwise appeared catatonic. "Is he okay?" She stopped the car and ran to stop a woman who was rifling through his pockets.

"You about to rob this man while he's laying flat on his back!" April scolded the woman, encouraging her to think about her own survival. "Every time you disrespect yourself or someone else, it stays with you. It makes recovery harder." The woman protested, then lingered for a few minutes before walking away.

April stayed until the ambulance came. "I used to be this person," she told the accompanying police officer, as if trying to convince him of the man's humanity. She watched them load the man onto a stretcher. Then April got back into her car, lit a Newport, and drove home.

CHAPTER NINETEEN

Larry Ley

2019

The old man formerly known as Dr. Larry Ley shrugged off his wool overcoat and shuffled over to a wooden bench next to the metal detector. He had been dizzy getting out of the cab. He'd had five cups of coffee that morning. He reeked of cigarettes. It was 8 a.m.

"I got an hour of sleep," he said, through a raspy cough. His voice sounded deep but broken, like marbles rolling across crumpled cellophane. He sat down on the bench on the ground floor of the Dirksen Federal Building, a sparse and busy federal courthouse and skyscraper in downtown Chicago. Larry pulled out his cellphone and opened texts from his friends in AA.

"Today is the day," he read aloud. "Seeing is believing is conceiving is achieving."

"Praying for you," another text said.

Andrew Dollard, Larry's friend and former business partner, wasn't there yet. He wanted to walk from the hotel to calm down and clear his head in the 10-degree air. "Wanted to ogle women, is what he means," Larry said, raising a bushy eyebrow. When Andrew arrived, they would go upstairs to

Rehab

the Seventh Circuit Court of Appeals. It was November 5, 2019. It would be the day, Larry hoped, that would finally clear his name.

Several years had passed since Larry and his staff were arrested in a DEA raid on DORN. Larry was the only person to go to trial. Prosecutors had charged him with nine counts of dealing in a Schedule III controlled substance. As the basis for these charges, they claimed he had failed to prescribe Suboxone for a legitimate medical purpose and that he and other doctors had pre-signed prescriptions without seeing patients.

The trial had lasted seven days and featured dozens of witnesses, including Larry himself, who seemed to relish the opportunity to show off his knowledge of addiction medicine. Prosecutors emphasized DORN's hefty patient rolls and the fact Larry had prescribed Suboxone for pain to get around the patient limit. But they failed to acknowledge that—right before the trial—the federal government had again increased the patient limit, rendering Larry's violation of the prescribing regulations practically meaningless. Following the bench trial, the judge said the state had not proven its case beyond a reasonable doubt. "People were asking to be treated," Judge Steve Nation said in his ruling. "The drug that was issued was appropriate for what they were being asked to be treated for." He decided to acquit. Prosecutors promptly dropped the charges against everyone else.

But the damage was done. Between his arrest and the trial, Larry had been arrested for two DUIs. He lost his medical license and all of DORN's patients had moved on, some to overdose. Dr. Luella Bangura had become so distressed by the charges that she stopped practicing all together.

Following his acquittal, Larry and his former employees decided to sue. They alleged their arrests had been politically motivated, pushed by a mayor who didn't like seeing his wealthy city associated with Larry's high-profile addiction practice. The lawsuit failed, prompting Larry and his former employees to appeal. Now, they were in Chicago for the federal appellate court hearing, during which Larry's attorney, Jim Fisher, would argue their case.

Andrew arrived. He was 46 years old—a much younger man than Larry—and he wore a trim suit and a purple tie. Andrew had started out as a probation officer and worked his way through law school to become a contract public defender before becoming Larry's right-hand man at DORN, where he made more money than he had ever made before. He was from a farm town in Indiana. He had never been to Chicago or a federal courthouse. "Come on, let's go," Andrew said, eying the security line. He was anxious to get upstairs, even though the hearing did not begin for another hour.

On the other side of the metal detector, the two made their way to the elevators. Andrew paced ahead, taking long and fast strides. Larry, with a chronic back condition, shuffled behind. Andrew realized they were going in the wrong direction and turned around. "Just follow the people," Larry suggested. "That's the best thing to do in large cities, I've found." They turned left, then right, and they made their way to another set of elevators. The building was enormous. It turned out there were four sets of elevators, each going to different sets of floors. They didn't know which one to take. Andrew found a thick stack of paper at a security podium and began flipping through it, looking for their case.

"Wait a second, that's the wrong date," Andrew said, flicking the stack. He flagged down a security guard, who directed them to another elevator. Andrew forged ahead.

"If you'd had done your job, you'd be prepared," Larry said, as they stepped into the elevator.

"You see what I have to put up with?" Andrew said. "You're like Trump. An angry old man."

They rode the elevator up to the 27th floor and stepped out into an empty corridor of floor-to-ceiling granite. There were glass doors on either side. Both were locked. Andrew turned to a blue touch screen embedded in a metal frame on the wall. "Court schedule by party/attorney," the screen said.

Andrew perked up. "Oh, let's try this. This is interesting." He typed his last name into the system, then stepped back. "Got to take a picture of this," he said, pulling out his phone. It was 8:28 a.m.

On the way to Chicago, a three-hour drive, Larry had told what he claimed was a funny story. It was from the height of his drinking days, he said, in the mid-'90s. "This is a really good story. One of Larry's truly great stories," Andrew had said, from the driver's seat. The story began with Larry getting drunk. He was driving his beloved Lexus at 110 miles per hour when he lost control around a curve in the road and catapulted over a grassy knoll. "So the car's sitting, you know, belly up—"

"In a ditch," Andrew piped in.

"And sure enough, fairly soon, here comes Indiana State Police. I kicked my window out and the trooper comes up. I can see his name tag. I was sober enough to read that. He says, 'Sir, seems like we've got a problem here.'"

"Officer McDowell," Larry slurred back, peering up at the officer through the window. "I was just fixing to come ashore."

The officer hadn't heard that one before. Couldn't stop himself from laughing. "'I'll see your ass at the hospital,' he said.

"Sure enough, they loaded me up in an ambulance and took me to the hospital. And sure enough, he comes walking into the room and says, 'Well, you made it ashore!'" Larry laughed a belly laugh.

"Run into him two or three times since then. He still remembers me," Larry said. His smile faded. By that time, Larry had quit practicing surgery. He wasn't allowed to drive anymore. "That's when I started going to AA."

Following his arrest, Larry had developed PTSD. He was now in therapy and taking medications to help with the insomnia and flashbacks. He felt guilty about the DORN raid and how the case had affected his former employees' lives, but he did not regret his choices, even as he admitted that not all the care he provided was up to par. He had not done physical exams. He had not followed the professional standards laid out by organizations like the American Society of Addiction Medicine. But Larry was proud that he had refused to follow professional recommendations. He believed they were not necessary. He believed that he knew better.

People were overdosing and dying all over the country, every day. And most still did not have access to treatment. In fact, Larry emphasized, outside of big cities with hospital and university networks and big managed-care organizations, treatment medications were still hard to come by, especially in some of the rural areas where Larry had chosen to open clinics.

For much of history, addiction treatment in the United States had been punitive and prescriptive. Many programs and recovery homes, like the one in which April Lee and Chris Koon had found themselves, still operated that way. In these programs, patients were never asked what they wanted, or given opportunities to choose their own path. At best, they were presented with the program and punished for breaking the rules. At worst, they were required to study the bible regardless of their religious views, or forced to work without pay as a form of "therapy." It was common for a program administrator to tell a patient what they needed, rather than help the patient determine their motivation for recovery and what was best for them.

However questionable his business choices, Larry had offered his patients something they often didn't get in other treatment programs. He encouraged patients to go to therapy, to attend 12-step meetings, to bring their families and friends into their recovery process, to find a support group. But he also didn't erect onerous requirements that might have caused patients to drop out of treatment or feel like they were failing in it. He had given them the opportunity to make their own choices.

Larry had used his program, as he had his medical career, to make money and attain status. And yet, the sad reality of the treatment landscape meant that he had still done a better job of facilitating his patients' survival than many other treatment programs. Amid his legal troubles, new studies were showing the importance of easy access to medications like Suboxone, and how staying connected to a program—even with continued drug use—kept people alive. Larry wanted the federal court to acknowledge the important role he had played and allow his lawsuit to proceed.

A clerk unlocked one of the glass doors and Andrew swung open the door, stepping into an expanse of dull blue-gray carpeting. He charged ahead, turning left down a hallway. "Where's he leading us?" Larry said, the soles of his orthopedic shoes rubbing against the carpet like sandpaper.

Rehab

Larry rounded the corner. At the end of the narrow hall stood a line of green leather chairs. A sign outside the courtroom door read "Court in Session. Quiet Please." And: "Cell phones & pagers must be turned off."

"Larry, turn your fucking phone off," Andrew said.

"It is off," Larry said, clutching his phone. It dings: "How may I help you?"

"It doesn't sound like it's off." Andrew took a picture of the courtroom door, then sat down.

Larry tucked his phone into his pocket and headed toward the bathroom. Andrew leaned over and whispered to me. "As you can see, Larry is a strange man. He was an excellent surgeon. In charge of life and death. And he just has this he-knows-best mentality. He won't listen to anybody else. If he had, we wouldn't be sitting here right now. He doesn't like to follow the rules."

Larry returned from the bathroom, and the courtroom door opened. Andrew jumped up. "I'm going in and powering down my phone. I would advise my colleagues to do the same," he said, glaring at Larry.

The two walked into the courtroom. Gigantic portraits of judges hung on the walls. The ceiling towered above them, a metal grid emitting a white light that accentuated every wrinkle in clothes and on faces. Larry sat down and leaned forward. He rubbed his leg. Beneath his shirt, a deep scar nearly a foot long ran down his back, the result of decades of surgeries to repair his eroding spinal cord. The wooden bench was already making his back ache.

Larry's attorney intended to poke holes in the DEA's case and argue his client's innocence. But as the hearing began, the judges seemed inclined to believe that the evidence agents collected was more than enough to justify their arrests, even if it wasn't enough ultimately to ensure their convictions. "Patients did not have to present IDs," noted Judge Ilana Rovner. "Didn't they show up and there was no doctor and they still got a 'script?" asked Judge Joel Flaum. Nearby, Ron Vierk, one of the DORN doctors, dropped his face into his hands. "I think we're about 50/50," Larry said, after the hearing.

Several weeks later, Larry and Andrew would finally receive word of the decision. Only Joseph Mackey, the part-time parking lot attendant, had standing to sue the DEA, the police department, and the city of Carmel. The State Supreme Court, their only other recourse, had no interest in hearing the case. For Larry, this was the end of the road.

A YEAR AFTER Larry's appeal was rejected, the U.S. Department of Justice (DOJ) announced a big win. After years of activism and anger from parents like Wendy McEntyre, the agency had finally begun pursuing cases against drug distributors and manufacturers such as Purdue Pharma. And now the DOJ was announcing their biggest win in the war against opioids yet—a criminal case against the manufacturer of Suboxone.

While the company had played a significant role in confronting the opioid epidemic, the government's case exposed the machinations of a pharmaceutical company intent on maximizing profits. The problem began in 2002, when the U.S. Food and Drug Administration (FDA) granted the company orphan drug status, a designation that ensured the government would not approve any generic versions of Suboxone or Subutex for seven years. With this monopoly in place, the company's profits quickly poured in. And as the expiration date neared, the company decided it would aim to protect those profits from generic competition by launching a new product: Suboxone Sublingual Film, a paper-thin patch that melted when placed under the tongue.

The company—now known as Indivior—began a campaign to undermine generic versions of the tablets, claiming they were a safety hazard for kids, and that the film, once dissolved in the mouth, could not be as easily diverted. By convincing everyone that the tablets were unsafe, the company would drive business to Suboxone film instead of the generic, allowing them to maintain their monopoly on the market. Sales reps began lobbying doctors and directors of healthcare programs to switch their patients to the film, citing falsified data on the safety risks to children. When healthcare agencies balked, a doctor associated with Indivior attempted to place letters in newspapers that accused them of "engaging in 21st century biological warfare, no different than giving small pox infected blankets to Indians." After receiving FDA approval, Indivior's CEO ordered a "Full Blitz campaign" to convert doctors to Suboxone film before generics could hit the market.

The DOJ's case resulted in a $1.4 billion settlement, and for seemingly the first time in the government's opioid fight against Big Pharma, an executive received a prison sentence. While none of the Sacklers would ever serve prison time for their role in the opioid epidemic, Indivior CEO Shaun Thaxter would plead guilty to a misdemeanor charge, receive a sentence of six months in federal prison, and be ordered to pay $600,000.

Several lawsuits followed the DOJ's case, including by the attorney general in Larry's home state of Indiana, who would win $4.3 million for the state while blaming Indivior for helping to "sustain drug addiction in this country at the very time they claimed to be helping eradicate it." But the charges and the lawsuit did not hinder Indivior's growth, and the company continued to expand, launching Sublocade—an injectable version of Suboxone—in 2018; then, in 2023, acquiring Opiant Pharmaceuticals, the makers of the overdose-reversal drug Narcan.

Amid escalating death rates, the same kind of profiteering and regulatory bureaucracy that had surrounded and slowed Suboxone distribution had expanded to include the overdose-reversal drug. Originally approved by the FDA in 1971, naloxone had long ago lost patent protection, preventing companies from monopolizing the market, the way Suboxone once had. So, companies began developing new ways of delivering the drug, like auto-injectors and nasal sprays, and obtained new patents. Some of these patents are not due to expire until 2035, ensuring prohibitively high prices. In 2022, researchers found that only one state in the entire country had enough naloxone to stem the overdose death crisis.

Finally, in 2023, the FDA approved the first naloxone nasal spray for over-the-counter purchase. But at about $45 per box, it remained out of reach for many who might need it.

Larry Ley

IN 2020, LARRY LEARNED he had cancer. His prognosis was not good. After several rounds of radiation, the doctors told him he had little time left. He began making plans to sell his house.

It was 10 degrees outside in February when a house painter arrived. As usual, Larry had hired only the best. "I found the finest painter in the world," Larry told me over the phone. He chose the colors himself: lemongrass green for the hallway and living room; a soft gray for the kitchen. A "bastard white" he had concocted for the ceilings; "I just had the guy at the paint store make some mixes until it got to the point I liked it," he said, delighting in his talent. "I probably should have gone into the construction business."

Most days now Larry spent resting. He was dizzy and unstable on his feet. His speech was even slower than before. His hands shook too much to write or text. He couldn't stomach the thought of food. He drank Core Power protein shakes (his favorite was chocolate), coffee, and ginger ale. He watched reruns of crime shows, *Dateline*, and *20/20*.

His son had moved out several months earlier and hadn't been by much since. His daughter was still refusing to talk to him. His brother sometimes came by, but in February he was snowbirding in Florida with his girlfriend. Most days, it was just Larry and his dog, George.

DORN's staff had moved on, in some ways. Andrew Dollard had his own law firm in downtown Noblesville, although he said he still had nightmares about his arrest. George Agapios had returned to medicine. Though she managed to retain her medical license, Luella Bangura had not resumed her practice. Larry's office manager Cassy Bratcher struggled to find work for years and eventually landed a job at another Suboxone clinic. "This one felt different from Larry's," she said. She worked closely with the nurse who ran it, who sat in on the one-on-one meetings with every patient. Cassy found herself wondering if she would have done some things differently at Larry's. But for some reason that clinic closed and Cassy found herself out of work yet again. Eventually, she entered a different field altogether.

Rehab

In the years since DORN had been shut down, the state of Indiana—and the towns where DORN used to operate—had changed. Carmel began deploying a quick-response team to every overdose scene, to help connect people with recovery support. In 2017, Kokomo announced it was joining a massive lawsuit against the country's three largest wholesale drug distributors. In a press release, the city accused the distributors of "dumping millions of dollars' worth of prescription opiates into its community" and of being "responsible for the opioid epidemic." Of course, the press release made no mention of the fact that the city had played a key role in preventing people from accessing treatment for years. Further, Suboxone clinics seemed to be spreading across the United States, some of them bearing a remarkable similarity to DORN.

Back in 2014, the year of DORN's raid and Larry's arrest, a former Dartmouth medical student teamed up with a doctor in New Hampshire to start a Suboxone clinic based on his thesis—what would later become the for-profit company Groups: Recover Together. "Our goal is to provide effective, evidence-based care to the largest group of people possible. Rather than exorbitantly expensive, bespoke care to those with means," the founder, Jeff De Flavio, told the tech website *The Verge*.

De Flavio said his company's model targeted two barriers to treatment—proximity and price—by opening up low-cost facilities in small towns and rural communities. Each office provided a Suboxone prescription and group therapy at a cost of $65 per week, which was $25 more than the cost of Larry's program. They strove to keep the program affordable and accessible, he said, by hiring minimal staff, contracting with doctors, and opening offices in rural places. "My interest, as an entrepreneur, is to bring private financing to bear on a huge social problem that has destroyed millions of lives," De Flavio told CNBC. The financial prospects involved would lead one board member to dub Groups a potential "unicorn"—a term for private companies valued at $1 billion or more. The company would ultimately grow to 142 offices in 16 states and would raise more than $60 million in funding. More programs just like it would soon follow, some charging more than $300 a month.

Larry Ley

"Hell, yes, they copied me," Larry said. "What I was doing was pioneering. I proved that it worked."

In 2022, the federal government—following years of advocacy—did away with patient limits and mandatory training. But doctors still remained hesitant about prescribing the medication, with a laundry list of concerns that ranged from lack of institutional support and burdensome insurance-approval processes to fear of DEA overreach and even the patients themselves. In the year immediately after these changes, buprenorphine prescriptions actually declined.

Methadone, too, remained hard to access. In 2024, the Biden administration loosened some regulations applying to methadone, including the requirement that a patient have experienced opioid addiction for at least a year before receiving a prescription. But policymakers stopped short of expanding access to methadone through other addiction-treatment programs or pharmacies—two efforts that have helped reduce overdose deaths in other countries. This is in part due to the influence of methadone clinics themselves. As overdose deaths have escalated, the private equity–backed industry has lobbied hard against reforms that might expand access to more people. "They don't want to surrender the profits that come from having a monopoly," Massachusetts Senator Ed Markey told *STAT*.

For a time, Larry returned to addiction treatment—as a patient. In 2017, he enrolled in an outpatient program for people with histories of addiction and PTSD. He began taking medication for anxiety, going to group therapy, and seeing an individual therapist twice a week. His life took on a different rhythm. He got a puppy, a Portuguese water dog with wavy black hair that he named George, after his father. He found enjoyment in George's penchant for stealing whole steaks and blocks of cheddar cheese off the kitchen counter, or jumping from couch to couch in the living room.

He began reading the Bible and going to church. He tried to find work. He took a word-processing class and prepared a résumé. He even applied for a job as a medical reporter at a local television station. In an application letter, he touted his schooling, communication skills, and areas of medical expertise before addressing his arrest. "Recently, extensive experience in the legal system of the United States and the State of Indiana has been acquired," Larry wrote. "Unfortunately I, as well as my entire staff, were wrongfully arrested and subsequently acquitted from all charges related to our efforts to adequately treat the ongoing 'opiate epidemic.' The only positive result of this experience is a better understanding of laws and regulations with respect to the medical field." Larry attached his list of references and his résumé and signed the letter, "Cordially yours, Larry J. Ley, MD, FACS, MBA." He never heard back.

In late 2022, Larry passed away. He was 77 years old.

CHAPTER TWENTY

Wendy McEntyre

2022

It was about 2:30 p.m., on March 21, 2022, when Cheryll's phone rang. Her sister, Wendy, was on the other end. Cheryll could not make out what Wendy was saying. She was screaming, talking a mile a minute. "Wait," she said. "What?"

"The police," Wendy told her. "They're outside."

The police were ringing her doorbell—pounding, trying to get in. They had been there for hours. At one point, a sheriff's deputy had peered in through the sliver of window at the front door and made eye contact with Wendy as she was crawling up the stairs from the living room. As soon as Wendy had spotted him, she fled back downstairs.

"Get back up here and open the door," Wendy had heard the deputy say. "Answer the door or we're kicking it in." Another grabbed a nearby pickaxe and blocked her Ring camera's view.

Wendy was shaking, her heart racing. She began frantically assembling boxes of evidence. *This will explain everything*, she thought. "They don't have a warrant," she told Cheryll.

Rehab

Cheryll told Wendy to let them in. "Wendy, these are San Bernardino cops and they're not going to give a shit what you have to say. Turn the kid over."

For a month, Wendy had been communicating daily with Diana Veles, the former medical assistant from Above It All Treatment Center, who long ago had fed her information on the facility's medication practices. The two had been out of touch for years when Diana reached out to Wendy about her new job at a local juvenile treatment program. Diana, who was finishing her bachelor's degree in psychology, was appalled at the conditions in the home, which provided therapeutic services and housing for adolescents. She had no idea what to do. A facility that served troubled youth was not Wendy's typical target. But the program was supposed to help vulnerable kids, including those with substance-use issues. Wendy told Diana not to quit. She should stay, report the information, and help stop what was going on.

Diana started feeding Wendy audio and photos. She sent pictures of metal filing cabinets that contained medications, padlocks dangling unlocked, and a photo of a staff member who was supposed to be watching the kids, but who had instead appeared to have fallen asleep. Diana noted that if a kid went missing, the facility was supposed to report it within two hours—but she said she saw kids run away and no one was called. Diana noted that one house manager consistently spent the entire morning playing video games in his office rather than watch the kids.

In California, mental health programs, group homes, and facilities for foster youth are overseen by the Department of Social Services (DSS). Wendy navigated to the DSS website, where she looked up the dozens of complaint investigations that had been filed and concluded since 2017. One by one, she printed them out and added them to a three-ring binder. Then she put on a blue fleece blanket with a hood and made herself a drink—vodka, ice, and Fruity Pebbles–flavored creamer—and sat down to review the reports with her notebook and highlighter in hand. Her takeaway was that the program had been plagued by serious complaints for years—allegations that the staff allowed youth to use drugs, that the staff were sleeping during work shifts, that staff had been physically violent or engaged in sexual activity with a minor. But many of the complaints had been unsubstantiated. This seemed to Wendy worthy of investigation. Diana agreed. "These kids are not lying," Diana texted Wendy.

The program claimed to serve the needs of LGBT youth. But soon, Diana told Wendy about how the facility was refusing to place a transgender teenager, who identified as a girl, in the girls' housing. Instead, she was being housed with boys, where she was being ridiculed and beaten up. After one of the kids hit the teenager with a belt, the facility had simply moved her to another boys' house, where a different kid promptly punched the teenager. Diana tried to support the teen by buying pink nail polish and perfume, but she felt the facility was failing to protect her. "WE SERIOUSLY NEED TO GET ____ OUT OF HERE!!!!," Diana texted Wendy. "The boys are so disrespectful to her way of being."

Wendy began her campaign in typical Wendy fashion. She contacted anyone and everyone, again and again, heading her emails in all caps, threatening legal action when she didn't hear back. "YOU ARE BEING WILLFULLY IGNORANT," she wrote. The teen "IS IN DANGER AND THERE IS NO SAFETY PLAN IN PLACE FOR HER." While Diana filed reports with DSS, Wendy reached out to social workers and urged the agency, for the kid's safety, to place the teenager somewhere else.

Finally, on March 15, ten days after the incident, an investigator with DSS reached out to Diana, who shared all the materials she'd gathered. Wendy spoke with a caseworker, who seemed disturbed that Wendy knew specific details about a child in state care—information that, by law, was supposed to be kept confidential. The caseworker assured her: "The state is involved. We actually have a meeting tomorrow," she said. "Thank you so much for your care and sharing this information with me."

But despite Wendy's aggressive efforts, the teen was still at the facility a week later, when Diana learned that she had been attacked again. Diana watched and recorded as an employee threatened to slam the teenager against the wall. "Keep on fucking with me," the employee said. "You're going to meet your mother-fucking maker." Diana took the teen to the hospital for a hand injury and called Wendy, who immediately alerted the authorities. "She needs to be placed somewhere safe IMMEDIATELY," Wendy wrote.

At first, the hospital said they would try to keep the kid overnight. But then, Diana learned, the hospital was planning to release her, and she would have to go back to the home. Diana said when the teenager overheard this, she ran out the door.

Text messages between Diana and Wendy seemed to show more detailed coordination:

"Update: we are up the street at a gas station."

"Please tell me your almost there. They're sending more people to search. He's in that Starbucks across the street. From the hospital."

"Ok, I'm going in. Hurry!! Put [her] in your vehicle, we are next door at 711 [sic]." Wendy's plan was to get the kid somewhere safe and then take her to a new facility the next day. "So the story is going to be [kid] called my 24/7 emergency hotline . . . from a pay phone and I came and got her," she wrote.

"Ok!" Diana wrote back.

At 9:30 p.m., Wendy told Diana that they were at home safe. She sent victorious messages to everyone, including child welfare authorities, and me. "I just got home . . . With the blessing of the social worker, I coordinated a rescue. I'll tell you more tomorrow. All I know is that [the facility] is shitting their pants." But by 1 p.m. the next day, Wendy was frantically texting everyone. "2 cop cars in front of my house for 30 minutes. . . . Do you think the facility called the cops on me?" And, "Emergency. I have cops at my door. They are going to arrest me. Please call me. They said they will brake my door down."

Finally, Wendy came out with her hands up. An officer placed her under arrest and put her in the back of a patrol car. As he drove her to the police station, Wendy launched into her life story, telling him about her son's death, how she'd created Jarrod's Law, how she had made it her mission to shut down abusive facilities. The deputy all but nodded, then interrupted Wendy to tell her she was under arrest for felony kidnapping.

The sheriff's office would later interview the teen's CPS caseworker, who would deny ever approving of the rescue. She told the deputy that she had received a call "randomly" from Wendy on March 15, during which Wendy had identified herself as a public safety advocate before going "on a rant for about 20 minutes" about trying to get the teenager transferred to another group home. The deputy asked the caseworker if she had ever told Wendy she would assist her in getting the teenager transferred. She said she had not.

The deputy told the teenager they planned to take her back to the facility. And then he took Wendy to jail.

THE NEXT TIME I heard from Wendy was the day after she got out of jail. Her mother and sister had gathered the funds to post her $250,000 bail and they picked her up. "Well, you know every activist has to go to jail at least once," her mother said on the ride home, trying to revive Wendy from shock. Usually, Wendy would be happy to pick up the phone and talk for hours. But this time she didn't have it in her. "I am not OK," Wendy wrote to me. "I am still in severe shock. Can't put words together to describe the horror of what I went through."

Wendy had never been inside a jail before. She felt guilty that she had ever wanted Jarrod to end up in such a place, even if it was to keep him from using. The woman she had been transported with to jail seemed to be losing her mind. The toilet in her cell was overflowing with blood and feces. She could see several women pounding on the glass, requesting tampons, but the guards were ignoring them. Eventually, Wendy was strip-searched and placed in a cell with another woman. She hadn't eaten or slept in over a day, and she soon needed to use the toilet. "I'm sorry I'm about to shit in front of you," Wendy said.

"That's OK. We're in a shitty situation. We're up shit's creek," the woman replied, then offered Wendy a bite of apple after she had finished. The little bit of humor and kindness made Wendy sob.

After several hours, attorney Karen Gold arrived and met with Wendy in a tiny visitation booth. Karen took her hand and began singing the Shema, a Jewish prayer of faith in God. Eventually, Wendy's mother and sister came to pick her up.

"She's a wreck," Cheryll told me the following morning. She didn't understand why Wendy would think it was a good idea to pick up a child. She was perplexed by her sister's choices. "But as Karen said to me, this is one of the things she really respects about Wendy. In those certain moments, you make these hard choices because it saves a life."

WENDY'S ARREST FOLLOWED years of small victories and persistent failures. She had been trying since 2005 to have Jarrod's Law passed, which would require the state to regulate sober-living homes, but every time she worked with a lawmaker to introduce the legislation, it stalled or was vetoed. Other laws did move forward, though, including one that finally permitted detox facilities—if certified—to employ medical staff. But Wendy continued to see rehabs across the state overmedicating and poorly monitoring patients, leading to more deaths.

In 2019, the day after she appeared at the State Capitol to testify in support of Jarrod's Law, Wendy learned about a death at Creative Care, a Malibu-based rehab that was heavily featured on the *Dr. Phil* show, despite a lengthy history of problems with the state.

Wendy launched an investigation and a campaign filled with lengthy emailed diatribes and Facebook posts; she got on the phone with *Dr. Phil*'s lawyers, who told her the show was cutting ties with the program. Then

Creative Care filed a libel lawsuit. Wendy felt like she was drowning under her mounting legal battles. In 2022, the latest version of Jarrod's Law—which would have required residential and sober-living facilities that distribute prescription drugs to be licensed—died in committee.

Wendy had always dreamed of seeing the Avarells in court. She had gleefully attended many of the depositions, lugging into the conference room her many boxes and binders full of her investigative findings. On one portable file box she'd scrawled "Evil Doers." This box was crammed with her evidence against the Avarells and their "henchmen," as she called them. The other box was labeled "Angels," and this included all the information she'd amassed on the people who had died. She even had a folder she'd marked "Devils or Angels"; this was for the employees—some complicit—who had turned against the Avarells and fed Wendy information.

The depositions expanded Wendy's understanding of Above It All's operations and unearthed evidence she had not been able to find. The evidence in the James Dugas case was so strong that, in 2019, Above It All admitted—on the record—to giving him the wrong medications and to not monitoring him "as often as he should have been after the drugs were administered," the rehab said. "The defendant admits that it was negligent but denies that the negligence was a substantial factor in causing the death of James Robert Dugas." In Matthew Maniace's case, Above It All agreed that a jury would likely find it was negligent and had substantially contributed to his death.

But in the end, all the wrongful-death lawsuits against Above It All were settled out of court. Wendy would not get to see the Avarells questioned on the stand. And when Lynn Maniace and Wendy contacted the District Attorney's office, a prosecutor told Wendy that he had previously looked into Above It All and been "unable to find enough proof to continue with any inquiry." By then, struggling under a mountain of debt, Above It All and its associated treatment programs had voluntarily closed their doors.

Rehab

ABOUT A WEEK after Wendy's arrest, Diana Veles was arrested, too. A mother of four, living on food stamps, she had been on the verge of obtaining her master's degree, and was looking forward to full-time employment and higher pay as a therapist. Now, she and her family and friends were hosting bake sales and selling tamales to fund her legal fees. She had to repay $800 monthly to the bail bondsman—something she could scarcely afford on her pay from Home Depot.

Wendy was trying to find a lawyer for Diana when she was hit by another restraining order, this time from the group home. Once again, Wendy found herself depicted as dangerous and "unhinged" from years of unresolved grief. The organization noted that Wendy had started her nonprofit after her son passed away at an unlicensed facility. But since then, "her tactics have become aggressive and increasingly menacing towards care facilities," the petition said. "McEntyre's vigilantism has turned criminal and her actions are completely unpredictable."

The facility would eventually drop the restraining order. But the San Bernardino District Attorney's office—the same agency that had repeatedly dismissed her complaints about Above It All—moved forward with the felony kidnapping charge against her. As the case wended its way toward a trial, Wendy found herself more introspective. Attorney Karen Gold gave her a book to read called *Feeling Good*, about developing a more positive outlook on life. She read another book titled *Nonviolent Communication* and watched *Stutz*, Jonah Hill's Netflix documentary about his psychiatrist. Wendy was thinking about her impulsiveness and her anger.

"I'm tired of people trying to paint me as a crazy person. I'm not," she told me. "Being emotionally intelligent is challenging at times when you're hurt. Trying to communicate with people when you're hurt without coming across in a negative, aggressive way, it's challenging. Because it's fucking maddening." She'd spent almost 20 years of her life trying to expose the dangers of a healthcare and treatment system grounded in profits. She'd led one-woman campaigns to shutter dozens of facilities. She had interviewed hundreds, perhaps thousands, of people and dispatched thousands of emails. She'd testified at the State Capitol and written to the U.S. House of Representatives. But in the end, many of the places she'd investigated remained open, or others arrived to take their place. Maybe, she thought, it was time to take a step back. She disconnected her 24/7 hotline. The network of grieving moms receded. "No more Rodger Dodger," Wendy said. "If you bury your child, you bury the man you love; nothing else matters." She bought a kayak and spent more time on Lake Gregory, and more time with her daughter and grandchildren.

CYNDI DOYLE WAS starting to move on, too. When she and her husband had stopped investigating, a well of grief opened up. Shannon attempted suicide. Cyndi fell into deep depression. "What kept us going was trying to figure out what happened," Cyndi told me. "I don't think I was mourning until I stopped." She and Wendy had once spent every day on the phone together. Now, months passed between their calls.

Matthew Maniace's mother, Lynn, continued her fight. She rarely slept more than three or four hours, even though she was seeing a therapist and took medication to help her sleep. Her husband, Bill, had no idea the extent to which she was still trying to get justice for their son. In 2021, she filed complaints with the nursing board in California, and she hoped that some way, somehow, the probe would lead to arrests. If that happened, Lynn said, she believed the nurses would give up the owners of Above It All. "And if they do, it will be the first time I could say I'm happy in years. Because somebody needs to pay for this. Because I want justice for Matthew, but also I don't want to see this thing keep happening. It's not just this facility. Other facilities are doing the same thing." In 2023, the nursing board finally declared its intent to take disciplinary action against the nurse who had ordered Matthew's prescription. But by 2025—eight years after Matthew's death—she still had her license.

Rehab

IN NOVEMBER 2022, I visited Wendy McEntyre. The small wooden house, perched on the edge of the mountain, was something of a fortress, with only one door for in and out. She invited me inside and showed me around. We passed the bathroom on the left—what Wendy referred to as "the cat's bathroom" because she'd taught her cat to urinate into the toilet during the pandemic. She walked through the hall into the kitchen, which opened up, three steps down, into the carpeted living room, where Wendy was growing fresh herbs under pink lights. Photographs of her son Jarrod and husband Dean were everywhere.

She'd hung plastic ivy vines around the windows, which framed a beautiful view of the sky over the San Bernardino Mountains. In her bedroom, she had a loaf of bread, a toaster, and a coffee machine on a table at her bedside. She seemed content to live this solitary life.

When I returned the next day, the screen door was open and music was blasting. Horizontal sheets of rain blew into the entryway. The howling wind was shaking the trees, which threatened to drop the limbs that were already dangling precariously from previous storms. Inside, Wendy was dancing in bright pink boots that looked like a cross between Crocs and Uggs. She was sweating, her hair swept to the side in a plastic orange clip. "I got *great* news this morning," she said, giddily. The DSS had substantiated Wendy's complaint. The juvenile facility was losing its short-term residential therapeutic program license. "You're fucking with the wrong chick, man," Wendy said. Then she pumped her fist and yelled into the ceiling, mimicking Dean's SpongeBob SquarePants urn. "I feel empowered!"

Wendy was still facing criminal charges, but the news validated her rescue effort. Despite her arrest, and the program's attempts to discredit her, the Department of Social Services had taken action more quickly than Wendy had ever seen from the Department of Health Care Services. After two years, in 2024, a judge would resolve the criminal case by ordering Wendy and Diana to complete 25 hours of community service, which Wendy promptly devoted to Jarrod's Law. If Wendy avoided any further arrests, the judge said, he would consider wiping the case off her record.

In this moment, in her house, Wendy felt victorious. None of the deaths or disappointments or heartaches mattered. She pumped her shoulders up and down, dancing around the living room. "I got goosebumps," she told me. Then she looked up at the sky again and yelled: "I FEEL EMPOWERED!"

Epilogue

At the beginning of 2025 came some stunning news: a nearly 24 percent drop in overdose deaths. It was the first year since 2021 that the number of estimated overdose deaths fell below 100,000—to 86,882.

The news was met with cautious optimism and confusion. What could have caused the drop? Are we simply seeing a return to pre-pandemic levels of deaths or is the drop in fatal overdoses reflective of a generational shift? As this book describes, many of the strategies the United States has employed to combat the epidemic have been in place for years, including expanded access to naloxone and addiction treatment programs. Many groups jockeyed to take the credit, with legitimate victories to show for it. Harm-reduction efforts, for example, have placed Narcan in the hands of more people than ever before, allowing people to come to the aid of those who are overdosing, without having to wait for police or paramedics. A more than 40 percent increase in Narcan use has ostensibly translated to fewer overdose deaths.

Others concluded the positive results must be from a combination of factors. Fentanyl use has been around for years, beginning on the East Coast and migrating slowly across to the West. Its reputation is now well known,

Rehab

and its spread into the drug supply and its deadly consequences are well reported. "People know they're selling fentanyl. They know they are buying fentanyl," said Stanford professor Keith Humphreys, a former Obama advisor. In the era of fentanyl, drug users have become smarter about the way they consume drugs, such as using them in the company of others and employing Narcan in case of overdose.

The other potential factor is especially grim: many users have already died. When epidemics or pandemics such as COVID-19 hit, it is the most marginalized who reap the worst consequences. "And a lot of vulnerable people who are buying fentanyl are already dead," Humphreys said.

While the cause of the drop is not totally clear, we can say with some certainty what the drop does not mean. More than two-thirds of American families—the vast majority of the American public—say they or a family member have struggled with addiction, to the point of homelessness or overdose. Overdose death rates provide us with little insight into the experiences of the millions of people in the United States who remain mired in addiction, stuck in the destructive cycle of drug use, who have survived overdose, and—especially—those who wish to stop. Surely, there's a better metric than not dying that can be used to measure the effectiveness of our epidemic response. Surely, people struggling with addiction deserve more than just survival.

This book highlights many problems in our system for treating addiction. Treatment helps people recover. But too often, people in need still have trouble accessing treatment, and when they do, it is often prohibitively expensive and short-lived, punitive and transactional. Despite the Biden administration's lifting of a waiver requirement for doctors prescribing buprenorphine, still too few doctors prescribe it, limiting access to the medication, including in some areas hardest hit by the epidemic. Routes to treatment are still largely funneled through the criminal justice system and through a profit-driven healthcare system that prioritizes profits over individualized patient care. And when rehabs exploit patients for profit, poorly equipped regulators are loath to stop it. Law enforcement agencies often view people with addiction as complicit in their own victimization, and they seldom put resources into

Epilogue

investigating those who harm them. Women in need of treatment—especially those who are pregnant or who have children—still can't access it, leading more and more children into foster care, and to a skyrocketing maternal overdose death rate.

People who are struggling with addiction benefit from treatment, particularly from programs that don't exploit or abuse them, or use them for profit. As Wendy McEntyre has pushed for decades, lawmakers and regulators are particularly key here, as they are the first line of defense against profit-hungry programs that don't keep patients safe. Treatment programs are especially effective when they are accessible and easy to enter, and when providers listen to a person's needs, support them in finding the motivation to get better, and continue that support in the long term.

Punishment can help people tap into motivation. The very concrete value of substances begins to erode when their use leads to consequences. Many people credit an arrest, or a loss of a child, relationship, or money, as a turning point that led them to recovery. But at a certain point, punishment stops working. As addiction-medicine doctor Barry Zevin once told me: "Drugs are compelling." Drugs offer benefits to the people who use them. They alleviate physical and mental pain. They offer routes to community, especially in a culture that encourages the relentless pursuit of pleasure, but demonizes those who appear to lose control or take it too far. If all anybody has to look forward to is punishment, or the relief of drugs, they're going to choose drugs. What research shows is that stopping needs to be reinforced and rewarded with hope and better, more positive alternatives. As long as using drugs remains more compelling than not using drugs, people will continue to use drugs.

Neuroscientist Dr. Carl Hart is among those who have conducted research demonstrating this fact. When Dr. Hart started his research career in the 1990s, he—like many before him—hoped to find a cure for addiction, some way to block the dopamine activity in the brain to stop the compulsive cravings. Hart ran ads in the *Village Voice* and offered addicts a chance to make $950 while smoking crack inside the confines of a locked hospital ward.

Rehab

Each day, the addicts started their day with varying amounts of crack. Then, later in the day, each participant received a choice: more crack or cash rewards. When the dose of crack offered was relatively small, most addicts decided to pass it up in favor of economic rewards. Dr. Hart repeated his experiment with methamphetamine and found the same result. Almost every drug user in the experiments passed up a dose of their drug of choice when they were offered $20 instead. "When they were given an alternative to crack, they made rational economic decisions," Dr. Hart would later say.

The experiments changed Dr. Hart's beliefs about addiction. It's not that addicts are physically incapable of stopping; it's that many simply don't have better alternatives, and the pathways to attaining those alternatives are less than clear. Since Dr. Hart's experiments, scores of studies have found *contingency management*—a type of treatment in which patients receive consequences and rewards for behavior—highly effective at treating addiction. Studies have also found that people who have more resources to support their recovery—something known as *recovery capital*—are more successful at maintaining their recovery.

This echoes another surprising and important fact that I discovered while researching this book. Tens of millions of people in the United States have reported recovering from addiction. And 60 percent of those people got there without any treatment at all. Most people recover after only two attempts. Studies of people who experience "natural recoveries" provide some insight into these findings: Those who recover without treatment typically have access to financial and social resources that help them overcome obstacles, facilitate life change, and allow them to find alternatives to drug use. And these people also are more likely to be white, with higher levels of education, social networks, and opportunity.

This is not to say that white people do not succumb to debilitating addictions, and the lack of opportunity that comes with it. The marginalization that causes or accompanies addiction defeats white people, too. Addiction can lead to trauma, incarceration, the loss of civil rights and government benefits. Addiction can prevent someone from obtaining housing, food

Epilogue

stamps, jobs, and loans. If there were no consequences for drug addiction, many people would never find the motivation to recover. But at some point, the consequences of addiction become as much a barrier to recovery as the addiction itself. Those obstacles become impossible to overcome, keeping many people in the cycle of addiction, without the resources and ability to climb out.

This problem seems clear when comparing April Lee's and Chris Koon's trajectories. Chris was able to move on so much more quickly than April or other members of her family, in part because he had greater financial resources and social support to fall back on. April, also, was able to move on, but in some ways it was a stroke of luck. Her talent for words opened doors to larger networks she could tap to help her at her lowest moment. April is the first to acknowledge she is the exception rather than the rule. The fact that Black residents of Philadelphia account for a growing and disproportionate number of overdose deaths underlines this fact.

This is fundamentally the problem with our treatment system, and the key component missing from current U.S. drug policy, that might help solve this crisis of drug addiction. Despite how Suboxone was sold to U.S. lawmakers and to the American public, there is no magic cure for addiction. Treatment is useless unless it is accompanied by life change, and for growing generations of people who live in the United States—even those not struggling with addiction, that kind of change is out of reach. In 2023, 36.8 million people lived in poverty in the United States. More than half of Americans struggled to pay basic bills. The American Dream does not materialize for the vast majority of people. Yet the "pull yourself up by the bootstraps" mentality that pervades American culture and politics also remains the dominant mentality in treatment and recovery. If you want it enough, if you try hard enough, you'll succeed.

While many people do eventually climb out—on their own, or often after multiple stints at treatment—the fentanyl coursing through the drug supply has so significantly increased the risk of overdose death that many people succumb before they even have the chance to get there. For tens of thousands of people per year, a treatment system that fails to address these larger challenges has become functionally a death warrant.

But there is also possibility on the horizon. Researchers continue to identify new methods of treating addiction—from psychedelic-assisted therapy to contingency management—and these are tools that may help many people. And while treatment may see more cuts, communities are starting to receive funds from an unlikely source: drug manufacturers, pharmacies, and distributors are paying out more than $50 billion over two decades as restitution for the harm caused by the opioid epidemic. Some of those funds have already been spent on police patrol cars, on balancing county budgets, and on paying old bills, but there is real potential for communities to invest the money in programs that could truly help people recover.

It's too soon to predict the impacts of the federal approach to the crisis. President Donald Trump has promised a reprisal of extreme drug-war policies, from mandatory minimum sentences to the death penalty for drug dealers. There's a possibility of cuts to grant funding and Medicaid, which would imperil treatment for an estimated 40 percent of adults with opioid addictions. Emboldened by a U.S. Supreme Court decision, cities and towns across the country are embracing a new crackdown on addiction and homelessness. The opioid epidemic has become politicized once again, with the Trump Administration using the fentanyl crisis to advance its tariff agenda, even as overdose deaths decline. Whereas once politicians embraced the universality of addiction and treatment as the cure, now their focus is on the border, on immigration, and on crime. Profit and punishment have ruled our treatment system, but it is these same concepts that seem to rule the United States.

It is an addiction, since the founding of this country, that we just can't seem to quit.

ACKNOWLEDGMENTS

Thank you to April Lee, Chris Koon, Wendy McEntyre, Larry Ley, and your friends and families for opening up your lives to me and spending hundreds of hours with me on the phone and in person, so that I could tell your stories. These conversations have had an indelible impact on me, stretching far beyond the confines of this book.

I began writing this book shortly after having a baby at the start of the COVID-19 pandemic. Nothing could have made me understand better the importance of having community, love, and support in one's life than trying to write an artful sentence while also trying to find an N-95 mask, get a baby to sleep, and hush addled nerves (mostly my own).

I am lucky to have an abundance of that support in my life. My deepest gratitude goes to my husband and best friend Jesse Rhodes, who took on far more than his fair share of the household work and childcare to allow me time to hold on to my day job while working on this book. I am eternally grateful for my own parents, Terri and Alan Walter, and sister, Arielle, who not only gave me the strength and confidence to pursue this long held dream, but

Acknowledgments

reviewed legal documents, provided reporting advice, read multiple versions of the proposal and then the draft, and provided comfort and encouragement at every anguish-filled turn. My immense gratitude goes, also, to my in-laws, Joni Pascal and Ted Rhodes, two miracles of human beings, who took us in during the pandemic, and then continuously pitched in at the drop of a hat to take care of their grandson and his exhausted parents without once ever asking for anything in return. My wonderful sister-in-law Rachel Rhodes gave me multiple crash courses in organization, took my headshot, and—along with Jeff Young—made for wonderful company.

Thank you to Eamon Dolan, Lisa Rivlin, and the entire Simon & Schuster team. Thank you to Ethan Bassoff for believing that I could write a book before I did. This wouldn't have happened without you. Thanks also to Aaron Glantz, who pushed me for years to write a book before I finally committed, and then provided invaluable guidance and support.

I am grateful to Amy Julia Harris, Ike Sriskandarajah, Laura Starecheski, and Narda Zacchino, my former collaborators and friends from the Center for Investigative Reporting whose reporting I relied on heavily for parts of this book. Thank you, also, to CIR, for giving me my dream job, and granting me time to pursue this book and long-form investigative journalism.

Thank you to therapist Ty DeChambeau. My dearest friends, Victoria Baranetsky and Ariel Schwartz, and several group chats added such light to my life and cheered me on at every turn. Thank you to many other friends who read parts or all of this book, and provided guidance and support, including Jesse Rhodes, Ariel Schwartz, Amy Julia Harris, Jennifer LaFleur, Erik Hetzner, Mya Frazier, Chris Leonard, and Megan Reed. Many loved ones put up with me disappearing and complaining and still provided endless encouragement and support.

Immense thanks to the Watchdog Writers Group, led by the wonderful Chris Leonard, for providing me with generous financial support, research help, and most importantly—a reporting and writing community in Mya Frazier, Alisa Roth, Pam Colloff, Michael Grunwald, and Sarah Smarsh.

Acknowledgments

Thanks to Cianna Morales and especially Kelly Deureck for her incredibly thorough research, and to fact checkers, Gabriel Baumgartner, Graham Hacia, and Hilary Mclellen. Thank you to the Alumnae Association of Mount Holyoke College for your generous support of this book.

My gratitude to Ben Platt for his editing/therapy sessions; I'll never look at a Samurai sword the same way again. I'm also grateful to the authors who offered valuable advice and encouragement, including Beth Macy, Aaron Glantz, Martha Ackmann, Bob Kolker, Bernice Yeung, Ebony Reed, Eric Eyre, and Melissa Segura. Special thank you to Gabrielle Glaser, who gave me a starter addiction-research library. I'm also grateful for early conversations with Ko Bragg and Duaa Eldeib that helped shape my approach to reporting on marginalized sources.

Much of this book was informed by my reading, and I am especially grateful for the work of the following authors and researchers: Nancy Campbell, David Courtwright, Carl Hart, Helena Hansen, Jules Netherland, Robert Granfield, Dorothy Roberts, and William Cloud. A special debt is owed to Teri Sforza, legendary investigative reporter at the Orange County Register who has documented and probed abuses in California's rehab industry for years. She was the first to report on Above It All and the death of Matthew Maniace, and her stories are what led me to Wendy.

I produced a lot of reporting that did not make it into the book, but informed it immensely. The staff of the Bridge Clinic at Highland Hospital in Oakland, California—including Christian Hailozian, Dr. Monish Ullal, Dr. Erik Anderson, and the peer navigators—allowed me to shadow providers for several months, meet patients, and witness firsthand the immense challenges and benefits of ethical, low-barrier addiction treatment. When I was pregnant, the then-staff of HEPPAC (HIV Education and Prevention Project of Alameda County)—including Denise Lopez, Sabrina Fuentes, and others—invited me on multiple ride-alongs as they distributed clean needles and other harm reduction supplies, and spent many hours answering my questions and introducing me to clients. I am

Acknowledgments

grateful to the other providers who granted me access to their addiction treatment programs and patients.

Finally, and most importantly, I interviewed hundreds of people in and out of recovery for this book, some of whom passed away before it could be published. Thank you for sharing your lives and hard-earned wisdom. Your stories matter. I'll carry them with me forever.

NOTES

INTRODUCTION

ix *They were looking*: Robert Hunter, Coroner investigation, Case 701404054, Decedent: Donavan William Doyle, San Bernardino Cty. Sher. (Cor. Div. June 4, 2014).

x *Donovan had started*: Cyndi Doyle v. Above It All Treatment Center, CIVDS 1419415, Sup. Ct. Cal., San Bernardino Cty., video. dep. of Christopher Ted O'Keefe (November 20, 2015), vol. 1, at 82.

x *But it wasn't until*: Cyndi Doyle, text message to Shannon Doyle, October 7, 2013.

x *By that point*: BlueCross BlueShield BluePlus of Minnesota, Explanation of Benefits Summary Statement, Patient Name Donavan Doyle, Patient ID XZ1180107, Claims Summary Period: September 1, 2013–November 1, 2013.

x *Then Donavan walked off*: Doyle, CIVDS 1419415, video. dep. of Christopher Ted O'Keefe, vol. 1, at 26–27.

x *thudded rapidly in the 90-degree heat*: "Climate & Weather Averages." Timeanddate.com, May 26, 2014. https://doi.org/1004254/tadcom_300x600; Shannon Doyle, interview with author, March 4, 2024.

xi *"When you're in pain"*: Cyndi Doyle, interview with author, December 11, 2022.

xi *They had bought it at*: Doyle, CIVDS 1419415, dep. of Shannon Doyle (December 18, 2015), vol. 2, at 172.

xii *The coroner ruled*: Robert Hunter, Coroner Investigation, Case 701404054, Decedent: Donavan William Doyle, Sher. San Bernardino Cty. (Cor. Div., June 4, 2014).

xii *The case was closed*: Hunter, Coroner investigation.

xii *Her own son's*: Betsy Magdaleno, Coroner investigation narrative, Case 2004-09117, Decedent: Jarrod Levi Autterson, Los Angeles Cty., Dep. of Coroner (December 1, 2004).

xiii *It could happen*: Barack Obama, Remarks and Question-and-Answer Session at Community Forum on Prescription Drug Abuse and Heroin Use, Charleston, West Virginia (October 21, 2015), https://www.govinfo.gov/content/pkg/DCPD-201500742/html/DCPD-201500742.htm.

Notes

xiv *The villain responsible*: Purdue Pharma L.P., "Purdue Pharma Announces Agreement in Principle on Landmark Opioid Litigation Settlement," news release, September 16, 2019, https://www.purduepharma.com/news/2019/09/16/purdue-pharma-announces-agreement-in-principle-on-landmark-opioid-litigation-settlement/.

xiv *First, the federal government*: "FDA Approval of Buprenorphine/Naloxone," Government Publishing Office, October 9, 2002, https://www.congress.gov/crec/2002/10/17/modified/CREC-2002-10-17-pt2-PgS10655-3.htm.

xiv *Today, addiction treatment*: John LaRosa, "$42 Billion U.S. Addiction Rehab Industry Poised for Growth, and Challenges," MarketResearch.com, blog, February 5, 2020, https://blog.marketresearch.com/42-billion-u.s.-addiction-rehab-industry-poised-for-growth-and-challenges.

xiv *for that year in the United States*: "European Drug Report 2023: Trends and Developments," European Monitoring Centre for Drugs and Drug Addiction, 2023, https://www.emcdda.europa.eu/publications/european-drug-report/2023_en.

xiv *In total, more than*: "Nearly One-Third of U.S. Adults Know Someone Who's Died of Drug Overdose," Johns Hopkins University, Bloomberg School of Public Health, May 31, 2024, https://publichealth.jhu.edu/2024/nearly-one-third-of-us-adults-know-someone-whos-died-of-drug-overdose.

xv *In just two*: Josh Katz, Margot Sanger-Katz, and Eileen Sullivan, "Some Key Facts about Fentanyl," *New York Times*, October 5, 2023, https://www.nytimes.com/2023/10/05/upshot/fentanyl-opioids-mexico-explainer.html.

xvi *patients are more likely to overdose and die*: John Strang, Jim McCambridge, David Best, Tracy Beswick, Jenny Bearn, et al., "Loss of Tolerance and Overdose Mortality after Inpatient Opiate Detoxification: Follow up Study," *BMJ* 326, no. 7396 (2003): 959–60, https://doi.org/10.1136/bmj.326.7396.959.

CHAPTER ONE

3 *Chris was 15*: Chris Koon, interview with author, March 24, 2019.

3 *He was born*: Chris Koon, interview.

4 *In 1989, John Koon*: John Koon, interview with author, November 29, 2021.

4 *When he turned four*: Carrie Tolbert, interview with author, March 27, 2019.

4 *Chris's grandparents became*: John Koon, interview.

4 *"They just knew"*: Chris Koon, interview.

4 *Next, Chris tried*: Chris Koon, interview.

5 *That tactic didn't work*: Steven L. West and Keri K. O'Neal, "Project D.A.R.E. Outcome Effectiveness Revisited," *American Journal of Public Health* 94, no. 6 (June 2004): 1027–29, https://ajph.aphapublications.org/doi/full/10.2105/AJPH.94.6.1027.

5 *only 10 percent*: Chris Ringwalt, Sean Hanley, Amy A. Vincus, Susan T. Ennett, Louise A. Rohrbach, et al., "The Prevalence of Effective Substance

Notes

Use Prevention Curricula in the Nation's High Schools," *Journal of Primary Prevention* 29, no. 6 (2008): 479–88, https://doi.org/10.1007/s10935-008-0158-4.

5 *From 2006 to 2019*: Steven Rich, Paige Moody, and Kevin Schaul, "How Deeply Did Prescription Opioid Pills Flood Your County? See Here," *Washington Post*, September 12, 2023. https://www.washingtonpost.com/investigations/interactive/2023/opioid-epidemic-pain-pills-sold-oxycodone-hydrocodone/.

5 *For many of those patients*: Shoshana Walter, "Officers See More Sick and Elderly Selling Prescription Drugs," *New York Times*, September 18, 2010, https://www.nytimes.com/2010/09/19/us/19bcdealers.html.

6 *"Are you sure?"*: Chris Koon, interview.

6 *In 1960*: Andrew L. Yarrow, "The Male Non-Working Class A Disquieting Survey," *Milken Institute Review*, July 30, 2020, https://www.milkenreview.org/articles/the-male-non-working-class.

6 *By 2009*: U.S. Bureau of Labor Studies, "Unemployment remains high in 2010," *Monthly Labor Review*, March 2011, https://www.bls.gov/opub/mlr/2011/03/art1full.pdf.

6 *Amid the high rates*: Kristoffer Rehder, Jaimie Luck, and Jason I. Chen, "Deaths of Despair: Conceptual and Clinical Implications," *Cognitive Behavioral Practice* 28, no. 1 (2019): 40–52, https://doi: 10.1016/jcbpra.2019.10.002; Amy Finkelstein, Matthew J. Notowidgdo, Frank Schilbach, and Jonathan Zhang, "Lives vs. Livelihoods: The Impact of the Great Recession on Mortality and Welfare," Becker Friedman Institute, Working Paper No. 2024-14 (2024), https://economics.mit.edu/sites/default/files/2024-11/FNSZ_Great_Recession_nov2024.pdf.

6 *In 1996*: John Temple, *American Pain: How a Young Felon and His Ring of Doctors Unleashed America's Deadliest Drug Epidemic* (Lyons Press, 2015), 41.

6 *This pain pill revolution*: "15-Minute Doctor Visits Take a Toll on Patient-Physician Relationships, *PBS News Hour*, April 21, 2014, https://www.pbs.org/newshour/health/need-15-minutes-doctors-time.

6 *Purdue Pharma deployed*: Sam Quinones, *Dreamland: The True Tale of America's Opiate Epidemic* (Bloomsbury Press, 2015), 97.

7 *When President Nixon*: Nick Miroff, Scott Higham, Steven Rich, Salwan Georges, and Erin Patrick O'Connor, "Cause of Death: Washington Faltered as Fentanyl Gripped America," *Washington Post*. December 12, 2022, https://www.washingtonpost.com/investigations/interactive/2022/dea-fentanyl-failure/.

7 *By 2008*: Quinones, *Dreamland*, 43; "Drug Poisoning Deaths in the United States, 1980-2008," NCHS Data Brief, No. 81, Centers for Disease Control, December 2011, https://www.cdc.gov/nchs/data/databriefs/db81.pdf.

7 *Prescription narcotics*: Temple, *American Pain*, 47.

Notes

7 *With every 1 percent*: Alex Hollingsworth, Christopher J. Ruhm, and Kosali Simon, "Macroeconomic Conditions and Opioid Abuse," National Bureau of Economic Research, Working Paper 23192, February 2017. https://www.nber.org/papers/w23192.

8 *As parish leaders fought*: Art Harris, "Louisiana Busing Face-off Defused as State Judge Accepts U.S. Plan," *Washington Pos,*. January 16, 1981, https://www.washingtonpost.com/archive/politics/1981/01/16/louisiana-busing-face-off-defused-as-state-judge-accepts-us-plan/22e34ac0-65a6-430d-944a-16324e532803/.

8 *As employers closed plants*: Linette Lopez, "The White House Is Only Telling You Half of the Sad Story of What Happened to American Jobs," *Business Insider*, July 25, 2017, https://www.businessinsider.com/what-happened-to-american-jobs-in-the-80s-2017-7.

8 *By 2008*: Jeff Matthews. "What Does Pineville Plan for Its Downtown?," *The Town Talk*, August 14, 2018, https://www.thetowntalk.com/story/news/local/2018/08/14/pineville-louisiana-downtown/9807250.

8 *With so much*: Ruth Simon, "U.S. Cities Battle Each Other for Jobs with $45 Billion in Incentives," *Wall Street Journal*, March 16, 2017, https://www.wsj.com/articles/u-s-cities-battle-each-other-for-jobs-with-45-billion-in-incentives-1489675343.

8 *But attracting new business*: Tommy Carnline (Chief of Staff, Rapides County Sheriff's Office), interview with author, October 19, 2021.

8 *One day, not long*: Chris Koon, interview.

10 *The sum total*: Chris Koon, Alexandria Police Department arrest reports, October 29, 2010 and March 23, 2015.

10 *Chris was an adult*: Chris Koon, interview.

10 *By now, heroin*: "National Drug Threat Assessment 2010," Intelligence Center, U.S. Department of Justice, February 2010, https://www.justice.gov/archive/ndic/pubs38/38661/movement.htm.

11 *And unlike OxyContin*: Jennifer R. Velander, "Suboxone: Rationale, Science, Misconceptions," *Oschner Journal* 18, no. 1 (Spring 2018): 23–29, https://pmc.ncbi.nlm.nih.gov/articles/PMC5855417/.

11 *"So lucky to"*: Chris Koon, excerpt from Facebook post, November 22, 2014.

11 *Even amid all*: Pat Koon, interview with author, February 2, 2020.

11 *At first, Chris had*: Chris Koon, interview.

12 *Chris wrote on Facebook*: Chris Koon, excerpt from Facebook post, February 21, 2015.

CHAPTER TWO

15 *In 2001, as the opioid epidemic*: April Lee, interview with author, February 1, 2021–February 28, 2025.

15 *Nadine had been*: April Lee, interview.

Notes

16 *Her favorite was*: Louis Sachar, *Holes* (Bloomsbury, 2015).
16 *The Lee family*: April, Ashley, and Derrick Lee, various interviews with author.
16 *For generations, the family*: Jake Blumgart, "How Redlining Segregated Philadelphia," WHYY news, December 10, 2017, https://whyy.org/segments/redlining-segregated-philadelphia/.
16 *As in Chris's*: "Mapping the Impact of Structural Racism in Philadelphia." Philadelphia City Controller's Office, report, 2020, https://controller.phila.gov/wp-content/uploads/2020/01/redlining_report-1.pdf.
16 *It wasn't just the drugs*: Donovan X. Ramsey, *When Crack Was King: A People's History of a Misunderstood Era* (Random House, 2023).
16 *And it was the government's*: Aaron Morrison, "50-Year War on Drugs Imprisoned Millions of Black Americans," *PBS News Hour,* July 26, 2021, https://www.pbs.org/newshour/nation/50-year-war-on-drugs-imprisoned-millions-of-black-americans; Ashley Nellis, "Mass Incarceration Trends," The Sentencing Project, report, May 21, 2024, https://www.sentencingproject.org/reports/mass-incarceration-trends/.
17 *Crack addiction did not*: Jesse Borke, "Cocaine Withdrawal," *MedlinePlus Medical Encyclopedia*, 2016, https://medlineplus.gov/ency/article/000947.htm; Fred Berger, "Opiate and Opioid Withdrawal," *MedlinePlus Medical Encyclopedia*, 2016, https://medlineplus.gov/ency/article/000949.htm.
17 *In 1990, less than*: "Drug Exposed Infants: A Generation at Risk," Statement by Charles A. Bowsher, Comptroller General of the U.S. General Accounting Office, before the Senate Committee on Finance, June 28, 1990, https://www.gao.gov/assets/t-hrd-90-46.pdf.
17 *Despite the politicized concerns*: "Punishing Women," Center for Reproductive Rights.
18 *But without childcare*: Dorothy Roberts, "Welfare Reform and Economic Freedom: Low-Income Mothers' Decisions About Work at Home and in the Market," *Santa Clara Law Review* 44 (2004): 44, https://scholarship.law.upenn.edu/faculty_scholarship/584/.
19 *Those were the*: Scott O. Lilienfeld and Hal Arkowitz, "Why 'Just Say No' Doesn't Work," *Scientific American*, January 2014, https://www.scientificamerican.com/article/why-just-say-no-doesnt-work/.
20 *In her mind, she was lucky*: Joshua H. Tamayo-Sarver, Susan W. Hinze, Rita K. Cydulka, and David W. Baker, "Racial and Ethnic Disparities in Emergency Department Analgesic Prescription," *American Journal of Public Health* 93, no. 12 (2003): 2067–73, https://doi.org/10.2105/ajph.93.12.2067.
20 *But like many people*: Jie Zhou, Ruijie Ma, Ying Jin, Junfan Fang, Junying Du, et al., "Molecular Mechanisms of Opioid Tolerance: From Opioid Receptors to Inflammatory Mediators," *Experimental and Therapeutic Medicine* 22, no. 3 (July 15, 2021): 1004, https://doi.org/10.3892/etm.2021.10437.

Notes

21 *More than 70 percent*: "Family-Centered Treatment for Women with Substance Use Disorders: History, Key Elements, and Challenges," Substance Abuse and Mental Health Services Administration, working paper, 2007, https://www.samhsa.gov/sites/default/files/family_treatment_paper508v.pdf.

21 *it's one of the top reasons*: "Drug-Exposed Infants," Government Accounting Office, report, June 1990, https://www.gao.gov/assets/hrd-90-138.pdf.

21 *Time and again, studies*: H. W. Clark, "Residential Substance Abuse Treatment for Pregnant and Postpartum Women and Their Children: Treatment and Policy Implications," *Child Welfare* 80, no. 2 (2001): 179–98, https://pubmed.ncbi.nlm.nih.gov/11291900/.

21 *number of treatment programs*: "National Survey of Substance Abuse Treatment Services (N-SSATS): 2003 Data on Substance Abuse Treatment Facilities," Substance Abuse and Mental Health Services Administration, report, 2004, https://www.samhsa.gov/data/sites/default/files/2003_nssats_rpt.pdf.

21 *By 2020, there would be*: "National Survey of Substance Abuse Treatment Services (N-SSATS): 2020 Data on Substance Abuse Treatment Facilities," Substance Abuse and Mental Health Services Administration, report, 2021, https://www.samhsa.gov/data/sites/default/files/reports/rpt35313/2020_NSSATS_FINAL.pdf.

21 *Further, some states*: Hanh Dau (researcher, Children and Family Futures), interview with author, October 27, 2022.

22 *But, studies have shown*: Pooja A. Lagisetty, Ryan Ross, Amy Bohnert, Michael Clay, and Donavan T. Maust, "Buprenorphine Treatment Divide by Race/Ethnicity and Payment," *JAMA Psychiatry* 76, no. 9 (2019): 979, https://doi.org/10.1001/jamapsychiatry.2019.0876.

CHAPTER THREE

23 *Dr. Larry Ley was*: Larry Ley, multiple interviews with author, April 2019–May 2021.

23 *had started as a way*: Dr. Elaine Ley, interview with author, October 15, 2020.

23 *Now, he was speaking*: Dana Knight, "Drugs Prove Costly: $4.5 Trillion Devoured in '97 by Addictions," *Noblesville Ledger*, April 2, 1998.

24 *Could Larry step in*: Larry also received a call from the Center for Substance Abuse Treatment, per confidential DEA report. U.S. Department of Justice, Drug Enforcement Administration, Report on Investigation, August 26, 2005, p. 43.

24 *Amid the growing*: Bradley D. Stein, Rosalie Liccardo Pacula, Adam J. Gordon, Rachel M. Burns, Douglas L. Leslie, et al., "Where Is Buprenorphine Dispensed to Treat Opioid Use Disorders? The Role of Private Offices, Opioid Treatment Programs, and Substance Abuse Treatment Facilities in Urban and Rural Counties," *Milbank Quarterly* 93, no. 3 (2015): 561–83, https://doi.org/10.1111/1468-0009.12137.

Notes

24 *In 1995, France had*: Anne Guichard, France Lert, Jean-Marc Brodeur, and Lucie Richard, "Buprenorphine Substitution Treatment in France: Drug Users' Views of the Doctor–User Relationship," *Social Science & Medicine* 64, no. 12 (2007): 2578–93, https://doi.org/10.1016/j.socscimed.2007.02.049.

24 *Now, the goal was*: Nguemeni Tiako, Max Jordan, Jules Netherland, Helena Hansen, and Marie Jauffret-Roustide, "Drug Overdose Epidemic Colliding with COVID-19: What the United States Can Learn from France," *American Journal of Public Health* 112, Suppl. 2 (2022): S128–32, https://doi.org/10.2105/ajph.2022.306763.

25 *The result was striking*: Marc Auriacombe, Mélina Fatséas, Jacques Dubernet, Jean-Pierre Daulouède, and Jean Tignol, "French Field Experience with Buprenorphine," *American Journal on Addictions* 13, Suppl. 1 (2004): S17–28, https://doi.org/10.1080/10550490490440780.

25 *Some users*: M. Fatseas and Marc Auriacombe, "Why Buprenorphine Is So Successful in Treating Opiate Addiction in France," *Current Psychiatry Reports* 9, no. 5 (2007): 358–64, https://doi.org/10.1007/s11920-007-0046-2.

25 *Doctors had been continually*: David F. Musto, *The American Disease: Origins of Narcotic Control* (Yale University Press, 1973), 61–68; Nat Hentoff, *A Doctor Among the Addicts* (Rand McNally, 1968), 71–73.

25 *In the 1960s*: David Courtwright, Don Des Jarlais, and Herman Joseph, *Addicts Who Survived: An Oral History of Narcotic Use in America, 1923–1965* (University of Tennessee Press, 1989), 331–37.

25 *Despite patients' high rates*: Courtwright et al., *Addicts*.

25 *Heroin, an "inner*: Matthew D. Lassiter, "Impossible Criminals: The Suburban Imperatives of America's War on Drugs," *Journal of American History* 102, no. 1 (2015): 126–40, https://www.jstor.org/stable/44286141.

26 *Senator Biden had long supported*: Marcia Lee Taylor (former Biden staffer), interview with author, November 20, 2020.

26 *NIDA proposed a partnership*: Nancy D. Campbell and Anne M. Lovell, "The History of the Development of Buprenorphine as an Addiction Therapeutic," *Annals of the New York Academy of Sciences* 1248, no. 1 (2012): 124–39, https://doi.org/10.1111/j.1749-6632.2011.06352.x.

26 *Reckitt hired former*: Charles O'Keeffe (former CEO of Reckitt Benckiser), interview with author, November 16, 2020; Robert Angarola identified as representing Purdue Pharma in State of Oklahoma v. Purdue Pharma, Judgment after bench trial, August 26, 2019, https://fm.cnbc.com/applications/cnbc.com/resources/editorialfiles/2019/8/26/1044673351-20190826-151346-.pdf.

26 *If passed, the*: Drug Addiction Treatment Act of 1999, Hearing before the Subcommittee on Health and Environment, House of Representatives Committee on Commerce, 106th Congress, July 30, 1999, https://www.govinfo.gov/content/pkg/CHRG-106hhrg58503/html/CHRG-106hhrg58503.htm.

Notes

26 *Biden threw his support*: Marcia Lee Taylor and Charles O'Keeffe, interviews.
26 *"It only makes"*: Drug Addiction Treatment Act of 1999, Hearing before the Subcommittee on Health and Environment, House of Representatives Committee on Commerce, 106th Congress, July 30, 1999, https://www.govinfo.gov/content/pkg/CHRG-106hhrg58503/html/CHRG-106hhrg58503.htm.
27 *Dr. Larry Alexander*: Drug Addiction Treatment Act, Hearing before Subcommittee.
27 *Bup "is expected"*: Drug Addiction Treatment Act, Hearing before Subcommittee.
27 *The head of*: Drug Addiction Treatment Act, Hearing before subcommittee.
27 *Doctors who adopted*: M. Fatseas and Marc Auriacombe, "Why Buprenorphine Is So Successful in Treating Opiate Addiction in France," *Current Psychiatry Reports* 9, no. 5 (2007): 358–64, https://doi.org/10.1007/s11920-007-0046-2.
28 *But the U.S. poverty rate*: Nguemeni Tiako et al., "Drug Overdose Epidemic Colliding with COVID-19."
28 *it was common to pay as much*: Bradley Stein, Maria Orlando, and Roland Sturm, "The Effect of Copayments on Drug and Alcohol Treatment Following Inpatient Detoxification Under Managed Care," *Psychiatric Services* 51, no. 2 (2000): 195–98, https://doi.org/10.1176/appi.ps.51.2.195.
28 *Congressional staffers saw no other*: Marcia Lee Taylor, interview.
28 *Pat Good, who was then*: Patricia Good (DEA Chief Liaison Officer), interview with author, October 9, 2020.
28 *O'Keeffe, the company's*: "Designating an Orphan Product: Drugs and Biological Products," U.S. Food and Drug Administration, report, July 8, 2022, https://www.fda.gov/industry/medical-products-rare-diseases-and-conditions/designating-orphan-product-drugs-and-biological-products.
28 *O'Keeffe claimed the company*: Charles O'Keeffe, interview.
28 *FDA's own analysis*: Kao-Ping Chua and Rena Conti, "Revocation of Orphan Drug Designation for Extended-Release Buprenorphine Injection: Implications and Next Steps," Forefront Group, report, March 2020, https://doi.org/10.1377/forefront.20200302.846103. The FDA later described its decision to grant orphan-drug status to Reckitt Benckiser as "erroneous," per a letter revoking the company's orphan-drug designation, November 7, 2019.
28 *But FDA staffers*: Marlene Haffner (former director, FDA Office of Orphan Product Development), interview with author, September 2, 2021.
29 *In 2000, the bill passed*: Campbell and Lovell, "History of the Development of Buprenorphine."
29 *One system was for poor people*: Jules Netherland and Helena Hansen, "White Opioids: Pharmaceutical Race and the War on Drugs That Wasn't," *BioSocieties* 12, no. 2 (2017): 217–38, https://doi.org/10.1057/biosoc.2015.46.

Notes

29 *But in these advertisements*: Jules Netherland, *Becoming Normal: The Social Construction of Buprenorphine and New Attempts to Medicalize Addiction* (Proquest, Umi Dissertation Publication, 2012).

29 *Among the original representatives*: Gail Groves Scott (Reckill Benckiser sales representative), interview with author, May 7, 2021.

29 *"It's very high pressure"*: Gail Groves Scott, interview.

31 *"some of them were"*: Gail Groves Scott, interview.

31 *By 2003, an estimated*: Julie Netherland, Michael Botsko, James E. Egan, Andrew J. Saxon, Chinazo O. Cunningham, et al., "Factors Affecting Willingness to Provide Buprenorphine Treatment," *Journal of Substance Abuse Treatment* 36, no. 3 (2009): 244–51, https://doi.org/10.1016/j.jsat.2008.06.006.

31 *but only 616*: Jonathan Bor, "Doctors, Drug Users Still wait on a Prescription of Promise; Shipping Delays, Stigma Hinder Pill's Availability," *Baltimore Sun*, January 15, 2003, https://advance.lexis.com/api/document?collection=news&id=urn:contentItem:47P7-R160-00BT-X4M1-00000-00&context=1519360.

32 *With his 6-foot, 3-inch frame*: Detail from an unpublished DEA briefing report.

32 *"I thought he was mean"*: Cameron Drury, interview with author, May 16, 2019.

32 *Larry's younger brother, a dentist*: Tom Ley, interview with author, October 7, 2020.

32 *Like the one time*: Tom Ley, interview.

32 *"In the middle of the night"*: Larry Ley, interview, September 9, 2019.

32 *In Indiana, there were*: Author analysis of all DATA-waived registrants, broken down by date and state, obtained via Freedom of Information Act, Drug Enforcement Administration, April 4, 2024.

32 *And many were*: Deborah Sontag, "Addiction Treatment with a Dark Side," *New York Times*, November 16, 2013, https://www.nytimes.com/2013/11/17/health/in-demand-in-clinics-and-on-the-street-bupe-can-be-savior-or-menace.html.

32 *The 30 people in*: Larry Ley, interview, July 7, 2019.

32 *"Opiate withdrawal"*: Larry Ley, interview.

33 *Katy Jo Dalton had*: Katy Jo Dalton, interview with author, September 17, 2020.

33 *"He was kind of"*: Katyl Jo Dalton, interview.

33 *But most doctors*: "Results from SAMHSA/CSAT's Evaluation of the Buprenorphine Waiver Program," National Alliance of Advocates for Buprenorphine, information sheet, 2005, https://naabt.org/documents/StantonCPDDhandout2.pdf.

34 *Across the country*: "Key Substance Use and Mental Health Indicators in the United States: Results from the 2023 National Survey on Drug Use and Health," Substance Abuse and Mental Health Services Administration,

report, 2023, https://www.samhsa.gov/data/sites/default/files/reports/rpt 47095/National%20Report/National%20Report/2023-nsduh-annual-na tional.pdf.

CHAPTER FOUR

35 *Wendy McEntyre learned*: Wendy McEntyre, multiple interviews with author, January 4, 19, 27, 2022.
35 *The younger of Wendy's*: Jamie Autterson, interview with author, January 25, 2022.
35 *Jamie was loud*: Wendy McEntyre, interview.
36 *That was when*: Jamie Autterson, interview with author, January 25, 2022.
36 *She gave him a folder*: Wendy McEntyre, interview.
37 *At Promises, which*: Lewis Pennock, "Malibu Compound that Was Once Home to A-List Rehab Promises Hits Market for $20M—but Buyer Will have to Honor Lease of Existing Treatment Facility Until it Expires," *Daily Mail*, July 18, 2023, https://www.dailymail.co.uk/news/article-12312351/Malibu-compound-home-list-rehab-Promises-hits-market-20M-buyer-honor-lease-existing-treatment-facility-expires.html.
37 *The nonprofit Betty*: Paul Pringle, "The Trouble with Rehab, Malibu-Style," *Los Angeles Times*, October 9, 2007, https://www.latimes.com/archives/la-xpm-2007-oct-09-me-rehab9-story.html.
37 *In 2000, in response*: "Analysis of the 2001-02 Budget Bill," Legislative Analyst's Office, California Health and Social Services, 2001, https://lao.ca.gov/analysis_2001/health_ss/hss_3_CC_Prop36.htm.
37 *Almost overnight, the law*: Proposition 36: Drug Treatment Diversion Program, California state ballot, 2000, https://lao.ca.gov/ballot/2000/36_11_2000.html.
37 *Longstanding programs began*: Yih-Ing Hser, Cheryl Teruya, David Huang, Elizabeth Evans, and Douglas Amglin, "Impact of California's Proposition 36 on the Drug Treatment System: Treatment Capacity and Displacement," *American Journal of Public Health* 97, no.1 (2007): 104–109, https://doi.org/10.2105/ajph.2005.069336.
37 *Treatment facilities and sober*: T. Peter Pierce, "Regulating Sober Living Homes and the Challenges of Implementing ADA and FHA," League of California Cities, General Session, May 4, 2016, https://www.cacities.org/Resources-Documents/Member-Engagement/Professional-Departments/City-Attorneys/Library/2016/2016-Spring/5-2016-Spring-Regulating-Sober-Living-Homes-and-th.
37 *"Jarrod will"*: Wendy McEntyre, Letter to Honorable Judge McKay, June 18, 2003.
38 *But when Jarrod appeared*: Wendy McEntyre, interview.
38 *He sat on*: Short Form Return of Organization Exempt from Income Tax

Notes

(2005 Form 990-EZ); Sober Living Network, Inc., Internal Revenue Service, Department of the Treasury; Rick Schoonover, "Alcohol & Drug Information," Safe Houses San Fernando Valley, 2004.

38 *Everyone was supposed*: Wendy Stone McEntyre v. Rick E. Schoonover, LC 076447, Sup. Ct. Cal., Los Angeles Cty., video. dep. of Rick Ernest Schoonover (March 13, 2009), vol. 1, at 100.
38 *Instead the program kicked him out*: McEntyre, LC 076447, video. dep. of Rick Schoonover, vol. 1, at 152.
39 *Jarrod mentioned*: Cynthia Kennedy, multiple interviews with author, October 26, November 4, 2024.
39 *Rick was Jarrod's sponsor*: McEntyre, LC 076447, video. dep. of Rick Schoonover.
39 *She called the house*: Cynthia Kennedy, interview.
39 *Finally, she called*: Cynthia Kennedy, interview.
40 *"When you lose a child"*: Wendy McEntyre, interview, January 19, 2022.
40 *He had personally*: McEntyre, LC 076447, video. dep. of Rick Schoonover, at 59.
40 *"It really bothered me"*: Wendy McEntyre, interview, January 27, 2022.
40 *He never cursed*: Betsy Magdaleno, Coroner Investigation Narrative, Case 2004-09117, Decedent: Jarrod Levi Autterson, Los Angeles Cty., Dep. of Coroner (December 1, 2004).
40 *For heroin use*: Schoonover, "Alcohol & Drug Information," 5.
40 *Jarrod was already dead*: Magdaleno, Coroner Investigation Narrative.
41 *According to house rules*: McEntyre, LC 076477, video. dep. of Rick Schoonover, at 102.
41 *A physician would*: Wendy Stone McEntyre v. Rick E. Schoonover, Safe House, Inc., Safe House Services, Inc. and Does I To 50, LC 076477, Sup. Ct. Cal. (2009), declaration of Marvin Pietruszka, M.D., M.S., J.D., F.C.A.P, in support of plaintiff's opposition to defendants' motion for summary judgment, at 4.
41 *There were even*: Association of Halfway House Alcoholism Programs of North America, Annual Conference, April 20–24 2002, https://web.archive.org/web/20021006084316/http://ahhap.org/pages/anncon.html.
41 *When she called*: Customer Service Request, CSR 146336, Los Angeles Dep. Building and Safety, Jarrod's Law, September 14, 2006.
42 *He, too, had*: Change of Occupancy Inspection, Los Angeles Dep. Building and Safety, 1966, 6825 Kester Ave., Van Nuys, CA.
42 *She had the*: Magdaleno, Coroner Investigation Narrative.
42 *The department told*: Wendy McEntyre, notes of conversation with Los Angeles Dep. Building and Safety, 2005.
42 *But by 2006*: Case Summary Report, Case 179973, Los Angeles Dep. Building and Safety (2006), 3.
42 *"She instantly reminded"*: Karen Gold (attorney for Wendy McEntyre), interview with author, January 22, 2022.

Notes

42 *"This is the first"*: Karen Gold, interview.
42 *They sat around*: Wendy McEntyre, interview; Cheryll McEntyre, interview with author, October 25, 2024.
43 *And longtime treatment*: "Why Rehab Doesn't Work: Part 1," NBC news, April 7, 2014, https://www.nbcnews.com/storyline/americas-heroin-epidemic/how-fix-rehab-expert-who-lost-son-addiction-has-plan-n67946.
43 *These savings were*: "Poll Finds Bipartisan Agreement on One Aspect of Health Care Reform: Addiction Treatment," Open Society Foundations, press release, September 22, 2009, https://www.opensocietyfoundations.org/newsroom/poll-finds-bipartisan-agreement-one-aspect-health-care-reform-addiction-treatment.
43 *In anticipation*: Brian Mann, "As Addiction Deaths Surge, Profit-Driven Rehab Industry Faces 'Severe Ethical Crisis,'" *Morning Edition*, National Public Radio, February 15, 2021, https://www.npr.org/2021/02/15/963700736/as-addiction-deaths-surge-profit-driven-rehab-industry-faces-severe-ethical-cris; Teri Sforza, "How Some Southern California Drug Rehab Centers Exploit Addiction," *Orange County Register*, May 21, 2017, https://www.npr.org/2021/02/15/963700736/as-addiction-deaths-surge-profit-driven-rehab-industry-faces-severe-ethical-cris.
43 *The program also*: Amy Kaufman, "Rehab Television Shows: Intervention or Exploitation?" *Los Angeles Times*, January 2, 2011, https://www.latimes.com/archives/la-xpm-2011-jan-02-la-ca-celebrity-rehab-20110102-story.html.
44 *She learned a*: Death Investigative Report, Department of Alcohol and Drug Programs, Program/facility ID 190250AP, Program/facility ID Pasadena Recovery Center, Complaint Investigation 12-091D, Cal. Dep. Health and Human Services (2013); Jason Henry, "State Shuts Down Pasadena-based 'Celebrity Rehab' Center over Death, Repeated Violations," *Pasadena Star News*, August 4 and 6, 2018, https://www.pasadenastarnews.com/2018/08/04/state-shuts-down-pasadena-based-celebrity-rehab-center-over-death-repeated-violations.
44 *"Jarrod's Law"*: Wendy Brockabitch McEntyre, business card for Jarrod's Law.

CHAPTER FIVE

47 *It started around*: Grant Parish Sheriff's Office arrest report for Chris Koon, July 30, 2015.
47 *After a brief*: John Koon, interview with author, November 29, 2021.
47 *The relapse was*: Chris Koon, interview with author, March 8, 2020.
49 *He had just*: John Koon, interview.
49 *For years, Louisiana*: "Louisiana Incarcerated," *Times Picayune*, May 13, 2012, https://www.nola.com/news/crime_police/louisiana-incarcerated-2012/article_4946aa9f-4a0e-50ea-8e95-35f945ce60e8.html.

Notes

49 *The Louisiana State*: Poet Wolfe, "'Bloodiest Prison in the US': Children Detained in Louisiana's Angola Prison Allege Abuses," *The Guardian*, October 30, 2023, https://www.theguardian.com/us-news/2023/oct/30/bloodiest-prison-in-the-us-children-detained-in-louisianas-angola-prison-allege-abuses.

49 *Bucking the national trend*: "Louisiana's 2017 Criminal Justice Reforms," Pew Trust, news brief, March 1, 2018, https://www.pewtrusts.org/en/research-and-analysis/issue-briefs/2018/03/louisianas-2017-criminal-justice-reforms; Bobbi-Jean Misick, "Louisiana still leads nation for state prisoners held in local jails," *Louisiana Illuminator*, January 24, 2024, https://lailluminator.com/2024/01/24/louisiana-local-jails/.

49 *In 2015, more than*: "Report to the United Nations on Racial Disparities in the U.S. Criminal Justice System," The Sentencing Project, April 19, 2018, https://www.sentencingproject.org/reports/report-to-the-united-nations-on-racial-disparities-in-the-u-s-criminal-justice-system/.

49 *Of the 277,000 people*: "Report to United Nations," Sentencing Project.

49 *And the racial disparities*: "Blueprint for Smart Justice," ACLU of Louisiana, https://www.laaclu.org/sites/default/files/field_documents/sj-blueprint-la_4.pdf.

50 *Just a few years before*: Nicole Lewis and Maurice Chammah, "Bernard Noble Is Released from Prison in Louisiana," *Marshall Project*, April 12, 2018, https://www.themarshallproject.org/2018/04/12/seven-years-behind-bars-for-two-joints-and-now-he-s-free.

50 *A couple hours*: Joe Gyan Jr., "Baton Rouge Judge Imposes Maximum Sentence to Man Convicted of Possessing Heroin with Intent to Distribute," *The Advocate*, March 16, 2016, https://www.theadvocate.com/baton_rouge/news/baton-rouge-judge-imposes-maximum-sentence-to-man-convicted-of-possessing-heroin-with-intent-to/article_0700b83b-db26-51df-b695-28a30120b51b.html.

50 *"When the penalty"*: Lev Facher, "'The Drug Bust Paradox': Study Shows Opioid Deaths Double After Police Action." *STAT*, June 13, 2023, https://www.statnews.com/2023/06/13/opioid-deaths-double-after-drug-arrests/. See also Amy S. B. Bohnert, Arijit Nandi, Melissa Tracy, Magdalena Cerdá, Kenneth J. Tardiff, et al., "Policing and Risk of Overdose Mortality in Urban Neighborhoods." *Drug and Alcohol Dependence* 113, no. 1 (2011): 62–68, https://doi.org/10.1016/j.drugalcdep.2010.07.008.

50 *But the algorithm assigned*: Julia Angwin, Jeff Larson, Surya Mattu, and Lauren Kirchner, "Machine Bias," *ProPublica*. May 23, 2016, https://www.propublica.org/article/machine-bias-risk-assessments-in-criminal-sentencing.

50 *In more recent years*: Scott Graves, "Criminal Justice Reform Is Working in California," California Budget and Policy Center, August 2020, calbudgetcenter.org/resources/criminal-justice-reform-is-working-in-california/.

50 *And programs like Cenikor*: Bill Bailey, "President's Message, Cenikor," Cenikor website, October 10,. 2024, www.cenikor.org/about-us/presi

dents-message/. See also "Recovering from Rehab: Work-Based Therapy in the US," *Al Jazeera*, April 24. 2019, www.aljazeera.com/program/fault-lines/2019/4/24/recovering-from-rehab-work-based-therapy-in-the-us.

50 *At least half*: Cenikor response to questions from *Reveal* reporters, March 21, 2019.

50 *1,000 clients*: Cenikor vocational services brochure.

50 *The program eagerly*: John and Kristin Carroll, interview with author, April 2, 2021.

50 *Judge Larry Gist*: Larry Gist, interview with author, December 2019.

51 *But about half of the*: Eric L. Sevigny, Brian K. Fuleihan, and Frank V. Ferdik, "Do Drug Courts Reduce the Use of Incarceration?: A Meta-Analysis," *Journal of Criminal Justice* 41, issue 6 (2013): 416–25, https://doi.org/10.1016/j.jcrimjus.2013.06.005; David Dematteo et al., "Outcome Trajectories in Drug Court: Do All Participants Have Drug Problems?," *Criminal Justice and Behavior* 36, no. 4 (2009): 354–68, doi:10.1177/0093854809331547.

51 *White defendants were*: Kerwin Kaye, *Enforcing Freedom: Drug Courts, Therapeutic Communities, and the Intimacies of the State* (Columbia University Press, 2019), 10.

51 *In some places*: David R. Lilley, "Did Drug Courts Lead to Increased Arrest and Punishment of Minor Drug Offenses?" *Justice Quarterly* 34, no. 4 (2016): 674–98, https://doi.org/10.1080/07418825.2016.1219760.

51 *In the U.S. criminal justice system*: Caroline Harlow, "Defense Counsel in Criminal Cases," Bureau of Justice Statistics, November 2000, https://bjs.ojp.gov/content/pub/pdf/dccc.pdf. See also Tiffany Costello, "A Comparison of Public Defenders vs. Private Attorneys," Merrimack Scholar Works, Merrimack College, 2021, scholarworks.merrimack.edu/honors_capstones/48.

51 *His parents were*: Carrie Tolbert, interview with author, March 27, 2019.

51 *If he rejected*: State of Louisiana v. Christopher Koon, 2015-CR-729, Order, August 26, 2015.

51 *He could end up*: "Louisiana Prisoner Suit Claims They're Forced to Endure Dangerous Conditions at Angola Prison Farm." AP news, September 16, 2023, apnews.com/article/louisiana-angola-prison-lawsuit-a091bf3375d0919 94d5814539dafb87f. See also Lois Ratcliff and Jamiles Lartey, "A Filthy New Orleans Jail Made My Son Sick: The 'Cruel and Unusual' Medical Treatment at Angola Prison Killed Him," *Marshall Project*, July 30, 2021, www.themarshallproject.org/2021/07/29/a-filthy-new-orleans-jail-made-my-son-sick-the-cruel-and-unusual-medical-treatment-at-angola-prison-killed-him.

CHAPTER SIX

53 *She squinted her eyes*: Account of April's time at the Blue Moon Hotel and in rehab is based on multiple author interviews with April Lee, January 1, 2022–September 9, 2022.

Notes

53 *Her cheek was pressed*: Danya Henninger, "City Inspectors Swear They're Not Trying to Stop the Party—Just Keep It Safe," Billy Penn at WHYY, December 11, 2016, https://billypenn.com/2016/12/11/city-inspectors-swear-theyre-not-trying-to-stop-the-party-just-keep-it-safe/. Additional information about the hotel's condition during this time is from Philadelphia's Department of Licenses & Inspections records.

55 *In the past decade*: "Medicaid Expansion in Pennsylvania: Transition from Waiver to Traditional Coverage," KFF, August 3, 2015, https://www.kff.org/medicaid/fact-sheet/medicaid-expansion-in-pennsylvania/; Matthew Buettgens, John Holahan, and Hannah Recht, "Medicaid Expansion, Health Coverage, and Spending: An Update for the 21 States that Have Not Expanded Eligibility," KFF, April 29, 2015, https://www.kff.org/medicaid/issue-brief/medicaid-expansion-health-coverage-and-spending-an-update-for-the-21-states-that-have-not-expanded-eligibility/; W. White, "The Struggle Continues, the Victory Is Certain: Transforming Addiction Treatment and Recovery Support in Philadelphia," interview with Roland Lamb (Chestnut Health Systems), https://www.chestnut.org/resources/78229cb8-a7b9-4b9e-8ef8-b3dbef6910d4/2012-Roland-Lamb-v2.pdf.

55 *Had April been*: Jillian Forstadt, "Study Finds Regional Disparities in Buprenorphine Distribution Across Pa," WHYY news program, January 5, 2023, https://whyy.org/articles/study-finds-regional-disparities-in-buprenorphine-distribution-across-pa/; "Medication for Opioid Use Disorder in Pennsylvania Jails and Prisons: A Report by the Pennsylvania Institutional Law Project," Vital Strategies, report, 2022, https://www.vitalstrategies.org/wp-content/uploads/MOUD-in-PA-Jails-2022-Report.pdf.

55 *Just like 12 years a slave*: Unpublished poem by April Lee.

56 *The practice had gained traction in*: Kenneth Anderson, "How 12-Step Programs Became Embedded in US Hospitals." *Filter*, September 7, 2022. https://filtermag.org/12-step-programs-hospitals/.

56 *But for many people*: Dr. John Kelly (professor of addiction medicine, Harvard Medical School), interview with author, October 21, 2021.

56 *Almost 60 percent*: John F. Kelly, Martha Claire Greene, Brandon G. Bergman, William L. White, and Bettina B. Hoeppner, "How Many Recovery Attempts Does It Take to Successfully Resolve an Alcohol or Drug Problem? Estimates and Correlates from a National Study of Recovering U.S. Adults," *Alcoholism: Clinical and Experimental Research* 43, no. 7 (2019): 1533–44, https://doi.org/10.1111/acer.14067.

56 *More than one in every ten*: Michael L. Dennis, Christy K. Scott, Rodney Funk, and Mark A. Foss, "The Duration and Correlates of Addiction and Treatment Careers," *Journal of Substance Abuse Treatment* 28, no. 2 (2005): S51–62, https://doi.org/10.1016/j.jsat.2004.10.013.

56 *This problem is especially acute*: Fabiola Arbelo Cruz, "Racial Inequities in Treatments of Addictive Disorders," Yale School of Medicine, news release,

October 1, 2021, https://medicine.yale.edu/news-article/racial-inequities-in-treatments-of-addictive-disorders/.

57 *Programs that last*: Shari Roan, "30-Day Myth," *Los Angeles Times*, November 10, 2008, https://www.latimes.com/archives/la-xpm-2009-nov-10-the-addiction10-story.html.

57 *One study found*: John Strang, "Loss of Tolerance and Overdose Mortality After Inpatient Opiate Detoxification: Follow up Study," *BMJ* 326, no. 7396 (2003): 959–60, https://doi.org/10.1136/bmj.326.7396.959; Anders Ledberg and Therese Reitan, "Increased Risk of Death Immediately After Discharge from Compulsory Care for Substance Abuse," *Drug and Alcohol Dependence* 236 (May 2022): 109492, https://doi.org/10.1016/j.drugalcdep.2022.109492.

57 *While families*: Paul J. Joudrey, Maria R. Khan, Emily A. Wang, Joy D. Scheidell, E. Jennifer Edelman, et al., "A Conceptual Model for Understanding Post-Release Opioid-Related Overdose Risk," *Addiction Science & Clinical Practice* 14, no. 1 (2019): 17, https://doi.org/10.1186/s13722-019-0145-5.

58 *April wrote a poem in her journal*: Unpublished poem by April Lee, July 12, 2014.

59 *"I just found out"*: Unpublished and undated entry from journal of April Lee.

CHAPTER SEVEN

61 *Cassy was the face*: Larry Ley, interview with author, September 13, 2019.

61 *Larry's face was perpetually*: Cassy Bratcher, interview with author, November 14, 2019.

62 *The local drug task force*: Ron Wilkins, "Burlington Doctor, 78, Admits Dealing Narcotics," *Journal and Courier*, May 30, 2014, https://www.jconline.com/story/news/crime/2014/05/29/burlington-doctor-admits-dealing-narcotics/9746203/.

62 *When patients got hooked*: Patrick Keith (EMT), interview with author, November 24, 2020.

62 *But many of the Wagoner patients*: Ryan Radford and other former DORN patients, interviews with author, November 17, 2020.

62 *By 2017, more than*: C. Holly, A. Andrilla, Cynthia Coulthard, and Eric H. Larson, "Barriers Rural Physicians Face Prescribing Buprenorphine for Opioid Use Disorder," *Annals of Family Medicine* 15, no. 4 (2017): 359–62, https://doi.org/10.1370/afm.2099.

62 *Suboxone was so*: Christopher Moraff, "Why Suboxone Diversion Is Nothing to Fear." Filter. February 10, 2020. https://filtermag.org/suboxone-diversion-street/.

62 *Some patients drove*: Cassy Bratcher, interview.

63 *to no more than 100 patients*: Christian Heidbreder, Paul J. Fudala, and Mark K. Greenwald, "History of the Discovery, Development, and FDA-

Notes

Approval of Buprenorphine Medications for the Treatment of Opioid Use Disorder," *Drug and Alcohol Dependence Reports* 6 (March 2023), https://doi.org/10.1016/j.dadr.2023.100133.

63 *And DEA investigators*: Dave Wickey (former DEA diversion investigator), interview with author, August 23, 2021.

63 *a Reckitt rep started contacting*: Larry Ley and George Agapios, interview with author November 3, 2019.

63 *Eventually, Larry had found*: Dr. Ron Vierk, interview with author, September 30, 2020. See also Derek Tislow, Andrew J. Dollard, Yvonne S. Morgan, Cassy L. Bratcher, Joseph A. Mackey, Jessica Callahan, Eric W. Ley, and Felicia Reid v. United States 1:16-cv-1721-LJM-DKL, dep. of Luella Bangura (March 8, 2018).

63 *They understood they*: Tislow et al., 1:16-cv-1721-LJM-DKL, dep. of George Agapios (May 9, 2018).

63 *It would be the wealthy*: Steve Cash (Carmel police officer), interview with author, October 30, 2020.

63 *"I thought we had"*: Dr. George Agapios, interview with author, December 15, 2020.

64 *Cassy was the person*: Cassy Bratcher, interview with author, June 5, 2019.

64 *DORN ramdomly tested*: Unpublished spreadsheet showing status of various patients, compiled from internal files of DORN.

64 *He told Cassy*: Unpublished DEA interview with Joseph Mackey, July 25, 2014.

64 *Ultimately, they would*: Cassy Bratcher, interview with author, March 6, 2025.

64 *There was no limit on prescriptions*: Patricia Good, interview with author, October 9, 2020.

64 *that is, as a treatment for chronic*: Howard A. Heit, Edward Covington, and Patricia M. Good, "Dear DEA," *Pain Medicine* 5, no. 3 (2004): 303–308, https://doi.org/10.1111/j.1526-4637.2004.04044.x.

64 *"I probably prescribe"*: Report of investigation, U.S. Department of Justice, Drug Enforcement Administration, April 26, 2007, p. 26.

65 *While Larry was*: Scott Higham, Sari Horwitz, Steven Rich, and Meryl Kornfield, "Inside the Drug Industry's Plan to Disarm the DEA," *Washington Post*, September 13, 2019, https://www.washingtonpost.com/graphics/2019/investigations/drug-industry-plan-to-defeat-dea/.

65 *vastly outnumbered*: Review of the Drug Enforcement Administration's Regulatory and Enforcement Efforts to Control the Diversion of Opioids, Office of the Inspector General, U.S. Department of Justice, 2019, https://oig.justice.gov/reports/2019/e1905.pdf.

65 *Suboxone-prescribing doctors*: David Wickey, James Rafalski, and James Geldhof, and others (various diversion investigators), interviews with author, August 17–23, 2021.

Notes

65 *The stance mimicked*: David Courtwright. "A Century of American Narcotic Policy." *Treating Drug Problem,: vol. 2: Commissioned Papers on Historical, Institutional, and Economic Contexts of Drug Treatment* (National Academies Press, 1992), https://www.ncbi.nlm.nih.gov/books/NBK234755/.

65 *Multiple studies had found*: Theodore J. Cicero, Matthew S. Ellis, and Howard D. Chilcoat, "Understanding the Use of Diverted Buprenorphine," *Drug and Alcohol Dependence* 193 (December 2018): 117–23, https://doi.org/10.1016/j.drugalcdep.2018.09.007.

65 *But internally, it seemed*: DEA administrator (granted on condition of anonymity), interview with author, August 5, 2021.

65 *In Ohio, one Suboxone*: David Singer, "Addiction Clinic Ceases Offering Medical Supplements, Opioid Treatments to Patients," WTOV news, July 12, 2017, https://wtov9.com/news/local/addiction-clinic-ceases-offering-medical-supplements-opioid-treatments-to-patients.

66 *The DEA had never explained*: Dr. Thomas Reach, unpublished email to numerous treatment providers and colleagues, May 1, 2014.

66 *Even pharmacists were*: Dennis R. Lewis (president of West Virginia Board of Pharmacy), unpublished letter to West Virginia pharmacies, March 31, 2017; unpublished correspondence between Kentucky Board of Pharmacy, pharmacists, and complainants, January 1, 2018 through January 6, 2021; Neda J. Kazerouni, Adriane N. Irwin, Ximena A. Levander, Jonah Geddes, Kirbee Johnston, et al., "Pharmacy-Related Buprenorphine Access Barriers: An Audit of Pharmacies in Counties with a High Opioid Overdose Burden," *Drug and Alcohol Dependence* 224 (July 2021): 108729, https://doi.org/10.1016/j.drugalcdep.2021.108729.

67 *"Why are we"*: James Geldhof, interview with author, August 20, 2021.

67 *"It made no sense"*: Anonymous diversion investigator, interview with author, August 17, 2021.

67 *When one doctor visited*: Information here is from various confidential, unpublished reports of investigations by U.S. Department of Justice, Drug Enforcement Administration.

67 *"But nobody's"*: Tislow et al., 1:16-cv-1721-LJM-DKL, dep. of Larry Ley (September 26, 2017), at 12.

67 *Each time the DEA*: Howard Heit, letter to the DEA, October 14, 2013.

67 *the DEA confirmed*: Report of investigation, U.S. Department of Justice, Drug Enforcement Administration, April 26, 2007.

67 *One day in 2014*: Report of investigation, U.S. Department of Justice, Drug Enforcement Administration, March 26, 2014.

CHAPTER EIGHT

70 *It was a hot*: "Wendy/Rick Confrontation," unpublished video, 2014.

71 *Eventually, Wendy would plead*: State of California v. Wendy McEntyre,

Notes

RIM 1410895, Sup. Ct. Cal., Riverside Cty., sentencing memorandum (May 29, 2015), 1.

71 *And so, when*: Much of the background on Donavan comes from depositions by Shannon and Cyndi Doyle, in addition to author interview with Cyndi Doyle.

71 *Now, he felt that experience*: Doyle, CIVDS 1419415, dep. of Shannon Doyle (November 13, 2015), at 6.

72 *To pay for*: Doyle, CIVDS 1419415, dep. of Cynthia A. Doyle (August 21, 2015), at 29–31.

72 *His mother took*: Doyle, CIVDS 1419415, dep. of Shannon Doyle (November 13, 2015), at 7–11.

72 *They spent Christmas*: Doyle, CIVDS 1419415, dep. of Cynthia A. Doyle, at 17–20.

72 *It was going*: Doyle, CIVDS 1419415, dep. off Cynthia A. Doyle, at 19.

73 *The shift started during*: Rachel Hammer, Molly Dingel, Jenny Ostergren, Brad Partridge, Jennifer McCormick, et al., "Addiction: Current Criticism of the Brain Disease Paradigm," *AJOB Neuroscience* 4, no. 3 (2013): 27–32, https://doi.org/10.1080/21507740.2013.796328; David T. Courtwright, *Dark Paradise: A History of Opiate Addiction in America* (Harvard University Press, 2001), 123–25, https://doi.org/10.2307/j.ctvk12rbo; Nancy D. Campbell and Anne M. Lovell, "The History of the Development of Buprenorphine as an Addiction Therapeutic," *Annals of the New York Academy of Sciences* 1248, no. 1 (2012): 124–39, https://doi.org/10.1111/j.1749-6632.2011.06352.x.

73 *The industry grew again*: Mental Health Parity and Addiction Equity Act (MHPAEA), Centers for Medicare and Medicaid Services, September 10, 2024, https://www.cms.gov/marketplace/private-health-insurance/mental-health-parity-addiction-equity.

73 *And again, when Barack*: Patient Protection and Affordable Care Act, H.R.3590, 111th Cong. (2009–2010) (enacted March 23, 2010), https://www.congress.gov/bill/111th-congress/house-bill/3590.

73 *Prior to "Obamacare"*: "Affordable Care Act Expands Mental Health and Substance Use Disorder Benefits and Federal Parity Protections for 62 Million Americans," Office of the Assistant Secretary for Planning and Evaluation, Office of the Assistant Secretary of Health and Human Services for Planning and Evaluation, report, February 19, 2013, https://aspe.hhs.gov/reports/affordable-care-act-expands-mental-health-substance-use-disorder-benefits-federal-parity-protections-0.

74 *Public addiction-treatment*: Janet R. Cummings, Hefei Wen, Michelle Ko, and Benjamin G. Druss, "Race/Ethnicity and Geographic Access to Medicaid Substance Use Disorder Treatment Facilities in the United States," *JAMA Psychiatry* 71, no. 2 (2014): 190, https://doi.org/10.1001/jamapsychiatry.2013.3575; "Black Communities Hit Hardest by Lack of Public Addiction Treatment Facilities," Recovery Research Institute, report, https://

Notes

www.recoveryanswers.org/research-post/black-communities-hit-hardest-by-lack-of-public-addiction-treatment-facilities/; Janet R. Cummings, Helen Wen, Michelle Ko, and Benjamin Druss, "Race/Ethnicity and Geographic Access to Medicaid Substance Use Disorder Treatment Facilities in the United States," *JAMA Psychiatry* 71, no. 2 (2014): 190, https://doi.org/10.1001/jamapsychiatry.2013.3575.

74 *Almost overnight*: Dan Munro, "Inside the $35 Billion Addiction Treatment Industry," *Forbes*, April 27, 2015, https://www.forbes.com/sites/danmunro/2015/04/27/inside-the-35-billion-addiction-treatment-industry/.

74 *Most for-profit rehabs*: "'Buyer Beware': Treatment Admissions Practices and Costs of Residential Treatment for Opioid Use Disorder," Recovery Research Institute, report, https://www.recoveryanswers.org/research-post/treatment-admissions-practives-costs-residential-treatment-opioid-use-disorder/.

74 *Looking to help*: Cyndi Doyle, interview.

74 *Cyndi learned the*: Cyndi Doyle, interview with author, March 4, 2025; Doyle, CIVDS 1419415, dep. of Cynthia A. Doyle, at 32–33.

74 *Shane was not*: "Sean the Body Broker Who Brokered Donovan Doyle," interview with Wendy McEntyre, Jarrod's Law, 7.

74 *In fact, Cyndi's*: Doyle, CIVDS 1419415, dep. of Shannon Doyle, at 13; BlueCross BlueShield, BluePlus of Minnesota, Explanation of Benefits Summary Statement, Patient Name Donavan Doyle, Patient ID XZ1180107, Claims Summary Period September 1, 2013–November 1, 2013.

74 *The Above It All Treatment Center*: Above It All Treatment Center estimate for Matthew Maniace, February 26, 2017, p. 29.

75 *That was more*: Zohra D. Yaqhubi, "Harvard Net Tuition Cost Lowest in Ivy League, Reveals College Scorecard," *Harvard Crimson*, February 21, 2013, https://www.thecrimson.com/article/2013/2/21/harvard-tuition-lowest-league/.

75 *A waived co-pay*: Lisa Riordan Seville, Anna Schecter, and Hannah Rappleye. 2017. "Fatal Overdoses, Fraud Plague Florida's Booming Drug Treatment Industry." NBC News. June 26, 2017. https://www.nbcnews.com/feature/megyn-kelly/florida-s-billion-dollar-drug-treatment-industry-plagued-overdoses-fraud-n773376.

75 *She trusted what Shane*: Drug Rehab Blog–Information on Addiction and Recovery, Above It All Treatment Center, https://web.archive.org/web/20130530114701/http://www.aboveitalltreatment.com/.

75 *Owner Kory Avarell*: "About the Above It All Treatment Team—Meet Our Caring Staff," Above It All Treatment Center, https://web.archive.org/web/20130424235321/http://www.aboveitalltreatment.com/about/team/.

75 *"Dude, this is"*: Doyle, CIVDS 1419415, dep. of Shannon Doyle, at 12.

76 *"I am praying"*: Shannon Doyle, text message to Cyndi Doyle, September 23, 2013.

76 *"I wouldn't rather"*: Donavan Doyle, letter to Benjamin Doyle.

Notes

76   *"It is easy"*: Cyndi Doyle, text message to Kory Avarell, October 2, 2013.
76   *Kory Avarell in fact*: Doyle, CIVDS 1419415, video. dep. of Kory Karis Avarell (February 29, 2016), at 12–34; Kory Avarell, interview with the author.
77   *"And he's like"*: Doyle, CIVDS 1419415, dep. of Cynthia A. Doyle, at 38.
77   *"His counselor broke"*: Kory Avarell, text message to Cyndi Doyle, October 3, 2013.
77   *"I'm glad you"*: Kory Avarell, text message to Cyndi Doyle, October 3, 2013; Doyle, CIVDS 1419415, video. dep. of Richard Lawrence Hughes (December 14, 2015), at 83–83.
77   *"I'll do anything"*: Doyle, CIVDS 1419415, dep. of Cynthia A. Doyle, at 39–40.
77   *By running away, he had*: Kory Avarell, text message to Cyndi Doyle, October 3, 2013.
77   *If Donovan didn't*: Cyndi Doyle, text message to Shannon Doyle, October 7, 2013.
78   *And if that happened*: Cyndi Doyle, text message to Shannon Doyle, October 7, 2013.
78   *The program was*: Cyndi Doyle, text message to Shannon Doyle, October 7, 2013.
78   *I'm sacred [sic]*: Cyndi Doyle, text message to Kory Avarell, October 8, 2013.
78   *He said that*: Doyle, Doyle, CIVDS 1419415, dep. of Cynthia A. Doyle, at 90.
79   *A snowstorm had*: Cyndi Doyle, interview.
79   *Shannon went to work*: Shannon Doyle, text message to Cyndi Doyle, October 10, 2013.
79   *He had to*: Doyle, CIVDS 1419415, dep. of Shannon Doyle, at 17–18.
79   *"I knew something"*: Doyle, CIVDS 1419415, dep. of Shannon Doyle, at 25.
79   *All he found*: Doyle, CIVDS 1419415, dep. of Shannon Doyle, at 29.
79   *"I'm scared, Cyndi"*: Shannon Doyle, text message to Cyndi Doyle, October 12, 2013.
79   *"Could he be feeling"*: Kory Avarell, text message to Cyndi Doyle, October 2013.
79   *Cyndi repeatedly asked*: Doyle, CIVDS 1419415, dep. of Cyndi A. Doyle (October 9, 2015), at 312.
80   *He said Donavan was considered*: Richard Camacho, emails to Cyndi Doyle, November 5, 2013–April 14, 2014.
80   *"It did not"*: Leslie Parrilla, "Parents Explain Discovery of Son's Remains, Criticize Investigators," *San Bernardino Sun*, June 2, 2014, https://www.sbsun.com/2014/06/02/parents-explain-discovery-of-sons-remains-criticize-investigators/.
80   *Two months after*: Richard Camacho, email to Cyndi Doyle, December 2, 2013.
80   *They had said, again*: Sheriff's Department, County of San Bernardino, missing person report, May 9, 2014.
80   *The detective suggested*: Richard Camacho, email to Cyndi Doyle, January 20, 2014.

Notes

80 *"You know"*: Search party footage, videotape by Wendy McEntyre, May 26, 2014.
80 *One of the men*: Doyle, CIVDS 1419415, video. dep. of Sean Kenneth Bly (November 2, 2015), 32.
81 *That morning, he said he had*: Sean Bly, in videotape by Wendy McEntyre, May 26, 2014.
81 *What's more*: Sean Bly, videotape.
81 *"Nobody ever said"*: Sean Bly, videotape.

CHAPTER NINE

83 *On a sweltering*: Chris Koon, Criminal Bond, Grant Parish, Louisiana.
83 *It was a two*: Chris Koon, interview with author, April 8, 2020.
83 *Carrie, too, felt*: Carrie Tolbert, interview with author, March 27, 2019.
84 *Now, he was charged*: Based on interviews with former Cenikor participants James Dyer, Justin Marshall, and John Potter.
84 *highest success rates*: Chris Koon, interview with author, April 8, 2020. See also Cenikor's vocational services brochure, which says: "Since 1967, Cenikor has been one of the most successful substance use disorder treatment centers...."
84 *The program provided*: Based on numerous accounts provided by former counselors, including Tara Dixon and Melanie Cefalu, interviews with author, January 7, 2019–March 27, 2019.
84 *They'd find Chris*: Cenikor Work Participation Agreement, Cenikor Foundation, 2017.
84 *It sounded really good*: Carrie Tolbert, interview with author, March 27, 2019.
84 *Cenikor had multiple*: "A Place for Change: 2016 Annual Report," Cenikor Foundation, 2016.
84 *They had accreditation*: Cenikor Foundation 210286, CARF International assessment, 2024.
84 *Cenikor's website*: See Cenikor's website, 2015.
84 *The coordinator told Chris*: This account of Chris's experience is from Chris Koon, interview with author, unless otherwise noted.
85 *The building was sprawling*: Timothy Boone, "Former Cenikor Facility in Baton Rouge Sells for $4.1M to New Orleans Investment Firm," *The Advocate*, February 5, 2021, https://www.theadvocate.com/baton_rouge/news/business/article_fe85fd7e-67ff-11eb-9e57-e3ca25d521b9.html. See also the marketing brochure from 2414 Bunker Hill.
85 *Participants complained of holes*: Michael and Kim Ludiker, "Illegal Activity and Great Concern for Residents of Cenikor Foundation," Complaint to Texas Attorney General, Louisiana Department of Justice, Medicaid Fraud Control Unit, Case no. 19-00398, May 10, 2019.
86 *The number of people*: Maggie English, interview with author, March 3, 2021.
86 *Or, there was the "the dishpan"*: Various Cenikor participants and employees, interviews with author and Amy Julia Harris, 2018–2020.

Notes

87 *Or, there was the "verbal haircut"*: See the description in the 1969 Cenikor handbook, detailing the haircut, signs around the neck, pull-up: "Any behavior which helps bring discredit upon Cenikor may be corrected by a simple 'pull-up,' which is a verbal chastisement and may be administered by any member of Cenikor such conduct and at any time."

87 *These were called*: Jason Maye, interview with author, Amy Julia Harris and Laura Starecheski, March 25, 2019. See also author interviews with Chris Koon, April 8, 2020, and Kristin Carroll, April 1, 2021.

87 *Cenikor staff called*: Tyrone Evans, interview with Laura Starecheski, April 27, 2019.

87 *Chris heard women*: Kristin Carroll, interview with author, April 1, 2021.

87 *Even some of the employees participated*: Tara Dixon, interview with author, January 7, 2019.

87 *Hundreds of such programs*: Shoshana Walter, "At Hundreds of Rehabs, Recovery Means Work Without Pay," *Reveal*, July 7, 2020, https://revealnews.org/article/at-hundreds-of-rehabs-recovery-means-work-without-pay/.

87 *At a program in*: Amy Julia Harris and Shoshana Walter, "She Said She'd Free Them from Addiction. She Turned Them into Her Personal Servants," *Reveal*, May 21, 2018, https://revealnews.org/article/drug-users-got-exploited-disabled-patients-got-hurt-one-woman-benefited-from-it-all/.

87 *Behavior modification*: Individual Rights and the Federal Role in Behavior Modification: A Study Prepared by the Staff of the Subcommittee on Constitutional Rights of the Committee on the Judiciary, U.S. Senate, 93rd Congress, Senate Committee on the Judiciary, November 1974 (15). https://survivingstraightinc.com/SeedFloridaGovernmentDocs/Individual-Rights-Seed-1974-part1.pdf.

88 *Henry Anslinger, the bombastic head*: Stanley Meisler, "Federal Narcotics Czar," *The Nation*, February 20, 1960, https://www.thenation.com/article/archive/federal-narcotics-czar/; Gerald D. Adix, "Addicts' Ranks Tripled Since World War II End," *San Bernardino County Sun*, June 4, 1958.

88 *The only way to stop*: "Miracle on the Beach," episode 2, *American Rehab*, July 4, 2020, https://revealnews.org/podcast/american-rehab-chapter-two-miracle-on-the-beach/.

88 *And the best way to do that*: Erin M. Weiss, "A New Deal for Junkies," *Philologia* 3, no. 1 (2011), https://vtechworks.lib.vt.edu/server/api/core/bitstreams/c70ed2d7-8e02-4abd-bb9c-be697f4b9ffd/content.

88 *One of the earliest homes*: Ralph Friedman, "Fight for their Lives: They're Wrestling Dope, Drink," *Miami News*, June 14, 1959.

88 *Early meetings resembled*: Kandy Latson, interview with Ike Sriskandarajah, October 9, 2019.

88 *After one participant*: John Stallone, interview with Ike Sriskandarajah, June 2019.

88 *Those for whom*: Claire Clark, *The Recovery Revolution* (Columbia University Press, 2017), 38.

Notes

89 *"Yeah, we brainwash"*: Kandy Latson, interview with Ike Sriskandarajah.
89 *In the counterculture*: "Overview: The 1970s," *Washington Post*, 1997, https://www.washingtonpost.com/wp-srv/national/longterm/cult/overview70s.htm; Lewis Yablonsky, *Confessions of a Criminologist* (Indiana University Press, 2010).
89 *"A tunnel back into the human race"*: Greg Villet, "A Tunnel Back into the Human Race," *Life*, March 9, 1962.
89 *After abolishing slavery*: Shane Bauer, "Why Do Inmates Fight Wildfires for Dollars a Day? The Origins of Prison Slavery in America," *Slate*, October 2, 2018, https://slate.com/news-and-politics/2018/10/origin-prison-slavery-shane-bauer-american-prison-excerpt.html.
89 *"Hard honest work"*: "Cowboy Conman," episode 4, *American Rehab*, July 18, 2020.
89 *As it turns out*: Clark, *Recovery Revolution*, 38.
89 *Studies would later*: William L. White and William R. Miller, "The Use of Confrontation in Addiction Treatment History, Science, and Time for Change," William White Papers, 2007, http://www.williamwhitepapers.com/pr/2007ConfrontationinAddictionTreatment.pdf.
89 *And in 1967*: Spec. Subcom. on Alcoholism and Narcotics, Senate Comm. on Labor and Public Welfare, 91st Cong. (September 29, 1969), testimony by James Lucas Austin.
90 *Austin was speaking*: Spec. Subcom. on Alcoholism and Narcotics.
90 *Two months after that*: Bill Peters, "Governor Discusses Policy of State Parole Board," Getty Images, 1969, https://www.gettyimages.it/detail/fotografie-di-cronaca/governor-discusses-policy-of-state-parole-board-fotografie-di-cronaca/161992204.
90 *Cenikor had a*: "Cowboy Conman," episode 4, *American Rehab*, July 18, 2020.
90 *Austin even founded*: As per KHOU film reel, December 3, 1974.
90 *By the early*: "Cowboy Conman," *American Rehab*.
91 *Just living off of us"*: "Cowboy Conman," *American Rehab*.
91 *All this information*: Jim Cicconi, memo to Michael Deaver, April 27, 1983.
91 *"I'm going to kill"*: Maria Micah Bleecher, interview with Laura Starecheski, April 23, 2019.
91 *Six months later*: "Cowboy Common," *American Rehab*; Ken Barun, interview with Laura Starecheski, March 22, 2019; Clark, *Recovery Revolution*; "News Digest," *Valley Morning Star*, July 30, 1978, https://www.newspapers.com/clip/1249765/cenikors-founder-luke-austins-mother/.
91 *By the time of*: Paul Morantz, "Change Partners and Dance," Paul Morantz website, https://web.archive.org/web/20200924115321/https://www.paulmorantz.com/the_synanon_story/change-partners-and-dance/.
91 *Synanon now let*: "A Venomous Snake," episode 3, *American Rehab*, July 11, 2020, https://revealnews.org/podcast/american-rehab-chapter-three-a-venomous-snake/.

Notes

91 *He banned sugar*: Richard Ofshe, "The Social Development of the Synanon Cult: The Managerial Strategy of Organizational Transformation," *Sociological Analysis* 41, no. 2 (1980): 114, https://doi.org/10.2307/3709903.

92 *One attorney*: Ronald J. Ostrow, "U.S. Indicts Nine From Synanon in Tax-Exemption Effort," *Los Angeles Times*, October 2, 1985.

92 *For the murder*: "Charles Dederich, Synanon Founder," *Tampa Bay Times*, March 4, 1997, https://www.tampabay.com/archive/1997/03/04/charles-dederich-synanon-founder/.

92 *The agency stripped*: "The Internal Revenue Service Has Filed Tax Liens to . . . ", UPI, February 16, 1984.

92 *They kept it going*: "Reagan with the Snap," episode 5, *American Rehab*, July 25, 2020, https://revealnews.org/podcast/american-rehab-chapter-5-reagan-with-the-snap/; Dan McNamara, letter to President Ronald Reagan, August 2, 1983.

92 *The arrangement was good timing*: Peter T. Kilborn, "Achievements, But Failures, Too, for Reaganomics: Economic Analysis," *New York Times*, July 1, 1983, https://www.nytimes.com/1983/07/01/business/achievements-but-failures-too-for-reaganomics-economic-analysis.html; "Reported Federal Drug Abuse Expenditures—Fiscal Years 1981 to 1985," Report by the U.S. General Accounting Office, June 3, 1985, https://www.ojp.gov/pdffiles1/Digitization/99775NCJRS.pdf.

92 *In 1983, President Ronald*: "The Daily Diary of President Ronald Reagan," The White House, April 29, 1983, https://www.reaganfoundation.org/ronald-reagan/white-house-diaries/diary-entry-04291983/.

92 *"I was glancing through"*: President Ronald Reagan, Remarks at the Cenikor Foundation Center in Houston, Texas, April 29, 1983, https://www.reaganlibrary.gov/archives/speech/remarks-cenikor-foundation-center-houston-texas.

92 *For Reagan, Cenikor*: David F. Musto, *The American Disease: Origins of Narcotic Control* (Yale University Press, 1973), 267–68; David T. Courtwright, *Dark Paradise: A History of Opioid Addiction in America* (Harvard University Press, 2009), 175–76.

92 *As the years passed*: Walter, "At Hundreds of Rehabs."

93 *Then in 2004*: Bill Bailey, interview with Kevin Price, *Price of Business*, January 2, 2015.

93 *Unlike the organization's*: Bailey interview, *Price of Business*.

93 *He hired licensed*: Anthony Boydston (former Cenikor employee), interview with author, March 15, 2019; Christina Hughes Babb (former participant), email to author, March 2, 2021; investigative reports, Louisiana Department of Justice, Medicaid Fraud Unit, May 10, 2019.

93 *Upon arriving at*: Chris Koon, interview with author, April 8, 2020; Cenikor Foundation admissions documents.

93 *"I also understand"*: Timothy Klick, Wilton Chambers, et. al. v. Cenikor Foundation, U.S. Court of Appeals, Fifth Cir., August 16, 2023.

Notes

94 *For example*: Cenikor admission paperwork, Matthew Oates, February 1, 2019.

94 *Earn 72 points*: Cenikor admission paperwork, Oates.

94 *Everyone's points*: Marc and Kayla Roussel, interview with author, December 4, 2018.

94 *In the years following the end of the Great*: Tian Luo, Amar Mann, and Richard J. Holden, "What Happened to Temps? Changes Since the Great Recession," *Monthly Labor Review*, February 2021, https://www.bls.gov/opub/mlr/2021/article/pdf/temp-help.pdf.

94 *Temp workers allowed*: Michael Grabell, "The Expendables: How the Temps Who Power Corporate Giants Are Getting Crushed," *ProPublica*, June 27, 2013, https://www.propublica.org/article/the-expendables-how-the-temps-who-power-corporate-giants-are-getting-crushed.

95 *Cenikor seized on this*: Walter and Harris, "They Worked in Sweltering Heat." This account also based on dozens of interviews with former participants, staff, and business partners.

95 *With jail or prison*: Wes Pope (former assistant vice president), interview with author, February 5, 2019.

95 *Every night, at each*: Joshua Campbell, interview with author, October 16, 2018; line-out sheet, Cenikor Foundation, January 2019.

95 *Some worked at*: Walter and Harris, "They Worked in Sweltering Heat."

95 *They built scaffolding*: Chris Koon, interview with author, December 12, 2018.

95 *Cenikor's corporate headquarters*: Paul Porche, interview with author, October 28, 2018.

95 *The vocational office*: Stephanie Collins, David Dupuis, Cody Collins, Chris Payne, and other vocational services workers, various interviews with author and with Amy Julia Harris, 2018–2020. The description of duties is from Patrick Odom's LinkedIn account; see also Cenikor, "Acquisition and Mgmt. of Temporary Employment Contracts for Cenikor Personnel Direct to Hire Staffing Service."

95 *The more they collected*: Managers Incentive Plan spreadsheet, internal document.

95 *When corporate headquarters pressured*: Cody Collins, interview with author, 2019.

95 *But internal documents*: Facility income statement for the two months ending August 31, 2016, report, Cenikor Foundation, Baton Rouge.

95 *Between 2013 and 2018*: Return of Organization Exempt from Income Tax (Form 990), Cenikor Foundation, Houston, Texas, Department of the Treasury, Internal Revenue Service, 2013–2018.

96 *Meanwhile, the facility*: Walter and Harris, "They Worked in Sweltering Heat."

96 *Finally, after about*: Cenikor Foundation admissions documents.

96 *Chris wore his best*: Chris Koon, interview with author, April 8, 2020.

96 *He told his dad*: Chris Koon, interview with author, December 12, 2018.

Notes

97 *At first, they sent*: Chris Koon, interview.
97 *His sole pay*: Chris Payne, interview with author, December 8, 2018.

CHAPTER TEN

99 *When April Lee graduated*: Unless otherwise specified, this account of April's time post-rehab is based on multiple interviews by author with April Lee.
100 *Medicaid expansion in Pennsylvania*: M. Olfson, M. Wall, C. L. Barry, C. Mauro, and R. Mojtabai, "Impact of Medicaid Expansion on Coverage and Treatment of Low-Income Adults with Substance Use Disorders," *Health Affairs* (Millwood) 37, no. 8 (August 2018): 1208–15, https://doi: 10.1377/hlthaff.2018.0124, PMID: 30080455, PMCID: PMC6190698; C. E. Blevins, N. Rawat, and M. D. Stein, "Gaps in the Substance Use Disorder Treatment Referral Process: Provider Perceptions," *Journal of Addiction Medicine* 12, no. 4 (July/August 2018): 273–77, https://doi: 10.1097/ADM.0000000000000400, PMID: 29738347, PMCID: PMC6066414.
100 *Since 2002, the number*: J. R. Cummings, H. Wen, and M. Ko, "Decline in Public Substance Use Disorder Treatment Centers Most Serious in Counties with High Shares of Black Residents," *Health Affairs* (Milkwood) 35, no. 6 (June 1 2016): 1036–44.
100 *Studies have shown that*: John F. Kelly, Martha Claire Greene, Brandon G. Bergman, William L. White, and Bettina B. Hoeppner, "How Many Recovery Attempts Does It Take to Successfully Resolve an Alcohol or Drug Problem? Estimates and Correlates from a National Study of Recovering U.S. Adults," *Alcoholism: Clinical and Experimental Research* 43, no. 7 (2019): 1533–44, https://doi.org/10.1111/acer.14067.
100 *And entering rehab quickly*: William White, "Recovery Management and Recovery-Oriented Systems of Care: Scientific Rationale and Promising Practices," William White Papers, 2008, http://www.williamwhitepapers.com/pr/2008RecoveryManagementMonograph.pdf.
100 *People who experience delays*: J. Chun, J. R. Guydish, F. Silber, and A. Gleghorn, "Drug Treatment Outcomes for Persons on Waiting Lists," *American Journal of Drug and Alcohol Abuse* 34, no. 5 (2008): 526–33, https://doi: 10.1080/00952990802146340, PMID: 18618338, PMCID: PMC2766557.
100 *Starting on buprenorphine*: A. A. Herring, A. D. Rosen, E. A. Samuels, Chunging Lin, Melissa Speener, et al., "Emergency Department Access to Buprenorphine for Opioid Use Disorder," *JAMA Network Open*.7, no. 1 (2024): e2353771, https://doi:10.1001/jamanetworkopen.2023.53771.
101 *they wouldn't immediately cover*: A spokesperson for Community Behavioral Health said the organization "uses medical necessity criteria [MNC]

when making decisions about treatment." Email from CBH to Victoria Valenzuela, January 18, 2023.

101 *For decades, Philadelphia had*: Maureen Graham and Larry King, "How N.J. Freed Addicts at Pa.'s Expense; Parolees Were Sent Without Permission, They Got Aid but Little Treatment," *Philadelphia Inquirer*, October 1, 1995, https://advance.lexis.com/api/document?collection=news&id=urn:contentItem:473F-C4V0-01K4-9216-00000-00&context=1519360.

101 *The city itself*: Robert P. Fairbanks, *How It Works* (University of Chicago Press, 2009); "Recovery House Initiative," (Philadelphia) Department of Behavioral Health and Intellectual Disability Services, news release. August 27, 2024, https://dbhids.org/about/organization/behavioral-health-division/single-county-authority/recovery-house-initiative/.

101 *As a result*: Alfred Lubrano, "'Pimping Out' Drug Addicts for Cash," *Philadelphia Inquirer*, June 1, 2017, https://www.inquirer.com/health/opioid-addiction/inq/pimping-out-drug-addicts-cash-20170601.html-2.

102 *subsisted through other methods*: Aubrey Whelan, "A Leading Addiction Recovery Reformer in Philly Was on the Payroll of a Rehab Center Now Charged with Crimes," *Philadelphia Inquirer*, September 27, 2021, https://www.inquirer.com/news/fred-way-philly-recovery-houses-addiction-treatment-parr-southwest-nustop-20210927.html.

102 *work without pay*: Author notes for a Philadelphia city paper story on recovery homes, 2001, no longer available online.

102 *With so many jobs*: Kelly E. Moore, Robyn L. Hacker, Lindsay Oberleitner, and Sherry A. McKee, "Reentry Interventions that Address Substance Use: A Systematic Review," *Psychological Services* 17, no. 1 (2020): 93–101, https://doi.org/10.1037/ser0000293; Fairbanks, *How It Works*.

102 *Others subjected their residents*: Rebecca E. Stewart, Courtney Benjamin Wolk, Geoffrey Neimark, Ridhi Vyas, Jordyn Young, et al., "It's Not Just the Money: The Role of Ideology in Publicly Funded Substance Use Disorder Treatment," *Journal of Substance Abuse Treatment* 20 (October 2020): 108176, https://doi.org/10.1016/j.jsat.2020.108176.

102 *access to treatment*: Fabiola Arbelo Cruz, "Racial Inequities in Treatments of Addictive Disorders," Yale School of Medicine, news release, October 1, 2021, https://medicine.yale.edu/news-article/racial-inequities-in-treatments-of-addictive-disorders/.

102 *While the country's*: Eli Hager, "The Cruel Failure of Welfare Reform in the Southwest," *ProPublica*, December 30, 2021, https://www.propublica.org/article/the-cruel-failure-of-welfare-reform-in-the-southwest; Jennifer Ludden, "Child Poverty More than Doubles—A Year After Hitting Record Low, Census Data Shows," NPR news, September 12, 2023, https://www.npr.org/2023/09/12/1198923453/child-poverty-child-tax-credi-pandemic-aid-census-data.

102 *Medicaid barred*: "Interface with Behavioral Health Services," Medicaid

Notes

handbook, Substance Abuse and Mental Health Services Administration, HHS Publication no. SMA-13-4773, 2013, p. 9.
102 *The neighborhood*: Chris Palmer Griffin, Dylan Purcell, Anna Orso, John Duchneskie, and Jessica Griffin, "How Impacted You Are by Philly's Shootings Epidemic Can Depend on the Block You Live On," *Philadelphia Inquirer*, September 16, 2021, https://www.inquirer.com/news/a/philadelphia-shootings-homicides-redlining-kensington-20210916.html.
103 *As the drug trade*: Marcus Biddle, "Philly's Next Mayor Could Try to End Kensington's Open-Air Drug Market. How That Could Unfold Is Uncertain," WHYY news, April 24, 2023, https://whyy.org/articles/philadelphia-mayor-kensington-open-air-drug-market/.
103 *Under the shadow*: Jennifer Percy, "Trapped by the 'Walmart of Heroin,'" *New York Times*, October 10, 2018, https://www.nytimes.com/2018/10/10/magazine/kensington-heroin-opioid-philadelphia.html; other descriptions here are based on author's observations.

CHAPTER ELEVEN

105 *On August 19*: Ashley Taylor, email to Aaron Deitz, August 19, 2013.
105 *About a month earlier*: Coroner Summary Report, Case no. 2013-102, Madison Cty. Coroner's Office, July 20, 2013.
105 *"He has been on"*: Coroner Summary Report.
106 *She had seen*: Review of "Ashley R. Taylor | Part Time | Madison County, Indiana, 2015," *OpenPayrolls*, 2015, https://openpayrolls.com/ashley-r-taylor-34622521.
106 *"I'm so tired"*: "Ashley R. Taylor," *OpenPayrolls*.
106 *Eventually, his cause*: Drug test results, AIT Laboratories, August 1, 2013.
106 *Nonetheless, the coroner*: Unpublished notes of Carmel Police Department Intelligence Unit, August 19 through October 10, 2013.
106 *He'd trained at*: State of Indiana v. Larry J. Ley, Case no. 29D01-1407-FB-006027, dep. of Gary Whisenand (May 31, 2016), at 7–8.
107 *Aaron Deitz, the head*: Scott Smith and Kokomo Tribune, "Wagoner Pleads Guilty to Seven Felony Drug Dealing Charges," *Carroll County Comet*, June 4, 2014, https://www.carrollcountycomet.com/articles/wagoner-pleads-guilty-to-seven-felony-drug-dealing-charges/.
107 *A quick search*: Report of Investigation, U.S. Department of Justice, Drug Enforcement Administration, July 12, 2014.
107 *But now Whisenand*: Report of Investigation, U.S. Department of Justice, Drug Enforcement Administration, December 2, 2013.
107 *A sheriff's deputy*: Report of Investigation, U.S. Department of Justice, Drug Enforcement Administration, July 12, 2014.
107 *"Might as well"*: Report of Investigation, July 12, 2014.
107 *Research had found*: Saie Choi, Carrie Garland, Taylor Harmening,

Michelle Kimbell, Katie Pashalides, et al., "Introduction Results Design/ Sample Summary Further Study Acknowledgements," University of California, Davis, news report, https://health.ucdavis.edu/nursing/news/Events /PDF/June11/Garland_The%20Effect%20of%20Payment%20Method%20 on%20Suboxone%20Therapy.pdf.

108 *"I think when"*: Katy Jo Dalton, interview with author, September 17, 2020.
108 *The cash-pay practices*: Art Van Zee and David A. Fiellin, "Proliferation of Cash-Only Buprenorphine Treatment Clinics: A Threat to the Nation's Response to the Opioid Crisis," *American Journal of Public Health* 109, no. 3 (2019): 393–94, https://doi.org/10.2105/ajph.2018.304899, https://pmc.ncbi .nlm.nih.gov/articles/PMC6366517/.
109 *Within a few months*: Report of Investigation, July 12, 2014.
109 *The hundreds of hours*: Descriptions of videos based on author's review of hundreds of hours of undercover DEA footage.
109 *"Our goal is"*: Unpublished undercover footage from DEA investigation, March 25, 2014.
110 *I'm not racist*: Recording of DEA interview with former DORN patient.
111 *At another appointment*: Unpublished undercover footage, March 25, 2014.

CHAPTER TWELVE

113 *She and Cyndi*: Cyndi Doyle, interview by author, December 11, 2022.
113 *"We recently have"*: Kyle Avarell, email message to Above It All staff, August 28, 2014.
114 *And soon, employees*: Above It All employees, videotape by Wendy McEntyre, September 1, 2014.
114 *He sat down on a log*: Cyndi Doyle v. v. Hi-Land Mountain Homes, Inc. DBA Above It All Treatment Center, CIVDS 1419415, Sup. Ct. Cal., San Bernardino Cty., video. dep. of Christopher Ted O'Keefe (December 15, 2015), vol. 2.
114 *This procedure was laid*: Doyle, CIVDS 1419415, Expert Witness Report, Christopher Lewis, SUD Compliance & Consulting, LLC (October 2, 2019), 6.
115 *The next morning*: Doyle, CIVDS 1419415, dep. of Christopher Ted O'Keefe, vol. 1, at 19–23.
115 *"Please make sure"*: Cyndi Doyle, text message to Kory Avarell, October 8, 2013.
115 *AIA's own policies*: Quality Assurance Department, "Case Record Review," in *Above It All Treatment Center Policy & Procedures*, approved by Above It All Management Team, issued August 20, 2013, revised October 15, 2015, p. 155; *Doyle*, CIVDS 1419415.
115 *If Donavan was trying*: Detention of Persons with a Mental Health Condition for Evaluation and Treatment, https://leginfo.legislature.ca.gov/faces /codes_displaySection.xhtml?lawCode=WIC&sectionNum=5150.

Notes

115 *Above It All typically*: Kory Avarell, interview with author.
115 *Chris's supervisor told him not to call 911*: Doyle, CIVDS 1419415, video. dep. of Christopher Ted O'Keefe, vol. 1, at 22–23, 29–30.
116 *Avarell would later say he knew nothing*: Doyle, CIVDS 1419415, video. dep. of Kory Karis Avarell (February 29, 2016), 124–26.
116 *Chris had not*: Quality Assurance Department, "Case Record Review," 129; Doyle, CIVDS 1419415, video. dep. of Christopher Ted O'Keefe, vol. 1, at 9; Doyle, CIVDS 1419415, at 5.
116 *And if that happened*: Doyle, CIVDS 1419415, video. dep. of Richard Lawrence Hughes (December 14, 2015), 67–68, 76–77; Doyle, CIVDS 1419415, video. dep. of Kory Karis Avarell (February 29, 2016), 145.
116 *Soon after, Rick*: Doyle, CIVDS 1419415, video. dep. of Richard Hughes, 220–21.
116 *Avarell said he did not*: Avarell said he did not recall telling Rick not to call 911. Doyle, CIVDS 1419415, video. dep. of Kory Karis Avarell, 150.
116 *The program's own*: Doyle, CIVDS 1419415, at 10–11.
116 *fog and snow*: Doyle, CIVDS 1419415, video. dep. of Kory Karis Avarell, 150.
117 *"I am left"*: Cyndi Doyle, text message to Kory Avarell, October 8, 2013.
117 *She advertised the*: Wendy McEntyre, interview with author, October 25, 2024.
117 *It was a niche industry*: Dan Munro, "Inside the $35 Billion Addiction Treatment Industry," *Forbes*, April 27, 2015, https://www.forbes.com/sites/danmunro/2015/04/27/inside-the-35-billion-addiction-treatment-industry/; Michael T. French, Joana Popovici, and Lauren Tapsell, "The Economic Costs of Substance Abuse Treatment: Updated Estimates and Cost Bands for Program Assessment and Reimbursement," *Journal of Substance Abuse Treatment* 35, no. 4 (2008): 462–69, https://doi:10.1016/j.jsat.2007.12.008.
117 *And unlike many other forms*: Tami L. Mark, William N. Dowd, and Carol L. Council, "Tracking the Quality of Addiction Treatment over Time and Across States: Using the Federal Government's 'Signs' of Higher Quality," RTI Press Publication No. RR-0040-2007, July 2020, https://doi.org/10.3768/rtipress.2020.rr.0040.2007.
117 *the high failure rate*: Doyle, CIVDS 1419415, video. dep. of Sean Kenneth Bly (November 2, 2015), 37. Bly describes his role as an aftercare coordinator involved in calling former patients "to do whatever I had to do" to re-enroll them in the program if they had relapsed, especially if they had "good" insurance.
118 *"too many trips to rehab"*: "Can You Have Too Many Stints in Rehab?," Recovery Place, blog, 2024, https://www.recoveryplace.com/blog/can-you-have-too-many-stints-in-rehab/.
118 *Despite being one of the*: David Blumenthal, Evan D. Gumas, Arnav Shah, Munira Z. Gunja, and Reginald D. Williams, "Mirror, Mirror 2024: A Portrait of the Failing U.S. Health System," Commonwealth Fund, report, September 2024, https://doi.org/10.26099/taog-zp66.

Notes

118 *An estimated 10 percent*: "National Health Expenditure Data," Centers for Medicare & Medicaid Services, December 18, 2024, https://www.cms.gov/data-research/statistics-trends-and-reports/national-health-expenditure-data/historical; William C. Hsiao, "Fraud and Abuse in Healthcare Claims," California Health and Human Services, report, October 12, 2021, https://www.chhs.ca.gov/wp-content/uploads/2022/01/Commissioner-William-Hsiao-Comments-on-Fraud-and-Abuse-in-Healthcare-Claims.pdf.

118 *But insurers have*: Marshall Allen, "We Asked Prosecutors if Health Insurance Companies Care About Fraud. They Laughed at Us," *ProPublica*, September 10, 2019, https://www.propublica.org/article/we-asked-prosecutors-if-health-insurance-companies-care-about-fraud-they-laughed-at-us.

118 *For example, urine drug testing*: David Segal, "In Pursuit of Liquid Gold," *New York Times*, December 27, 2017, https://www.nytimes.com/interactive/2017/12/27/business/urine-test-cost.html.

118 *Soon after leaving*: MMR Services, Invoice no. 688232037, December 12, 2016, for $202,860.00, p. 3.

118 *one rehab went from*: Phil Drechsler and Carolyn Johnson, "Rehab Clinics Under Federal Scrutiny for Fraud, Neglect," *NBC Los Angeles*, September 6, 2017, https://www.nbclosangeles.com/news/rehab-clinics-under-federal-scrutiny-for-fraud-neglect/22655/.

119 *Some years later, though*: Arrest and Notice to Appear, Michael Lohan, Boca Raton Police Department, April 19, 2021.

119 *This practice, illegal in some states*: Roseanna Alacala, interview by author, January 3, 2022.

119 *Even high-profile members*: Letter from Addiction Treatment Advocacy Coalition to Commissioner Dave Jones at California Department of Insurance, May 5, 2016, 4; spreadsheet from internal files of EST Solutions, a marketing company owned by Josiah Shafer. This spreadsheet shows the company used body brokers to place patients at ATAC-affiliated treatment centers.

119 *Treatment programs paid hefty fees*: Josiah Shafer, interview with author, February 26, 2021.

119 *To find clients*: Shafer, interview.

119 *In coastal cities*: Teri Sforza, Tony Saavedra, Scott Schwebke, Lori Basheda, Mindy Schauer, Jeff Gritchen, Ian Wheeler, "How Some Southern California Drug Rehab Centers Exploit Addiction," *Orange County Register*, November 5, 2018, https://www.ocregister.com/2017/05/21/how-some-southern-california-drug-rehab-centers-exploit-addiction/; Jordan Graham, "Are Drug Rehab Centers Fueling Homelessness in Southern California?," *Orange County Register*, July 30, 2018, https://www.ocregister.com/2017/12/17/are-drug-rehab-centers-fueling-homelessness-in-southern-california/.

119 *And deaths at*: Teri Sforza, Tony Saavedra, Scott Schwebke, Lori Basheda, Mindy Schauer, et al., "How Some Southern California Drug Rehab Centers

Notes

Exploit Addiction," *Orange County Register*, November 5, 2018, https://www.ocregister.com/2017/05/21/how-some-southern-california-drug-rehab-centers-exploit-addiction/.
119 *It often took*: Drug and Alcohol Treatment Facilities, California State Auditor, report, October 2024, pp. 34, 39, 43, https://www.auditor.ca.gov/wp-content/uploads/2024/10/2023-120-Report.pdf.
120 *And when the complaints were*: Wendy McEntyre, interview with author, December 15, 2021.

CHAPTER THIRTEEN

121 *John Koon was starting*: John Koon, interview with author, November 29, 2021.
122 *His family—his mother*: Pat and Chris Koon, interviews with author, February 2, 2020.
123 *"Mind Control Techniques"*: Michael Powell, *Mind Games* (Fall River Press, 2011), 97.
123 *He never knew*: Chris Koon, interview with author, December 12, 2018.
123 *During the drill*: John and Kristin Carroll, interview with author, April 2, 2021.
124 *When Chris had*: Tara Dixon, interview with author, December 2019.
124 *The program had begun*: Numerous former Cenikor staff, interviews with author, 2018–2021; state investigative reports, Medicaid Fraud Unit, Louisiana Department of Justice, May 10, 2019, https://www.documentcloud.org/documents/6881819-Cenikor-Louisiana-AG-Medicaid-Fraud-investigation/?mode=document#document/p36/a562441.
124 *Chris quickly found*: Various accounts here are from interviews with Cenikor participants and counselors, 2018–2022, and from state investigative reports.
124 *At one point*: Melanie Cefalu (former counselor), interview with author, March 27, 2019.
124 *Not only was*: Melanie Cefalu, interview; Tara Dixon, interview with author, January 7, 2019.
124 *"Fine," Chris would*: Chris Koon, interview with author, March 24, 2019, and Melanie Cefalu, interview.
125 *She was miserable working at*: Peggy Billeaudeau, interview with author, October 22, 2018; Tara Dixon, interview with author; anonymous administrators at Cenikor, interviews with author, 2019–2020.
126 *Tara Dixon saw*: Tara Dixon, interview.
126 *"In order to see change"*: Tara Dixon, interview.
126 *Tara was especially alarmed*: Tara Dixon, interview.
127 *In addition to*: Melanie Cefalu, interview, and Justin Marshall, interview with author, July 19, 2018.

Notes

128 *At the Houston*: Investigative Report, Texas Health and Human Services Commission, Substance Abuse Compliance Group, February 5, 2018; various Cenikor participants, interviews with Amy Julia Harris and author, 2018–2019.
128 *After the hurricanes*: Peggy Billeaudeau, interview.
128 *The dull repetitive motion*: Cody Collins, interview.
129 *At Cenikor, none*: Melanie Cefalu, interview.
129 *Melanie Cefalu*: Melanie Cefalu, interview.
129 *In Louisiana, rehab*: Statement of Deficiencies and Plan of Correction, Cenikor Foundation, August 1, 2012, p. 27.
129 *One counselor on*: Statement of Deficiencies, Cenikor Foundation.
130 *In 2017, when Chris*: Return of Organization Exempt from Income Tax (Form 990), Cenikor Foundation, Houston, Texas, Department of the Treasury, Internal Revenue Service, 2017.
130 *No corporate executive or government*: Tara Dixon and Peggy Billeaudeau, interviews.
130 *Peggy pulled*: Peggy Billeaudeau, interview with author, October 22, 2018.
132 *One night, Chris*: Chris Koon, interview; Maggie English, interview.
133 *Patrick barely acknowledged*: Chris Koon, Kayla Roussel (nurse), and other Cenikor participants and staff, interviews with author, 2018–2020. The Louisiana Attorney General also found that Odom would routinely overrule the medical department's advice not to send participants out to work. "Odom would consistently send clients to work either sick or injured and on some occasions would delay clients from seeing medical so they could continue to work," investigative reports, Medicaid Fraud Unit, Louisiana Department of Justice, May 10, 2019.
133 *And there were even worse*: "The Work Cure," episode 7, *American Rehab*, August 1, 2020, https://revealnews.org/podcast/american-rehab-chapter-seven-the-work-cure/.
134 *Chris didn't know*: U.S. Department of Labor, Occupational Safety and Health Administration, worksheet, February 8, 1996.
134 *After a lengthy investigation*: U.S. Department of Labor, worksheet.
135 *It did so by*: Chris Nakamoto, "Amputee Learns He Has No Health Insurance After Employer Neglected to Pay Bills," WBRZ news, March 6, 2021, https://www.wbrz.com/news/amputee-learns-he-has-no-health-insurance-after-employer-neglected-to-pay-bills; Chris Nakamoto, "Contractor Behind Emergency Sunshine Bridge Repair Still Owes State Police Nearly $900K," WBRZ news, February 6, 2021, https://www.wbrz.com/news/contractor-behind-emergency-sunshine-bridge-repair-still-owes-state-police-nearly-900k/.
135 *Cenikor sent*: Letter to Judge Warren Willet, February 21, 2017.
136 *"Tell them to take"*: Carrie Tolbert, interview; Chris Koon, interview.
136 *A day later*: Email to Judge Warren Willet, February 19, 2017.

Notes

CHAPTER FOURTEEN

139 *At first, April*: April Lee, interviews with author, 2022–2023. Accounts of April's time on the street are also based on interviews with a former companion and a former treatment provider, and on author observations from multiple visits to Kensington.

140 *More than 77 percent*: Dana DiFilippo, "Funding Approved for Ex-Prostitutes' Halfway House," *Philadelphia Inquirer*, January 24, 2015, https://www.inquirer.com/philly/news/20150125_Funding_approved_for_ex-prostitutes__halfway_house.html.; Confirmed with court records of April's two prostitution arrests during this time.

140 *Only a few years*: Dana DiFilippo, "Wrongly Jailed as Kensington Strangler, Man Sues Philly and Pa. for Civil Rights Violations," WHYY news, March 9, 2017, https://whyy.org/articles/wrongly-suspected-as-kensington-strangler-man-sues-city-state-for-civil-rights-violations/.

141 *From time to time, she brought bread*: Derrick Lee, interview with author, February 20, 2022.

141 *Down the block*: "History of Prevention Point Philadelphia," Prevention Point Philadelphia, https://ppponline.org/about-us/history-prevention-point-philadelphia.

142 *By the time*: Nina Feldman, "Syringe Exchange Saved Billions in HIV-Related Costs in Philly, Study Finds," WHYY news, October 29, 2019, https://whyy.org/articles/syringe-exchange-saved-billions-in-hiv-related-costs-in-philadelphia-study-finds/.

142 *Although it was unlicensed*: Courtenay Harris Bond, "32 Years Ago, Philly Began Using Syringe Exchanges to Fight AIDS. With Funding Now in Doubt, Experts Fear an HIV Surge," *Philly Voice*, April 18, 2024, https://www.phillyvoice.com/syringe-exchange-hiv-aids-philadelphia-history-hepatitis/.

142 *Fentanyl, a synthetic*: United States Drug Enforcement Administration, "Fentanyl," Dea.gov, U.S. Department of Justice. October 2022, https://www.dea.gov/factsheets/fentanyl; "Fatal Overdoses: Unintentional Drug Overdose Deaths by Specific Drugs Involved, 2010–2021," Substance Use Philly, https://www.substanceusephilly.com/fatal-overdoses.

142 *April sold the works*: April Lee, interview. See also Emma Jacobs, "Needle Exchange Program Creates Black Market in Clean Syringes," NPR news, January 3, 2015, https://www.npr.org/2015/01/03/374560431/needle-exchange-program-creates-black-market-in-clean-syringes.

143 *The spires of*: Episcopal Hospital, Philadelphia Buildings, information sheet, 2024, https://www.philadelphiabuildings.org/pab/app/pj_display.cfm?RecordId=946707DF-5AB9-48B9-8C08038F52B9952A.

143 *Overcrowding became*: Mallory Locklear, "Emergency Department Crowding Hits Crisis Levels, Risking Patient Safety," *Yale News*, September 30,

Notes

2022, https://news.yale.edu/2022/09/30/emergency-department-crowd ing-hits-crisis-levels-risking-patient-safety.

143 *Ever since, amid*: Robert A. Barish, Patrick L. McGauly, and Thomas C. Arnold, "Emergency Room Crowding: A Marker of Hospital Health," *Transactions of the American Clinical and Climatological Association* 123 (2024): 304, https://pmc.ncbi.nlm.nih.gov/articles/PMC3540619/.

143 *A survey*: Barish, McGauly, and Arnold, "Emergency Room Crowding."

143 *This situation made the*: Dr. Joseph D'Orazio (associate professor of Clinical Emergency Medicine and director of the Division of Medical Toxicology & Addiction Medicine, Department of Emergency Medicine, Lewis Katz School of Medicine, Temple University), interview with author, August 2, 2022.

144 *"It's absolute"*: Dr. Joseph D'Orazio, interview with author, August 2, 2022.

144 *Nearly 4.5 percent*: Dr. Joseph D'Orazio, interview.

144 *In 2015, a study*: Gail D'Onofrio, Patrick G. O'Connor, Michael V. Pantalon, Marek C. Chawarski, Susan H. Busch, et al., "Emergency Department– Initiated Buprenorphine/Naloxone Treatment for Opioid Dependence," *JAMA* 313, no. 16 (2015): 1636, https://doi.org/10.1001/jama.2015.3474.

144 *Buprenorphine by this point*: Dr. Joseph D'Orazio, interview.

144 *But even at those that did*: Fabiola Arbelo Cruz, "Racial Inequities in Treatments of Addictive Disorders," Yale School of Medicine, news release, October 1, 2021, https://medicine.yale.edu/news-article/racial-inequities -in-treatments-of-addictive-disorders/.

145 *She knew there was a warrant*: Records show that April was found in contempt of court on February 3, 2015.

146 *Overdose deaths alone*: "Analysis of Drug-Related Overdose Deaths in Pennsylvania, 2015," Drug Enforcement Administration, report, July 2016, https://www.dea.gov/sites/default/files/2018-07/phi071216_attach.pdf.

146 *Some 200 recovery homes*: Alfred Lubrano, "'Pimping Out' Drug Addicts for Cash," *Philadelphia Inquirer*, June 1, 2017, https://www.inquirer.com /health/opioid-addiction/inq/pimping-out-drug-addicts-cash-20170601 .html-2.

146 *Many homes*: Gwen Shaffer, "Silent Treatment: Hundreds of Unregulated Drug-Recovery Houses Operate in Philadelphia Without Any Government Oversight," *Philadelphia City Paper*, November 15, 2001.

148 *The stakes were*: Lia N. Pizzicato, Rebecca Drake, Reed Domer-Shank, Caroline C. Johnson, and Kendra M. Viner, "Beyond the Walls: Risk Factors for Overdose Mortality Following Release from the Philadelphia Department of Prisons," *Drug and Alcohol Dependence* 189 (August 2018): 108–15, https:// doi.org/10.1016/j.drugalcdep.2018.04.034.

148 *April took a train*: Description is based on author's September 22, 2022, tour of Why Not Prosper, a grassroots nonprofit organization that supports women; April Lee, interviews; Michelle Simmons (founder of Why Not

Notes

Prosper), interview with author, September 19, 2022 and September 22, 2022.

CHAPTER FIFTEEN

- 151 *In June 2014*: State of Indiana v. Larry J. Ley, Case no. 29D01-1407-FB-006027, dep. of Gary Whisenand (May 31, 2016). Also based on private correspondence among Josh Minkler, Dennis Wichern, Matthew Brookman, and Barry Glickman.
- 151 *Federal charges made*: Tislow et al., 1:16-cv-1721-LJM-DKL, dep. of Aaron Dietz (October 12, 2017), 10.
- 151 *He said he*: Email from Aaron K. Dietz to Andre Miksha, July 7, 2014.
- 152 *Dietz decided*: Email from Kietz to Miksha.
- 152 *Josh Minkler felt*: Email from Josh Minkler to Dennis Wichern, June 25, 2014.
- 152 *"I trust you"*: Email from Minkler to Wichern.
- 152 *"After a careful"*: Email from Matthew Brookman to Dennis Wichern, July 3, 2014.
- 152 *And since the DEA*: Tislow et al., 1:16-cv-1721-LJM-DKL, dep. of Aaron Dietz, 36.
- 153 *As the DEA prepared*: Pete Smith, "Even Here: Heroin Use Growing in Carmel," *Current Publishing*, July 8, 2014, https://www.youarecurrent.com/2014/07/08/even-here/.
- 153 *The story centered*: Smith, "Even Here."
- 154 *The article soon*: Tislow et al., 1:16-cv-1721-LJM-DKL, dep. of Aaron Dietz, 31.
- 154 *"He's right!"*: Tislow et al., 1:16-cv-1721-LJM-DKL, dep. of Aaron Deitz.
- 154 *More than 70*: Operational plan, Drug Enforcement Administration, Chicago Field Division, July 25, 2014.
- 155 *In Noblesville, officers*: Report of investigation, U.S. Department of Justice, Drug Enforcement Administration, July 25, 2014.
- 155 *In Carmel, Ley's*: Andrew Dollard, interview with author, May 28, 2019.
- 155 *Office manager Cassy*: Cassy Bratcher, interview with author, May 22, 2019.
- 155 *"I don't understand"*: As per Drug Enforcement Administration recording of Luella Bangura's arrest.
- 155 *The sun was high*: Marie Doan, email announcing press conference, July 25, 2014.
- 155 *The officials, wearing*: "Doctors, Employees Arrested in DEA Raid," WRTV news (Indianapolis), July 25, 2014, https://www.youtube.com/watch?v=gvXxTzuu1OE.
- 157 *"This was a thorough"*: "Four Central Indiana Doctors Arrested in DEA Raid," WRTV news (Indianapolis). July 25, 2014, https://www.youtube.com/watch?v=ZdzTuw4V5x4.

Notes

158 *At home in Kokomo*: Ryan Radford, interview with author, November 17, 2020.
158 *"It's not the type of medication*: Sean Hays, interview with author, May 2, 2020.
159 *Across the country*: Rose A. Rudd, Puja Seth, Felicita David, and Lawrence Scholl, "Increases in Drug and Opioid-Involved Overdose Deaths: United States, 2010–2015," *Morbidity and Mortality Weekly Report* 65, no. 5051 (2015): 1445–52, https://doi.org/10.15585/mmwr.mm655051e1.
159 *In just six months*: George Myers, "More than 25 People Die from Drug Overdoses in Howard County this Year," *Indiana Economic Digest*, news report, 2015, https://indianaeconomicdigest.net/MobileContent/Most-Recent/Development-Economic/Article/More-than-25-people-die-from-drug-overdoses-in-Howard-County-this-year/31/121/81508.
159 *"If the 2015 trend"*: "Not Enough for Wagoner," editorial, *Kokomo Tribune*, July 5, 2015, https://www.kokomotribune.com/opinion/editorials/editorial-not-enough-for-wagoner/article_34ca07ea-217f-11e5-b006-1b02c99510c3.html.
159 *Around the same*: "Victim Identified in Crash East of Greentown," *Kokomo Tribune*, February 12, 2015, https://www.kokomotribune.com/news/local_news/updated-victim-identified-in-crash-east-of-greentown/article_178daf52-b2b6-11e4-a8be-cb3654ad47c0.html.
159 *His official cause*: Rachel Sherrill, interview with author, September 22, 2020.
159 *Dr. Ron Vierk posted*: Ron Vierk, interview with author, September 30, 2020.
159 *The court had set*: Larry Ley, interview with author, May 30, 2019.
159 *But not a single*: Kelly Reinke, "Boone County Jail Becomes First in State to Administer Suboxone for Addiction Treatment." *Fox 59*, news program, March 3, 2020. https://fox59.com/news/indycrime/boone-county-jail-becomes-first-in-state-to-administer-suboxone-for-addiction-treatment/.
160 *This was a potential*: P. R. Williamson and B. A. Whaley, "The Americans with Disabilities Act and Medication Assisted Treatment in Correctional Settings," *Forensic Science and Addiction Research* 6, no. 3 (2024): 491–93, https://doi: 10.31031/FSAR.2024.06.000641, PMID: 38770439, PMCID: PMC11103793.

CHAPTER SIXTEEN

161 *"Korey [sic] Avarell is scurrying"*: Wendy McEntyre, email message to Deputy Director Bruce Lim, August 11, 2014.
161 *"Your silence disturbs"*: Wendy McEntyre, email message to Daniel Gunther, July 29, 2014.
161 *These emails contained*: Bruce Lim, email message to Karen Baylor and Marlies Perez, August 11, 2014.
162 *She'd first heard about it*: Chris O'Keefe, interview with Wendy McEntyre, September 12, 2014.

Notes

162 *"There's more money"*: Doyle, CIVDS 1419415, video. dep. of Christopher Ted O'Keefe, vol.1, at 51–52.

162 *But several nurses and medical*: Chris O'Keefe, interview with Wendy McEntyre.

162 *"We don't destroy meds"*: Diana Veles, interview with Wendy McEntyre, August 28, 2014.

163 *The dismissal*: Diana Veles, interview with author, November 6, 2022.

163 *Numerous people complained*: Compilation of claims filed with the California Labor Commissioner or in San Bernardino Superior Court by numerous former Above It All employees.

164 *"I want you to know"*: Wendy McEntyre, text message to Brianna Moody, August 13, 2014.

164 *"Provider is violating"*: Marlies Perez, letter to Kyle Avarell, December 29, 2014, pp. 64–66.

164 *Instead, he claimed*: "Rehab Centers Under Attack," *Alpenhorn News*, June 4, 2015.

165 *"I don't want"*: Hi-Land Mountain Homes, Inc. v. Department of Health Care Services, CIVDS 1501769, Sup. Ct. Cal., San Bernardino Cty., reporter's transcript of oral proceedings (March 11, 2015), 24.

165 *"When I"*: Hi-Land Mountain Homes, CIVDS 1501769, reporter's transcript, 5.

165 *His son had applied for a new license*: License application for Mountain Village Treatment Center, 26163 Circle Dr., Twin Peaks, CA (March 19, 2015).

165 *About one month later*: "Above It All Treatment Center Featured in A&E's 'Intervention,'" PRWeb, press release, May 27, 2015, https://www.prweb.com/releases/2015/05/prweb12695111.htm.

165 *"So what"*: "Samantha," episode 22, season 14, *Intervention*, April 26, 2015, A&E, https://play.aetv.com/shows/intervention/season-14/episode-22.

165 *By July, Kyle*: "Big Changes Are in the Works for Above It All (AIA), the Drug and Alcohol Treatment Business that Operates Approximately 18 Facilities from Running Springs to Cedarpines Park," *Alpenhorn News*, July 2, 2015.

165 *"Several new patients"*: Wendy McEntyre, email to Task Force, July 31, 2015.

166 *James had attended two*: Julia Lurie, "America's Only Publicly Traded Addiction Treatment Chain Makes Millions Off Patients. What Could Go Wrong?" *Mother Jones*, April 22, 2019, https://www.motherjones.com/politics/2019/04/american-addiction-centers-publicly-traded-rehab/.

166 *He then went to*: Dugas, CIVDS 1618878, video. dep. of Patricia Dugas (April 17, 2019), vol. 1, 57.

166 *The first step*: Matthew Maniace report, Above It All Treatment Center, February 26, 2017, p. 31.

167 *Employees would fill*: Patricia Dugas v. Above It All Treatment Center, CIVDS 1618878, Sup. Ct. Cal., San Bernardino Cty., video. dep. of Robert Treuherz, M.D. (May 7, 2019), vol. 1, at 14.

167 *Although James had*: Dugas, CIVDS 1618878, dep. of David Harrell Griffin (April 29, 2019).

Notes

167 *The next day*: Dugas, CIVDS 1618878, records of James Robert Dugas, ordered by Trauma Law Center, APLC, Order Date: November 14, 2018, Injury Date: December 13, 2015, Record Location: Citrus Pharmacy, 511 Amigos Dr. Ste. B, Redlands, CA 92373.

167 *Despite the order*: Dugas, CIVDS 1618878, James Robert Dugas, Citrus Pharmacy Records.

168 *But for people who have*: Dugas, CIVDS 1618878, dep. trans. of Dr. Mario San Bartolome (July 18, 2019, unedited draft), 21.

168 *Soon after*: Expert witness report, Christopher Lewis, SUD Compliance & Consulting, LLC (July 2019), 10.

168 *Records showed*: Expert witness report, Christopher Lewis.

168 *Then an employee*: Dugas, CIVDS 1618878, dep. of David Harrell Griffin (April 29, 2019), 24; Citrus Pharmacy and prescription records for James Dugas, November 19, 2018.

168 *Under state requirements*: Certification for Alcohol and Other Drug Programs 1.0, Department of Health Care Services, October 2023, p. 37, https://www.dhcs.ca.gov/provgovpart/Documents/DHCS-AOD-Certification-Standards.pdf.

168 *The staff performed only 12*: Expert witness report, Christopher Lewis, 9.

168 *At about 3:40 a.m., after*: Expert witness report, Christopher Lewis.

168 *He was then airlifted*: Dugas, CIVDS 1618878, records of James Robert Dugas, Order Date: February 6, 2017, Injury Date: December 13, 2015, Record Location: San Bernardino Cty. Sher. Cor., 655 E. 3rd St., San Bernardino, CA 92415, at 13.

168 *"So, it was a day"*: Dugas, CIVDS 1618878, video. dep. of Patricia Dugas (April 17, 2019), vol. 1.

168 *For less than three days*: Ryan O'Connor, letter to James Dugas, February 20, 2016.

168 *But she had spoken*: Gladiz Melara v. Above It All Treatment Center, CIVDS 1602733, Sup. Ct. Cal., San Bernardino Cty., Complaint for Damages (February 24, 2016).

168 *A nurse had used*: Bryant Darling v. Hi-Land Mountain Homes, Inc., CIVDS 1509871, Sup. Ct. Cal., San Bernardino Cty., video. dep. of Harinder Grewal, M.D. (August 17, 2018), vol. 2, at 139, 156.

169 *And here was James*: Frank Sheridan, San Bernardino County Sheriff's Department Coroner Division Report, Coroner's Case 701404937, Autopsy A-0825-14, Name: Terri Lynn Darling (September 12, 2016).

169 *It was in all caps*: Wendy McEntyre, email to Marlies Perez at DHCS, December 14, 2015; Wendy McEntyre, email to Sheriff's Office Detective Michelle Brand, December 14, 2015.

169 *The DHCS then approved*: Complaint 15-244, Department of Health Care Services, California Health and Human Services Agency, n.d.

Notes

169 *After one insurer*: Addiction Treatment Advocacy Coalition, letter to Commissioner Dave Jones at California Department of Insurance, May 5, 2016.

170 *The DHCS ultimately*: Eli Richman, "California Files Order Against Health-Net for Stiffing Addiction Recovery Providers," *Fierce Healthcare*, August 2, 2018, https://www.fiercehealthcare.com/payer/california-files-notice-against-healthnet-for-resisting-addiction-recovery-facilities.

170 *Karen Gold, the attorney*: Karen Gold, interview.

170 *"If they want"*: Wendy McEntyre, interview with author, May 31, 2022.

170 *Wendy relished the chance*: Above It All Treatment Center v. Wendy McEntyre, CIVDS 1603633, Sup. Ct. Cal., San Bernardino Cty., reporter's transcript of Evidentiary Hearing Proceedings (May 9, 2016).

172 *Wendy was required*: Above It All, CIVDS 1603633, Case Summary, Court Access Portal, accessed November 23, 2024.

173 *The Avarells had also filed*: Hi-Land Mountain Homes, Inc. v. Wendy McEntyre, CIVDS 1703313, Sup. Ct. Cal., San Bernardino Cty., Complaint for Damages (February 24, 2017).

173 *But when he moved*: Lynn Maniace, interview with author, December 17, 2022.

173 *He told his mom*: Matthew Maniace, Facebook Messenger messages to Lynn Maniace, from October 28, 2016 through June 19, 2018.

173 *His urine test*: Matthew Maniace report, Above It All Treatment Center, p. 23.

174 *Even though the order*: Citrus Pharmacy and prescription records for Matthew Maniace, February 24–25, 2017.

174 *The U.S. Food*: Highlights of Prescribing Information, U.S. Food and Drug Administration, Information sheet, accessed January 12, 2025, https://www.accessdata.fda.gov/drugsatfda_docs/label/2022/020733s031s032lbl.pdf.

174 *Suboxone alone, if*: Todd A. Miano, Lei Wang, Charles E. Leonard, Colleen M. Brensinger, Emily K. Acton, et al., "Identifying Clinically Relevant Drug–Drug Interactions with Methadone and Buprenorphine: A Translational Approach to Signal Detection," *Clinical Pharmacology & Therapeutics* 112, no. 5 (2022): 1120–29, https://doi.org/10.1002/cpt.2717.

174 *Most patients who*: Lucinda A. Grande, Deborah L. Cundiff, Mark K. Greenwald, MaryAnne Murray, Tricia E. Wright, et al., "Evidence on Buprenorphine Dose Limits: A Review," *Journal of Addiction Medicine* 17, no. 5 (2023): 509–16, https://doi.org/10.1097/adm.0000000000001189.

174 *He told a sheriff's*: William Zerbe, Death Investigation of Matthew Maniace, Case 051700320, Sher. Dep. San Bernardino Cty. (February 26, 2017).

174 *the doctor wrote that the*: Mary Lynn Maniace v. Hi-Land Mountain Homes, Inc., CIVDS 1805405, Sup. Ct. Cal., San Bernardino Cty., report by Dr. Mario Bartolome, Addiction Medicine Expert Witness.

Notes

175 *When paramedics arrived*: Maniace, CIVDS 1805405, Expert witness report, Christopher Lewis, SUD Compliance & Consulting, LLC (January 2020), 5.
175 *The investigator also found*: Death investigative report, Department of Health Care Services, December 14, 2017.
175 *Kory Avarell would be allowed*: Death investigative report.
176 *Lynn called the investigator's supervisor*: Lynn Maniace, personal notes of phone calls and correspondence with DHCS.
176 *The next month*: Lynn Maniace, email to Marlies Perez, April 12, 2018.
176 *Soon after, a DHCS*: Lynn Maniace, personal notes.
176 *When the investigators*: Maniace, CIVDS 1805405, Plaintiff Mary Lynn Maniace's responses to request to produce documents at deposition (March 1, 2019), set 2, at 83.
176 *His son Kyle*: Agreement for admission to Lake Arrowhead Recovery Center. The program specified charges of $35,000 per week for incidental medical services and $28,000 per week for detox.

CHAPTER SEVENTEEN

179 *After almost two years*: Chris Koon, interview with author, March 24, 2019.
179 *Chris would serve*: Minutes report, 35th Dist., Grant. Case no. 2015-CR-729.
180 *It was a small*: Observations of author, from in-person visits with John and Chris Koon, March 23–25, 2019.
181 *As Chris tried*: Shoshana Walter and Amy Julia Harris, "They Worked in Sweltering Heat for Exxon, Shell and Walmart. They Didn't Get Paid a Dime." *Reveal*, April 24, 2019, https://revealnews.org/article/they-worked-in-sweltering-heat-for-exxon-shell-and-walmart-they-didnt-get-paid-a-dime/.
181 *Suddenly, companies began*: Shoshana Walter, "Drug Rehab Faces Investigations into Labor Practices and Medicaid Fraud," *Reveal*, May 16, 2019, https://revealnews.org/article/drug-rehab-faces-investigations-into-labor-practices-and-medicaid-fraud/.
182 *Several lawyers tracked*: Shoshana Walter, "Prominent Rehab Faces 3 Lawsuits for Sending Patients to Work Without Pay," *Reveal*, May 15, 2019, https://revealnews.org/blog/prominent-rehab-faces-three-lawsuits-for-sending-patients-to-work-without-pay/.
182 *They said that*: James Victorian, interview with author, April 10, 2020.
182 *No serious violations*: Walter, "Drug Rehab Faces Investigations."
182 *In 2018, he received*: Return of Organization Exempt from Income Tax (Form 990): Cenikor Foundation, Houston, Texas, U.S. Department of the Treasury, Internal Revenue Service, 2018.
182 *The state of Texas*: Consolidated Financial Statements and Uniform Guidance Reports, Cenikir Foundation Subsidiary, June 30, 2020 and 2019.

Notes

182 *Their investigations confirmed*: Investigation findings reports, Texas Health and Human Services, Division of Regulatory Services, Substance Abuse Compliance Group.

183 *Cenikor ultimately paid*: Executed Settlement Agreements, Cenikor Foundation, Texas Health and Human Services Commission; Thomas Vazquez (Texas Health and Human Services Commission), email to Gabriel Baumgaertner, February 28, 2025.

183 *"I'm struggling"*: Carrie Tolbert, interview with author, March 27, 2019.

184 *"You're gonna be"*: Carrie Tolbert, interview.

184 *The longer someone*: Marguerite Burns, Lu Tang, Chung-Chou H. Chang, Joo Yeon Kim, Katherine Ahrens, et al., "Duration of Medication Treatment for Opioid-Use Disorder and Risk of Overdose Among Medicaid Enrollees in 11 States: A Retrospective Cohort Study," *Addiction* (Abingdon, England) 117, no. 12 (2022): 3079–88, https://doi.org/10.1111/add.15959.

185 *He collected all*: John Koon, interview with author, March 24, 2019. Also based on author observations from in-person visits with John and Chris Koon.

185 *He started eating*: Chris Koon, interview with author.

CHAPTER EIGHTEEN

187 *Instead of family*: Unless otherwise stated, April's account of her experience with Why Not Prosper is based on author's in-person observations during a visit to the recovery home on September 22, 2022. April Lee accompanied author on the tour and described what was present during her stay; Michelle Simmons (founder of Why Not Prosper), interview with author, September 19, 2022 and September 22, 2022.

188 *"You don't deserve"*: Unpublished journal entry by April Lee.

188 *In one letter, she wrote*: Undated letter by April Lee to her son.

188 *"Prepare my mind"*: Yolanda Adams, "I'm Gonna Be Ready," from the album *Believe*.

189 *Studies have shown*: Erick G. Guerrero, Hortensia Amaro, Tenie Khachikian, Mona Zahir, and Jeanne C Marsh, "A Bifurcated Opioid Treatment System and Widening Insidious Disparities," *Addictive Behaviors* 130 (March 2022): 107296-96, https://doi.org/10.1016/j.addbeh.2022.107296; Julie Harris and Karen McElrath, "Methadone as Social Control," *Qualitative Health Research* 22, no. 6 (2012): 810–24, https://doi.org/10.1177/1049732311432718.

189 *"Don't really know"*: Journal entry by April Lee, January 29, 2016.

189 *"I wanted to snap"*: Journal entry by April Lee, January 30, 2016.

191 *the city had*: Erin Kelly, Megan Reed, Lara Weinstein, Robert Sterling, Tracy Camacho et al., "Map OUD—Mapping the Opioid Use Disorder Crisis in Philadelphia," accessed January 26, 2024, https://www.jefferson.edu

Notes

/content/dam/academic/skmc/departments/family-medicine/MAPOUD.pdf.

192 *"Try again tomorrow"*: Tracy Esteves Camacho, interview with author, January 22, 2025.

193 *For a long time*: Tim Henderson, "Overdose Deaths Are Rising Among Black and Indigenous Americans," *Stateline*, October 29, 2024, https://stateline.org/2024/10/29/overdose-deaths-are-rising-among-black-and-indigenous-americans/.

193 *In 2022, overdose deaths*: Nicole Leonard, "Overdoses Are Rising Among Black Philadelphians as Deaths Reach a Record Number," WHYY news, October 4, 2023, https://whyy.org/articles/philadelphia-overdose-deaths-record-racial-disparities-widen/.

193 *In 2023, for the first*: Nicole Leonard, "Philadelphia Sees a Decline in Drug Overdose Deaths Among Residents for the First Time in 5 Years, Data Show," WHYY news, October 2, 2024, https://whyy.org/articles/philadelphia-overdose-deaths-decline/.

194 *In Philadelphia, this*: Courtenay Harris Bond, "A Law-And-Order Approach to Philly's Overdose Crisis Will Have Grave Effects, Harm Reduction Advocates Say," *Philly Voice*, March 6, 2024, https://www.phillyvoice.com/addiction-overdose-philadelphia-kensington-drugs-harm-reduction-city-hall/; Lauren Rowello, "Syringe Service Provider Responds to Mayor Parker's Defunding," *Philadelphia Gay News*, July 22, 2024, https://epgn.com/2024/07/22/syringe-service-provider-responds-to-mayor-parkers-defunding/.

194 *Incentives and motivation*: Ethan Sahker, Maisha N. Toussaint, Marizen Ramirez, Saba R. Ali, and Stephan Arndt, "Evaluating Racial Disparity in Referral Source and Successful Completion of Substance Abuse Treatment," *Addictive Behaviors* 48 (September 2015): 25–29, https://doi.org/10.1016/j.addbeh.2015.04.006.

194 *But this expansion*: Emily Baumgaertner, "Medication Treatment for Addiction Is Shorter for Black and Hispanic Patients, Study Finds," *New York Times*, November 9, 2022, https://www.nytimes.com/2022/11/09/health/opioid-addiction-treatment-racial-disparities.html.

194 *who continue to have greater access*: Huiru Dong, Erin J. Stringfellow, W. Alton Russell, and Mohammad S. Jalali, "Racial and Ethnic Disparities in Buprenorphine Treatment Duration in the US," *JAMA Psychiatry* 80, no. 1 (2023): 93–95, https://doi.org/10.1001/jamapsychiatry.2022.3673.

194 *The longer someone*: Marguerite Burns, Lu Tang, H. Chang Chung-Chou, Joo Yeon Kim, Katherine Ahrens, et al., "Duration of Medication Treatment for Opioid-Use Disorder and Risk of Overdose among Medicaid Enrollees in 11 States: A Retrospective Cohort Study," *Addiction* (Abingdon, England) 117, no. 12 (2022): 3079–88, https://doi.org/10.1111/add.15959.

194 *But rates of*: Dong et al., "Racial and Ethnic Disparities."

Notes

194 *After Purdue Pharma*: Harrington, United States Trustee, Region 2 v. Purdue Pharma LP, et al., No. 23–124, U.S. Sup. Ct. (2024), https://www.supremecourt.gov/opinions/23pdf/23-124_8nko.pdf; Patrick Radden Keefe, "An Insider from the Purdue Pharma Bankruptcy Speaks Out," *The New Yorker*, September 20, 2021, https://www.newyorker.com/news/news-desk/an-insider-from-the-purdue-pharma-bankruptcy-speaks-out.

194 *"there was resistance to trying it"*: Ryan Hampton, interview with author, July 30, 2021.

195 *Having a criminal record*: Jamiles Lartey, "How Criminal Records Hold Back Millions of People," *Marshall Project*, April 1, 2023, https://www.themarshallproject.org/2023/04/01/criminal-record-job-housing-barriers-discrimination.

195 *Parents who are reported*: "How to Remedy Harm Caused by State Child Abuse Registries," Annie E. Casey Foundation, blog, November 10, 2023, https://www.aecf.org/blog/how-to-remedy-harm-caused-by-state-child-abuse-registries.

195 *Falling behind on*: Mark Puente and Tara Morgan, "No License to Drive: How Many Ohio Drivers Are Suspended, Mostly for Unpaid Fines," *Marshall Project*, August 10, 2023, https://www.themarshallproject.org/2023/08/10/ohio-drivers-suspended-for-unpaid-fines.

195 *positive drug screens*: "Trump Administration Considering Plan to Drug Test Some Food Stamp Recipients," *PBS News*, April 11, 2018.

195 *"How do we"*: Dr. John Kelly, interview with author, interview with author, October 21, 2021.

195 *In addiction-research circles*: "Does Recovery Capital Influence Treatment Benefit?," Recovery Research Institute, report, January 31, 2020, https://www.recoveryanswers.org/research-post/recovery-capital-treatment-benefit/.

CHAPTER NINETEEN

197 *The old man*: Dialogue and descriptions were personally witnessed and recorded by author, November 5, 2019.

198 *The trial had lasted*: State of Indiana v. Larry J. Ley, Case no. 29D01-1407-FB-006027, transcript of bench trial (August 8–16, 2016).

198 *Prosecutors emphasized DORN's*: Medication Assisted Treatment for Opioid Use Disorders, Final Rule, U.S. Department of Health and Human Services, July 8, 2016, https://s3.amazonaws.com/public-inspection.federalregister.gov/2016-16120.pdf.

198 *"People were asking"*: Indiana, Case no. 29D01-1407-FB-006027, transcript of bench trial, at 22.

198 *Prosecutors promptly dropped*: Mike Emery, "All Wayne County Charges Dropped in Drug & Opiate Recovery Network Drug Case," *Richmond*

Notes

Palladium, December 27, 2016, https://www.pal-item.com/story/news/crime/2016/12/27/all-local-charges-dropped-dorn-drug-case/95870382/.

198 *He lost his*: "Larry J. Ley," State of Indiana, license verification search, https://mylicense.in.gov/everification/Details.aspx?result=663ac584-0647-40f8-bebd-1fe186ef5e02.

198 *Dr. Luella Bangura*: Jeff McQuary, interview with author, October 27, 2020.

198 *He was 46*: Operational plan, Chicago Field Division, Drug Enforcement Administration, July 25, 2014.

198 *Andrew Dollard had started*: Andew Dollard, interview with author, May 17, 2019.

200 *Following his arrest*: Larry Ley, interview with author, June 10, 2019.

200 *He had not followed*: Indiana, Case no. 29D01-1407-FB-006027, transcript of bench trial (August 12, 2016).

200 *In fact, Larry emphasized*: E. Pullen and C. Oser, "Barriers to Substance Abuse Treatment in Rural and Urban Communities: Counselor Perspectives," *Substance Use & Misuse* 49, no. 7 (2014): 891–901, https://doi:10.3109/10826084.2014.891615, PMID: 24611820, PMCID: PMC3995852.

201 *still hard to come by*: "The Crisis in Indiana: Understanding the Crisis," Indiana University, Addictions, information sheet, https://addictions.iu.edu/understanding-crisis/crisis-in-indiana.html.

201 *Amid his legal*: S. Koser, S. Weiner, J. Suzuki, and C. Price, "23 Implementation of a Substance Use Disorder Bridge Clinic," *Annals of Emergency Medicine* 74, no. 4 (2019): S11, https://doi.org/10.1016/j.annemergmed.2019.08.026.

203 *After years of activism*: "Justice Department Announces Global Resolution of Criminal and Civil Investigations with Opioid Manufacturer Purdue Pharma and Civil Settlement with Members of the Sackler Family," U.S. Department of Justice, press release, October 21, 2020, https://www.justice.gov/opa/pr/justice-department-announces-global-resolution-criminal-and-civil-investigations-opioid.

203 *And now the DOJ*: "Indivior Solutions Pleads Guilty to Felony Charge and Indivior Entities Agree to Pay $600 Million to Resolve Criminal and Civil Investigations as Part of DOJ's Largest Opioid Resolution," U.S. Department of Justice, press release, July 24, 2020, https://www.justice.gov/opa/pr/indivior-solutions-pleads-guilty-felony-charge-and-indivior-entities-agree-pay-600-million.

203 *The problem began*: Abhimanyu Sud, Meghan McGee, Barbara Mintzes, and Matthew Herder, "Permissive Regulation: A Critical Review of the Regulatory History of Buprenorphine Formulations in Canada," *International Journal of Drug Policy* 105 (July 2022): 103749, https://doi.org/10.1016/j.drugpo.2022.103749.

203 *Sales reps began*: United States v. Shaun Thaxter, Case 1:20-cr-00024-JPJ-

Notes

PMS, U.S. Dist. Ct. West. Dist. VA, Abingdon, sentencing memorandum (March 8, 2021).

203 *When healthcare agencies*: United States v. Indivior Inc., Case 1:19CR00016, U.S. Dist. Ct. West. Dist. VA, Abingdon, indictment (April 9, 2019).

204 *After receiving FDA approval*: United States, Case 1:19CR00016.

204 *While none of*: "Suboxone Manufacturer Indivior's Former Chief Executive Officer Sentenced to Jail Time in Connection with Drug Safety Claims," U.S. Department of Justice, press release, October 22, 2020, https://www.justice.gov/usao-wdva/pr/suboxone-manufacturer-indiviors-former-chief-executive-officer-sentenced-jail-time; Brian Mann, "For the First Time, Victims of the Opioid Crisis Formally Confront the Sackler Family," *NPR News*, March 10, 2022, https://www.npr.org/2022/03/10/1085174528/sackler-opioid-victims.

204 *Several lawsuits followed*: "Attorney General Todd Rokita Secures $4.3 Million for Indiana in Settlement with Suboxone Distributor," State of Indiana, Localist Community Event Platform, 2021.

204 *then, in 2023, acquiring*: Sean Jones, "Richmond-based Pharma Company Indivior Buys Narcan Developer," *Richmond Times-Dispatch*, November 16, 2022, https://richmond.com/business/richmond-area-based-pharma-company-indivior-buys-narcan-developer-opiant-aims-to-launch-new-overdose/article_e959f12e-baf9-527a-9457-6f711ae203bf.html.

204 *In 2022, researchers*: Michael Irvine, Declan Oller, Jesse Boggis, Brian Bishop, Daniel Coombs, et al., "Estimating Naloxone Need in the USA Across Fentanyl, Heroin, and Prescription Opioid Epidemics: A Modelling Study," *The Lancet* 7, no. 3 (March 2022): e210–e218, https://www.thelancet.com/journals/lanpub/article/PIIS2468-2667(21)00304-2/fulltext.

204 *Finally, in 2023*: Sean Whooley, "Emergent BioSolutions Launches Over-the-Counter Narcan Spray," *Drug Delivery Business*, August 30, 2023, https://www.drugdeliverybusiness.com/emergent-biosolutions-launches-otc-narcan/.

204 *But at about*: Allie Volpe, "Narcan—the Opioid Overdose Medication—Will Finally Be Available over the Counter," *Vox*, September 1, 2023, https://www.vox.com/23855543/narcan-naloxone-over-the-counter-walgreens-cost-use-overdose-opioid.

205 *"I found the"*: Larry Ley, interview with author, February 2, 2021.

206 *Carmel began deploying*: Shari Rudavsky, "Hamilton County Residents Who Overdose from Opioids Will Get More Help than Just Narcan," *Indianapolis Star*, March 11, 2019, https://www.indystar.com/story/news/2019/03/11/opioid-crisis-prompts-launch-new-hamilton-county-quick-response-team/3106899002/.

206 *In 2017, Kokomo*: "Kokomo to Join the Fight against Opioid Distributors," City of Kokomo, press release, 2017, https://www.cityofkokomo.org/news detail_T2_R263.php.

Notes

206 *Back in 2014, the year*: Ben Popper, "How a Startup Hopes to Treat the Rural Opioid Epidemic, at a Profit," *The Verge*, September 20, 2017, https://www.theverge.com/2017/9/20/16335562/groups-recovery-addiction-treatment-heroin-opioid-epidemic-suboxone-medication-access.

206 *"My interest, as an entrepreneur"*: Josh Lipton, "Here's How New Technologies Are Tackling the Opioid Crisis," CNBC news, December 15, 2017, https://www.cnbc.com/2017/12/15/groups-takes-tech-start-up-approach-to-attacking-opioid-crisis.html.

206 *The company would*: "Groups Recover Together—Products, Competitors, Financials, Employees, Headquarters Locations," *CB Insights*, 2023, https://www.cbinsights.com/company/recover-together.

207 *"Hell, yes"*: Larry Ley, interview with author, April 16, 2019.

207 *did away with patient limits*: Kao-Ping Chua, Mark C. Bicket, Amy S. B. Bohnert, Rena M. Conti, Pooja Lagisetty, et al., "Buprenorphine Dispensing After Elimination of the Waiver Requirement," *New England Journal of Medicine* 390, no. 16 (2024): 1530–32, https://doi.org/10.1056/nejmc2312906.

207 *doctors still remained hesitant*: Lev Facher, "Providers Still Hesitate to Prescribe Buprenorphine for Addiction, Despite 'X-Waiver' Removal," *STAT*, July 21, 2023, https://www.statnews.com/2023/07/21/opioid-addiction-buprenorphine-suboxone-x-waiver/.

207 *In the year immediately after*: Pauline Anderson, "Despite X-Waiver Elimination, Buprenorphine Prescriptions Decline," *Medscape*, December 20, 2023, https://www.medscape.com/viewarticle/despite-x-waiver-elimination-buprenorphine-prescriptions-2023a1000w61?form=fpf.

207 *In 2024, the Biden*: Brian Mann, "With Opioid Deaths Soaring, Biden Administration Will Widen Access to Methadone," NPR news, February 2, 2024, https://www.npr.org/sections/health-shots/2024/02/02/1228349518/opioid-overdose-addiction-methadone.

207 *"They don't want"*: Lev Facher, "The Methadone Clinic Monopoly: Opioid Treatment Chains Backed by Private Equity Are Fighting Calls for Reform," *STAT*, March 19, 2024, https://www.statnews.com/2024/03/19/methadone-clinics-opioid-addiction-private-equity/.

208 *"Recently, extensive experience"*: Larry Ley, letter to WISH-TV, November 13, 2019.

208 *In late 2022*: Larry Ley obituary, December 21, 2022, Carmel, Indiana, Bussell Family Funerals, https://www.bussellfamilyfunerals.com/obituary/Larry-Ley.

CHAPTER TWENTY

209 *It was about 2:30 p.m.*: Wendy McEntyre, Ring camera video, March 21, 2022.

209 *"The police"*: Cheryll Stone, interview with author, March 23, 2022.

Notes

209 *"Get back up here"*: Wendy McEntyre, Ring camera footage, 14:29:31 through 14:36:25 PDT, March 21, 2022.
210 *For a month, Wendy*: Wendy McEntyre, text messages to Diana Veles, February 24 to March 30, 2022.
210 *Diana, who was finishing*: Diana Veles, text message to Pasami Savea, January 12, 2022.
210 *A facility that served troubled*: Return of Organization Exempt from Income Tax (2016 Form 990), Alpha Connection Youth & Family Services, U.S. Department of Treasury, Internal Revenue Service.
210 *She sent pictures*: Miscellaneous photos from Diana Veles, depicting various alleged issues at Alpha Connection.
210 *Wendy navigated to*: Alpha Connection, Inc. v. Wendy McEntyre, Case: CIV SB 2206135-01, Sup. Ct. San Bernardino Cty., respondent: Wendy McEntyre, attachment 10 (2022), exhibit 11, at 40–63.
210 *Then she put on*: Wendy McEntyre, interview with author, March 5, 2022.
210 *Her takeaway was*: Various complaint investigation reports from the California Department of Social Services, from June 25, 2020.
211 *"These kids are not"*: Diana Veles, text messages to Wendy McEntyre, March 9, 2022.
211 *The program claimed*: Alpha Connection, CIV SB 2206135-01, exhibit 23, at 167–70.
211 *"WE SERIOUSLY NEED"*: Diana Veles, text messages to Wendy McEntyre, March 12, 2022.
211 *The teen "IS IN DANGER"*: Wendy McEntyre, email to Christina Barnes, March 14, 2022.
211 *Finally, on March 15*: Diana Veles, "timeline," 4.
211 *"The state is involved*: Wendy McEntyre, transcript of call with social worker, March 15, 2022.
211 *an employee threatened*: Diana Veles, audio recording of Alpha Connection employee threatening teenager, March 20, 2022.
212 *Diana took*: Don Richard, recording of 911 call regarding teen's disappearance, accessed February 9, 2023.
212 *"She needs to be placed"*: Wendy McEntyre, email to DSS authorities, March 20, 2022.
212 *"All I know"*: Wendy McEntyre, email to author, March 20, 2022.
213 *The deputy all but*: Wendy McEntyre, interview with sheriff's deputy, March 21, 2022.
213 *The deputy told*: Unnamed teen, interview.
213 *"Well, you know"*: Cheryll Stone, interview.
213 *"I am not OK"*: Wendy McEntyre emails to author.
213 *The toilet in her cell*: Wendy McEntyre, interview with author, March 30, 2022.
214 *"She's a wreck"*: Cheryll Stone, interview with author, March 23, 2022.

Notes

214 *Other laws did*: Teri Sforza, "Detox Can End in Death at Some 'Non-Medical' Southern California Rehabs," *Orange County Register*, December 17, 2017, https://www.ocregister.com/2017/12/17/detox-can-end-in-death-at-some-non-medical-southern-california-rehabs/; Assembly Bill No. 848, "Alcoholism and Drug Abuse Treatment Facilities," California Legislative Counsel's Digest, October 10, 2015, https://leginfo.legislature.ca.gov/faces/billTextClient.xhtml?bill_id=201520160AB848.

214 *In 2019, the day*: "Bill to Strengthen Patient Protections in Alcoholism and Drug Abuse Treatment Advances. Department of Health Care Services to Play a Critical Role in New State Effort," Assembly Democratic Caucus, Assemblywoman Cottie Petrie-Norris, news release, July 3, 2019, https://a73.asmdc.org/press-releases/20190703-release-bill-strengthen-patient-protections-alcoholism-and-drug-abuse.

214 *Wendy learned about*: Gary Baum, "Meet the Controversial Doctor Behind the Dr. Phil Empire," *Hollywood Reporter*, February 27, 2022, https://www.hollywoodreporter.com/tv/tv-news/controversial-therapist-shaping-dr-phil-1281050/.

214 *Wendy launched an investigation*: Wendy McEntyre, "Creative Care Investigation Redacted Reports," Jarrod's Law, 2019; Bill Haggerty and Charles L. Babcock, phone conversation with Wendy McEntyre; Creative Care, Inc. and Dr, Morteza Khaleghi v. Wendy McEntyre, 2nd Civil Appeal B308643, Ct. of App. Cal., 2nd App. Dist. Div. 3, respondent's brief (February 24, 2022).

215 *Creative Care filed a libel lawsuit*: *Creative Care and Khaleghi*, B308643.

215 *In 2022, the latest*: "Jarrod's Law—Addiction Treatment Patient Protection," Assembly Democratic Caucus, video release, April 20, 2022, https://a73.asmdc.org/video/20220420-jarrods-law-addiction-treatment-patient-protection.

215 *She even had*: Wendy McEntyre, photo, November 15, 2015.

215 *The evidence in the*: Patricia Dugas v. Hi-Land Mountain Homes, Inc., CIVDS 1618878, Sup. Ct. Cal., San Bernardino Cty., def.'s proposed stip. re admitted negligence (September 25, 2019).

215 *"The defendant admits"*: *Dugas*, CIVDS 1618878, def.'s proposed state of case (September 25, 2019).

215 *In Matthew Maniace's*: Mary Lynn Maniace v. Hi-Land Mountain Homes, Inc., CIVDS 1805405, Sup. Ct. Cal., San Bernardino Cty., special verdict form (December 13, 2019).

215 *And when Lynn Maniace and Wendy*: Charles Miller, email to Wendy McEntyre, June 3, 2021.

215 *had voluntarily closed their doors*: *Dugas*, CIVDS 1618878, video. dep. of Kory Avarell (May 16, 2019), 21.

216 *She had to repay*: Diana Veles, interview with author, November 6, 2022.

216 *Wendy was trying*: *Alpha Connection*, CIV SB 2206135-01, WV-110 temporary restraining order, respondent: Wendy Beth McEntyre (April 6, 2022).

Notes

216 *Wendy was thinking about*: Wendy McEntyre, interview with author, April 9, 2022.
216 *"I'm tired"*: Wendy McEntyre, interview.
217 *Shannon attempted suicide*: Cyndi Doyle v. Above It All Treatment Center, CIVDS 1419415, Sup. Ct. Cal., San Bernardino Cty., dep. of Shannon Doyle (November 13, 2015), vol. 1, at 27.
217 *Cyndi fell into*: Cyndi Doyle, interview with author, December 11, 2022.
217 *If that happened*: Lynn Maniace, interview with author, December 17, 2022.
217 *"And if they"*: Lynn Maniace, interview.
217 *In 2023, the nursing*: Elaine Yamaguchi, "In the Matter of the Accusation Against: Jamie Michelle Eagle," Vocational Nurse License VN 205518, Case 4302022000586, Board of Vocational Nursing and Psychiatric Technicians, Department of Consumer Affairs, State of California (July 25, 2023).
217 *But by 2025*: Licensing Details for 205518, Board of Vocational Nursing and Psychiatric Technicians, accessed December 8, 2024.
218 *The DSS had substantiated*: Nicole Strickland, "Complaint Determination Notification: Substantiated," Complaint 19-CR-20220321113906, Community Care Licensing Division (December 21, 2022).
218 *the juvenile facility was losing*: Daniel Mena, "Facility Evaluation Report," Community Care Licensing Division (October 12, 2022).
219 *If Wendy avoided*: People of the State of California v. Wendy Beth McEntyre, MVI 22002442, Sup. Ct. Cal., San Bernardino Cty., Minute Order (May 18, 2024); People of the State of California v. Diana Verenise Veles, MVI 22002443, Sup. Ct. Cal., San Bernardino Cty., Portal Minute Order (May 18, 2024).
219 *"I got goosebumps"*: Wendy McEntyre, interview with author, November 8, 2022.

EPILOGUE

221 *At the beginning*: "CDC Reports Nearly 24% Decline in U.S. Drug Overdose Deaths," U.S. Centers for Disease Control and Prevention, press release, February 25, 2025, https://www.cdc.gov/media/releases/2025/2025-cdc-reports-decline-in-us-drug-overdose-deaths.html.
221 *Are we simply*: Keith Humphreys, interview with author, October 17, 2024.
221 *Harm-reduction efforts*: "Use of Opioid Overdose Antidote by Laypersons Rose 43% from 2020 to 2022, Study Finds," CNN news. October 14, 2024, https://www.cnn.com/2024/10/14/health/naloxone-bystander-usage/index.html.
222 *"People know"*: Keith Humphreys, interview with author, October 17, 2024.
222 *"And a lot"*: Keith Humphreys, interview.
222 *More than two-thirds*: Alex Montero and Isabelle Valdes, "KFF Tracking Poll July 2023: Substance Use Crisis and Accessing Treatment," *KFF*.

August 15, 2023, https://www.kff.org/other/poll-finding/kff-tracking-poll-july-2023-substance-use-crisis-and-accessing-treatment/.

222 *Treatment helps people*: Christy K. Scott, Michael L. Dennis, and Mark A. Foss, "Utilizing Recovery Management Checkups to Shorten the Cycle of Relapse, Treatment Reentry, and Recovery," *Drug and Alcohol Dependence* 78, no. 3 (2005): 325–38, https://doi.org/10.1016/j.drugalcdep.2004.12.005.

223 *Women in need*: "Overdose Deaths Increased in Pregnant and Postpartum Women from Early 2018 to Late 2021," National Institutes of Health (NIH), press release, November 22, 2023, https://www.nih.gov/news-events news-releases/overdose-deaths-increased-pregnant-postpartum-women-early-2018-late-2021.

223 *As addiction-medicine doctor*: Dr. Barry Zevin, interview with author, March 23, 2021.

223 *As long as*: Robert Granfield and William Cloud, *Coming Clean: Overcoming Addiction Without Treatment* (New York University Press, 1999), 53.

223 *Neuroscientist Dr. Carl Hart*: Dr. Carl Hart, interview with author, September 1, 2020.

224 *"When they were given"*: Quoted in John Tierney, "The Rational Choices of Crack Addicts," *New York Times*, September 16, 2013, https://www.nytimes.com/2013/09/17/science/the-rational-choices-of-crack-addicts.html.

224 *And 60 percent*: Christopher M. Jones, Rita K. Noonan, and Wilson M. Compton, "Prevalence and Correlates of Ever Having a Substance Use Problem and Substance Use Recovery Status among Adults in the United States, 2018," *Drug and Alcohol Dependence* 214 (September 2020): 108169, https://doi.org/10.1016/j.drugalcdep.2020.108169; Florian De Meyer, Amine Zerrouk, Clara De Ruysscher, and Wouter Vanderplasschen, "Exploring Indicators of Natural Recovery from Alcohol and Drug Use Problems: Findings from the Life in Recovery Survey in Flanders," *Substance Abuse Treatment, Prevention, and Policy* 19, no. 1 (2024), https://doi.org/10.1186/s13011-024-00604-y.

224 *Most people recover*: "How Many Tries Does It Take to Resolve a Substance Use Problem? Lessons from a National Study of Recovering Adults in the U.S.," Recovery Research Institute, https://www.recoveryanswers.org/research-post/recovery-attempts-review/.

224 *And these people*: Leonard A. Jason, Mayra Guerrero, Ted Bobak, John M. Light, and Mike Stoolmiller, "Reducing Health Disparities Among Black Individuals in the Post-Treatment Environment," *Journal of Ethnicity in Substance Abuse* December 30, 2020: 1–17, https://doi.org/10.1080/15332640.2020.1861497, PMID: 33380259, PMCID: PMC8649697.

225 *The fact that Black*: Aubrey Whelan, "Overdose Deaths Dropped in Philly for the First Time in Five Years. But Deaths Are Soaring among Black Men," *Philadelphia Inquirer*, October 2, 2024, https://www.inquirer.com

/health/overdose-deaths-philadelphia-2023-mortality-statistics-2024
1002.html.

225 *In 2023, 36.8 million*: Emily Shrider, "Poverty in the United States: 2023," U.S. Census Bureau, September 10, 2024, https://www.census.gov/library publications/2024/demo/p60-283.html.

225 *More than half of Americans*: Maria Clara Cobo, "Millions of Americans Struggle to Pay Bills, Save Money," Bloomberg.com, November 19, 2024, https://www.bloomberg.com/news/articles/2024-11-19/more-than-half-of-americans-struggle-to-pay-bills-and-save-money; Kassandra Martinchek and Dulce Gonzalez, "Many Families Are Taking on Debt to Pay for Groceries," Urban Institute, May 15, 2024, https://www.urban.org/urban-wire/many-families-are-taking-debt-pay-groceries.

226 *Researchers continue to*: Brendan Borrell, "The Next Big Addiction Treatment," *New York Times*, March 31, 2022, https://www.nytimes.com/2022/03/31/well/mind/psilocybin-mushrooms-addiction-therapy.html; Lev Facher, "Biden Administration Allows Larger Incentives for People Who Reduce Meth Use," *STAT*, January 8, 2025, https://www.statnews.com/2025/01/08/methamphetamine-use-white-house-incentives-contingency-management/.

226 *And while treatment*: Aneri Pattani, "$50 Billion in Opioid Settlement Cash Is on the Way. We're Tracking How It's Spent," *KFF Health News*, March 30, 2023, https://kffhealthnews.org/news/article/opioid-drugmakers-settlement-funds-50-billion-dollars-khn-investigation-payback/.

226 *Some of those funds*: Aneri Pattani, "Using Opioid Settlement Cash for Police Gear like Squad Cars and Scanners Sparks Debate," *KFF Health News*, October 23, 2023, https://kffhealthnews.org/news/article/using-opioid-settlement-cash-for-police-gear-like-squad-cars-and-scanners-sparks-debate/.

226 *President Donald Trump*: Dustin Jones, "Trump Wants the Death Penalty for Drug Dealers. Here's Why That Probably Won't Happen," NPR news, May 10, 2023, https://www.npr.org/2023/05/10/1152847242/trump-campaign-execute-drug-dealers-smugglers-traffickers-death-row.

226 *There's a possibility*: Stephan Lindner, Kyle D Hart, Brynna Manibusan, Dennis McCarty, and K. John McConnell, "State- and County-Level Geographic Variation in Opioid Use Disorder, Medication Treatment, and Opioid-Related Overdose Among Medicaid Enrollees," *JAMA Health Forum* 4, no. 6 (2023): e231574–74, https://doi.org/10.1001/jamahealthforum.2023.1574.

226 *Emboldened by a U.S. Supreme*: Berkeley Lovelace, "Millions at Risk of Losing Health Insurance After Trump's Victory," NBC news, November 7, 2024, https://www.nbcnews.com/health/health-news/millions-risk-losing-health-insurance-trumps-victory-rcna179146; Marisa Kendall, "One Issue Trump and Newsom Agree On? Homeless Encampments," *Cal Matters*,

November 8, 2024, https://calmatters.org/housing/homelessness/2024/11/trump-agenda-homelessness/.

226 *Whereas once politicians*: Trevor Hunnicutt, "Harris Promises Tougher Immigration, Fentanyl Controls at Border," *Reuters*, September 27, 2024, https://www.reuters.com/world/us/harris-visits-us-southern-border-trump-focuses-immigration-2024-09-27/; Trevor Hunnicutt, "Biden Calls for Bigger Penalties, More Controls to Fight US Fentanyl Crisis," *Reuters*, July 31, 2024, https://www.reuters.com/world/us/biden-calls-bigger-penalties-more-controls-fight-us-fentanyl-crisis-2024-07-31/.

INDEX

AA, *see* Alcoholics Anonymous
Above It All (AIA)
   Department of Health Care services investigation, 164
   dispensing of medications/controlled substances, 162–163
   Donavan Doyle's disappearance from, ix–xii, 79–81
   Donavan Doyle's treatment at, 74–81, 114–117
   James Dugas's death, 166–168
   fraud investigation spearheaded by Wendy McEntyre, 113–120
   Matthew Maniace's death, 173–175, 217
   Lynn Maniace's fight against, 217
   Wendy McEntyre's investigation of, 161–165, 169–170, 210, 215
   policies for suicide threat/attempt, 115–116
   reaction to denial of insurance claims, 170
   restraining order filed against Wendy McEntyre, 170–172
ACA, *see* Affordable Care Act
Adams, Yolanda, 188

Adderall, 4
Addiction Treatment Advocacy Coalition, 119, 169
Affordable Care Act (ACA), 73
   and expansion of for-profit rehab industry, x, xiv–xvi, 74, 117–118
   possibility of cuts under Trump administration, 226
   and shift to treatment approach to addiction, 43
African Americans, *see* race, ethnicity, and discrimination
Agapios, George, 63, 155, 159, 205
AIA, *see* Above It All
AIDS, 19, 54–55
Alcoholics Anonymous (AA)
   Chuck Dederich and, 88
   Larry Ley and, 24
   and "rock bottom" concept, 78
   see also 12-step programs
Alexander, Larry, 27
American Addiction Centers, 166
Americans with Disabilities Act, 160
Angola (Louisiana State Penitentiary), 49
Anslinger, Harry, 88

Index

Austin, Dottie, 90
Austin, James Lucas, 89–91
Avarell, Kory, 75, 161
   Department of Health Care Services investigation, 164
   Cyndi Doyle's phone calls with, 76–79, 115
   Donavan Doyle's suicide threats, 115–117
   Cyndi Doyle's suspicions of concealing information, 117
   libel lawsuit against Wendy McEntyre, 173
   and Matthew Maniace's death, 175, 176
   and prescriber ID misuse, 168
   reaction to denial of insurance claims, 170
   and wrongful-death lawsuits, 169
Avarell, Kyle, 164
   libel lawsuit against Wendy McEntyre, 173
   and Matthew Maniace's death, 176
   and prescriber ID misuse, 168–169
   restraining order against Wendy McEntyre, 170, 171

Bailey, Bill, 93, 129, 130, 182
Ball, Lucille, 89
Bangura, Luella, 155, 198, 205
Barun, Ken, 91
benzodiazepines, 110, 167, 174
Betty Ford Center, 37
Biden, Joe, and administration, xiv, 26, 222
Big Pharma, 204

Billeaudeau, Peggy, 125, 126, 128, 130–132
Black Americans, *see* race, ethnicity, and discrimination
Blue Cross Blue Shield, 74, 75
Blue Moon Hotel (Philadelphia), 53–55
Bly, Sean, 80–81, 163
body brokering, 119
brainwashing, 87, 89, 124
Bratcher, Cassy, 61–62, 64, 110–112, 155, 205
Brookman, Matt, 152
buprenorphine (bup)
   access problems for Black patients, 22
   chance of rehab success with, 100
   continued limited access to, 222
   correlation with addiction treatment, 144
   dangers of combining with benzodiazepines, 174
   and DEA's investigation of DORN, 110
   decline in prescriptions in 2022, 207
   and Drug Addiction Treatment Act, 27
   in France, 24, 25, 28
   and Matthew Maniace's death, 174
   racial disparities with access to, 194
   regulatory constraints on prescribers, 62–63
   see also Suboxone
Bush, George W., and administration
   Mental Health Parity Act, 73
   Suboxone prescription regulation, 108
   treatment approach to addiction, xiv

Index

California
  criminal justice reforms, 37
  difficulty of investigating fraud in, 119
  expansion of for-profit treatment industry, 43
  insurance fraud in, 118
  lax regulations of rehab facilities, 74, 77, 163
  unpaid labor from rehab participants, 93
California Department of Insurance, 169–170
CARF (Commission on Accreditation of Rehabilitation Facilities), 84, 164
Carmel, Indiana
  quick-response team, 206
  see also Drug and Opiate Recovery Network (DORN); Ley, Larry
Carmel Current, The (website), 153
Carmel Police Department, 105–106, 151
Cefalu, Melanie, 124–129
Celebrate Recovery, 72
Celebrity Rehab (TV show), 43, 44, 118
Cenikor
  author's investigation of, 181–183
  CARF accreditation, 165
  clients injured on jobs in Texas, 183–184
  and drug sentencing reform, 50–51
  effect on Chris Koon, 179–181
  founding and early years, 88–93
  investigation by Louisiana regulators, 182

  investigation by Texas regulators, 182–183
  Chris Koon at, 83–87, 93–97, 121–125, 127–137
  Chris Koon's assignment to, 49, 51, 52
  Chris Koon's departure from, 179
  oppressive rules at, 121–123
  Synanon as predecessor, 88–89
chronic pain, 6, 64
Coastal Bridge, 135
cocaine, 20
  see also crack
Cockrell, Tonda, 107
Collins, Cody, 95, 129
Commission on Accreditation of Rehabilitation Facilities (CARF), 84, 164
Congress, US
  James Lucas Austin's testimony before, 90
  Drug Addiction Treatment Act hearings, 26–29
  framing of addiction as disease, xiv
  and Suboxone regulation, 29, 108
consequences, of addiction, 224–225
contingency management, 224
Courtney, Aaron, 159
COVID-19 pandemic, 193, 222
crack
  addiction–economic rewards study, 223–224
  Chris Koon and, 4
  April Lee and, 20
  April Lee's mother and, 15–16

Index

crack (*cont.*)
    in Philadelphia, 16–17
    and treatment vs. punishment
        debate, xiv, 26
Creative Care, 214–215
criminal justice reform, 37, 50
criminal record, as barrier to
    post-recovery progress, 195
Cynthia (Jarrod's girlfriend), 42

Dalton, Katy Jo, 33, 108
DARE (Drug Abuse Resistance Education), 5
Dateline NBC, 25–26
DEA, *see* Drug Enforcement Administration
Dederich, Chuck, 88, 89, 91–92
De Flavio, Jeff, 206
Department of Health and Human Services, U.S. (DHHS), 182
Department of Health Care Services (DHCS, California)
    and insurance claim payments to for-profit rehab facilities, 170
    investigation of Matthew Maniace's death, 175, 176
    Wendy McEntyre's contacts with, 164, 169
Department of Justice (DOJ), US
    and Purdue Pharma settlement funds, 194
    Suboxone cases, 203–204
Department of Social Services (DSS), California, 210, 211, 218

detox
    at AIA, 166–169, 173–174
    Donavan Doyle, 115
    lax California regulations, 163
    April Lee's advocacy for others, 192–193
    April Lee's experiences, 55–56, 103
    programs prioritizing alcohol/opioid users over crack/meth users, 192
DHCS, *see* Department of Health Care Services, California
DHHS (Department of Health and Human Services, U.S.), 182
Dietz, Aaron K., 105–107, 151–158
Dilaudid, 10
Dirksen Federal Building (Chicago, Ill.), 197
disease, framing addiction as, xiv
diversion investigators, 64–67
Dixon, Tara, 126–127, 130–131
Dr. Phil show, 214
DOJ (Department of Justice), US
    and Purdue Pharma settlement funds, 194
    Suboxone cases, 203–204
Dollard, Andrew, 155, 197–202, 205
dopamine, 223–224
D'Orazio, Joseph, 144
DORN, *see* Drug and Opiate Recovery Network
Doyle, Cyndi, 161
    at AIA after Donavan's death, 114, 115
    and Donavan's son, 72
    end of investigations of Donavan's death, 217

Index

first visit to Donavan at AIA, 75–76
Wendy McEntyre and, 113
phone calls with Kory Avarell, 76–79
and search for Donavan after his
   disappearance from AIA, x–xiii,
   79–81
search for drug treatment center for
   Donavan, 74–75
Doyle, Donavan, 161
at AIA, 74–79, 114–117
contemplation of suicide, 78, 115–116,
   162
discovery of remains, 113
early attempts at rehab, 72
early drug abuse, 71–72
final hours of life, 114–117
Chris O'Keefe's account of Donavan's
   time at AIA, 114–116
San Bernardino County Sheriff's
   Office response to death, xi–xii
search for appropriate rehab
   program, 73–74
search for remains of, ix–xiii, 79–81
Doyle, Shannon, 161
at AIA after Donavan's death, 114
and Donavan's drug use, 71, 72
initial reaction to AIA, 75, 76
search for Donavan after his
   disappearance from AIA, x, xi,
   79, 81
Drug Addiction Treatment Act, 26–29,
   37
Drug and Opiate Recovery Network
   (DORN)
changes in Indiana after closure of,
   206

DEA investigation of, 67–68, 105–112,
   153–159
expansion after closure of Wagoner
   pain clinic, 61–64
Larry Ley's appellate court hearing
   after DEA closure of, 197–203
staff members' experiences after
   closure of, 205
drug courts, 50–51
Drug Enforcement Administration
   (DEA)
attitude towards Suboxone, 65–66
diversion investigators, 64–67
DORN investigation, xvi, 67–68,
   105–112, 153–159
opposition to treatment approach to
   addiction, 28
prosecution of Larry Ley, 151–153,
   155
and Suboxone clinics, 62–63
drug industry settlement funds, 226
drug prevention programs, 5
drug sales representatives, 23, 24
Drug Task Force, Hamilton County,
   Indiana, 106
drug testing, insurance fraud and,
   118
Drury, Cameron, 32
DSS (Department of Social Services),
   California, 210, 211, 218
Dugas, James, 166–168, 215

emergency rooms, 143–145
Erwin, Mike, 50
European Union, overdose deaths
   (2021), xiv

Index

"family meetings" (Cenikor), 126–127
FDA (Food and Drug Administration, U.S.), 203
fear, as Cenikor tactic, 123, 124, 126
fentanyl
   in Kensington, 142
   and overdose deaths, 225–226
   overdose deaths from, xv
   and overdose deaths in 2024, 221–222
   and racial disparities among death tolls during opioid epidemic, 193
   and Trump tariffs, 226
Fisher, Jim, 198
Flaum, Joel, 202
Food and Drug Administration, U.S. (FDA), 203
forced labor, 89
   see also unpaid labor
France, addiction treatment in, 24–25, 27–28
fraud, in rehab industry, 118
free labor, *see* unpaid labor

gabapentin, 167, 168, 174
"Game, The"
   at Cenikor, 87, 126–127
   at Synanon, 88, 89
Georgia, unpaid labor from rehab patients, 92–93
Gist, Larry, 50–51
Gold, Karen
   first meeting with Wendy McEntyre, 42
   reaction to Wendy's pursuit of AIA, 161–162, 170
   and Wendy's arrest after rescuing a child from juvenile treatment program, 214, 216
   and Wendy's business card, 44
   and wrongful-death lawsuits, 169
Good, Pat, 28
Great Recession, 94
Grewal, Harinder, 168
Groups: Recover Together, 206
gun violence, during COVID-19 pandemic, 193

Hampton, Ryan, 194–195
Harris, Amy Julia, 181–183
Hart, Carl, 223–224
Hart, Larry, 134
Hayes, David, 157–158
Hays, Sean, 158–159
healthcare reform, 43
health insurance
   April Lee and, 100
   US vs. France, 28
HealthNet, 169–170
heroin
   Jarrod and, 36
   Aaron Dietz's view of, 153, 156
   and DORN patients, 32–33
   harm reduction and, 24–26
   Chris Koon and, 10–13
   April Lee and, 22
   in April Lee's family, 17
   Justin Marshall and, 129
   methadone treatment for addiction, 27
   Suboxone treatment for addiction, 29–30

Index

in suburbia, 25–26
Kedric Williams case, 50
HIV, 142
Hogsett, Joe, 151–152
Holes (Sachar), 16
homelessness
   during crack epidemic, 17–18
   and rehab/relapse cycle, 119, 192, 195
Houston, Texas, 90
Hughes, Rick, 77, 78, 80
hydroxyzine, 167, 168

"Imperial Marines," 92
Indiana
   after DORN's closure, 159, 206
   Suboxone providers in, 32
   see also Drug and Opiate Recovery Network (DORN); Ley, Larry
Indivior, 203–204
insurance companies
   barriers to treatment coverage, xv
   denial of claims from for-profit rehab facilities, 169–170
   limits on rehab duration, 117–118
   and pain pill revolution, 6–7
Intervention (A&E show), 164

Jarrod (Wendy McEntyre's son)
   addiction struggles, 35–38
   death of, 39–41
   mother's activism after death of, 40–44, 69–71
   mother's reaction to his heroin addiction, 35–37
   in rehab system, 73
   at Safe House, 38–41
Jarrod's Law, 213–215, 219
Jones, Gene, 90–91

Kelly, John, 195–196
Kensington (Philadelphia neighborhood), 100, 102–104, 139–149, 191–193, 195
"Kensington Strangler," 140
Klein, Marc, 106
Klonopin, 173, 174
Kokomo, Indiana, 206
Koon, Chris
   after leaving Cenikor, 179–181, 183–185
   agreement to go to Cenikor, 49, 51, 52
   and Carrie (mother), 4, 9, 83–84, 136, 180, 183, 184
   at Cenikor, 83–87, 93–97, 121–125, 127–137
   cyst problems, 135–136, 181
   disillusionment with Cenikor, 96–97
   early drug experiences, 3–5, 10–13
   first arrest, 9
   first overdose, 12
   free labor at for-profit companies, xvi
   and heroin, 10–11
   incarceration, 48–49
   injury while on Cenikor job, 132–134
   and *Mind Games*, 122–124
   and Pat ("Granny"), 3, 4, 11, 12, 83–85, 93, 122, 180

Index

Koon, Chris (*cont.*)
  and Percocet, 181
  recovery trajectory compared to April Lee, 225
  relapse while at Cenikor, 135
  second arrest, 10
  and Suboxone, 11, 183–184
  third arrest, 47–48
  in welding school, 180
Koon, John, 4
  after Chris's release from Cenikor, 185
  and Chris's first run-in with the law, 9
  and Chris's maturity after Cenikor, 180
  visit to Chris at Cenikor, 96, 121–122

labor, *see* unpaid labor
Latinos, *see* race, ethnicity, and discrimination
Lee, April
  after graduating from 30-day rehab, 99–100
  after relapse, 139–149
  after treatment, 189–196
  assistance to people on the streets in Kensington after recovery, 191–194, 196
  attempts to revive overdose victims, 142–143
  at Blue Moon Hotel, 53–55
  and Chris (brother), 58–59, 99
  and Derrick (eldest son), 141, 189–190
  in detox and rehab, 55–59
  discharge from jail, 146–147
  early drug experiences, 20
  early years, 15–18
  financial state after recovery, 190
  and heroin, 17, 22
  in jail, 145–147
  letter to son, 188
  and Nadine (mother), 15–19, 54–55
  pregnancies, 15, 18, 21
  at Prevention Point, 141–142
  prostitution, 140, 145
  and racial barriers to treatment, xvi
  at recovery house, 100–104, 148–149, 187–189
  recovery trajectory compared to Chris Koon, 225
  relapse after rehab, 100
  reuniting with her children, 189–190
  skill at finding veins, 140–141
  and Tasha (sister-in-law), 99–101
  at Temple University Hospital emergency room, 143–145
Ley, Larry, xvii
  appellate court hearing, 197–203
  arrest of, 155
  cancer diagnosis, 205
  on companies copying DORN model, 207
  DEA investigation of DORN, 67, 105–111
  death of, 208
  early days as Suboxone prescriber, 23–24, 29, 31–34
  federal prosecution of, 151–160
  imprisonment after DEA raid, 159–160

Index

news coverage of arrest, 157
in outpatient addiction/PTSD program, 207–208
on punishment vs. treatment, 154
and Tom (brother), 32
Lohan, Lindsay, 37, 118
Lohan, Michael, 118–119
Long Beach, California, 90
Lortab, 67, 135
Los Angeles Department of Building and Safety, 41–42
Louisiana
incarceration rate, 49
lax investigations of rehab programs, 129
pain pill prescriptions in, 5–6
racial disparities in incarceration, 49–50
see also Koon, Chris
Louisiana State Penitentiary, 49
Love, John, 90
Luke Austin and Country Kingdom USA, 90

Mackey, Joe, 155, 202–203
Maniace, Bill, 217
Maniace, Lynn, 173, 175–176, 215, 217
Maniace, Matthew, 173–175, 215, 217
Marie (DORN patient), 111, 112
marijuana (weed), 4–6, 8, 19, 50, 72, 147
Markey, Ed, 207
Marshall, Justin, 127–129
MAT (medication-assisted treatment), 195

McEntyre, Wendy
activism following son Jarrod's death, 69–71
after James Dugas's death at AIA, 168–169
campaign against abuse in juvenile detention facility, 209–213
and Cheryll (sister), 42–43, 209–210, 214
court appearance for restraining order filed by AIA, 170–172
and Dean (husband), 42, 44
effects of AIA investigation on, 173
felony kidnapping arrest after rescuing a child from juvenile treatment program, 209–218
interviews with ex-employees of AIA, 163–164
investigation of AIA, 113–114, 116–120, 161–165, 169–170, 215
and Jamie (daughter), 35–36, 39, 42
mission to reform rehab industry, xi, xvi–xvii
news of Jarrod's heroin addiction, 35–37
reaction to Jarrod's death, 39–44
search for Donavan Doyle's remains, x–xiii, 80–81
search for treatment center for Jarrod, 73
see also Jarrod
Medicaid
barring of funding for important elements of recovery, 100, 101–102

- 293 -

Index

Medicaid (cont.)
   and Cenikor's counseling requirements, 124
   and Cenikor's expansion, 93, 96
   potential cuts under Trump administration, 226
   refusal of treatment to crack users on, 17
Medicaid expansion, 55, 100
Medicaid fraud, Cenikor and, 182
"medical cure," for addiction, 26
medication-assisted treatment (MAT), 195
Mental Health Parity and Addiction Equity Act of 2008 (MHPAEA), 73, 170
methadone
   for addiction treatment at Temple Episcopal Campus hospital, 144
   Jarrod and, 37
   chance of rehab success with, 100
   DEA and, 65
   difficulties in access to, 207
   Drug Addiction Treatment Act and, 27
   early studies of, 25
   Sean Hays and, 159
   as potential solution to Suboxone scarcity, 108
methamphetamine (meth), 35, 47, 48, 71–72, 128, 167, 224
MHPAEA (Mental Health Parity and Addiction Equity Act of 2008), 73, 170
Mind Games (book), 122–124
Minkler, Josh, 152
"mirror therapy," 86

Morgan, Yvonne, 62
MRSA, 136

naloxone, 142, 143, 204
Narcan, 204, 221–222
Nation, Steve, 198
National Football League, Cenikor's partnership with, 92
National Institute on Drug Abuse (NIDA), 26, 27
"natural recoveries," 224
needle exchange programs, 24, 27, 141–142, 194
New England Journal of Medicine, 6–7
NIDA (National Institute on Drug Abuse), 26, 27
Nimoy, Leonard, 89
Nixon, Richard M., 7
Noble, Bernard, 50
Noblesville, Indiana, 23
   see also Ley, Larry
nonprofit outpatient programs, decline in, 74
North Philadelphia, see Lee, April

Obama, Barack, and administration
   Affordable Care Act, 73
   and shift in treatment approach to addiction, xiv, 43
   speech on opioid crisis, xiii
Obamacare, 73
   see also Affordable Care Act (ACA)
Occupational Safety and Health Administration (OSHA), 134
Odom, Patrick, 95, 125, 132–133, 135
O'Keefe, Chris, 114–116, 162

Index

O'Keeffe, Charles, 26, 28–29
Opana, 10
Opiant Pharmaceuticals, 204
opioid crisis/epidemic
    Obama's speech on, xiii
    racial disparities as epidemic continued, 193–194
    shift in thinking on punishment vs. treatment, xiii
    and treatment vs. punishment debate, 26–27
orphan drug status, for Suboxone, 28–29, 108, 203
OSHA (Occupational Safety and Health Administration), 134
out-of-network providers, 74–75
overdose deaths, 144
    after incarceration, 148
    criminalization and, 50
    decline in 2024, 221–222
    fentanyl and, 142, 225–226
    in France, 25
    increase (1971–2008), 7
    increase in Indiana after DEA raid on DORN, 159
    increase since 1999, xiv
    racial disparities among death tolls during opioid epidemic, 193
    U.S. vs. EU (2021), xiv
overmedication, at rehab centers, xv, 118, 162–163, 175–176
OxyContin, xiv
    doctors' latitude in prescribing, 62
    heroin as cheaper alternative to, 10
    in Chris Koon's community, 5–7
    origins, 6–7
    overdose deaths (early 2000s), 7
    Suboxone as treatment for addiction to, 11
    see also Purdue Pharma

pain pills
    April Lee and, 20–21
    see also prescription narcotics; specific pills, e.g.: OxyContin
people of color, *see* race, ethnicity, and discrimination
Percocet, 20, 22, 181
Philadelphia, *see* Lee, April
Pineville, Louisiana, 7–8
Pinsky, Drew, 43
poverty
    and chronic pain, 6
    in Philadelphia, 16–17
    US rate (2023), 225
    US vs. France, 28
pregnant women, refusal of admission to treatment programs, 17, 22, 223
prescription narcotics, 29
    April Lee and, 20
    overdose deaths from, 7
    see also OxyContin
Prevention Point (Kensington nonprofit), 141–142
Promises (rehab center), 37
Propranolol, 167
prostitution, 140
Public Records Act, 44
"pull ups" (Cenikor practice), 87
punishment
    as motivation for treatment, 223
    as response to crack epidemic, 16–17

Index

punishment (*cont.*)
    treatment vs., xiii, xiv, 26–27, 43, 153–154
Purdue Pharma
    OxyContin sales campaign, 6–7
    sales tactics as model for Suboxone promotion, 30, 63
    use of settlement funds, 194
    as villain in opioid epidemic, xiv

race, ethnicity, and discrimination
    access to treatment, 192
    buprenorphine access, 144, 194
    disparities among addiction-treatment facilities, 74
    disparities among death tolls during opioid epidemic, 193–194
    drug rehab success rates, 56–57
    housing in Louisiana, 7–8
    incarceration rates, 49–50
    national drug policies, 26
    overdose deaths in Philadelphia, 225
    perception of addiction and recovery, 43
    response to addiction crisis, 25–27
    risk scores and, 50
    treatment vs. punishment debate, xiv
Radford, Ryan, 67–68, 158
Rapides Parish, Louisiana, 7–8
Reagan, Ronald, and administration, 5, 92
Reckitt Benckiser
    and DORN's business practices, 107–108
    and DORN's expansion, 63
    lobbying for orphan drug status for Suboxone, 28–29
    and NIDA legislation, 26
    sales call to Larry Ley, 23
    sales strategy, 29–31
"recovery capital," 196, 224
recovery houses, in Philadelphia, 100–104, 146–148, 193
relapse
    after short-term rehab programs, xv–xvi, 57
    cycle of, xvii
    due to insurers' limits on rehab duration, 117–118
    Synanon and, 88, 89
Robaxin, 173, 174
Rockefeller Institute, 25
Rovner, Ilana, 202
rules, mind control and, 123

Sachs, Michael, 171, 172
Safe House (Van Nuys, Calif.), 38, 40–42
sales representatives
    OxyContin, 6–7
    Suboxone, 23, 24, 30–31, 63, 203–204
SAMHSA (Substance Abuse and Mental Health Services Administration), 182
San Bernardino County Sheriff's Office, xi–xii
San Bernardino District Attorney's office, 216
San Bernardino Mountains, ix, 44, 71
Schoonover, Rick, 38–42, 69–71

Index

Scott, Gail Groves, 30–31
Seeley, Ken, 164
"self-efficacy," 5
Serling, Rod, 89
sexual abuse, 18, 21, 188, 211
sexual harassment, at Cenikor, 127, 183
Shalala, Donna, 27
Shane (Above It All employee), 74
Shintech, 97
slavery, 89
  see also unpaid labor
sleep deprivation, 123
sober-living homes
  Cenikor's transition from rehab centers to, 127
  Jarrod and, xi, xvi, 36, 38, 40–41
  Jarrod's Law and, 214
  rebranding of AIA facilities as, 164
  rebranding of Cenikor facilities as, 183
  see also specific facilities, e.g.: Safe House
Sober Living Network, 38
Spears, Britney, 37
structural racism, 16–17, 193
  see also race, ethnicity, and discrimination
Sublocade, 204
Suboxone
  Black patients and, 21–22
  and DEA investigation of DORN, 105–108, 110
  development and introduction of, xiv
  DOJ and criminal case against manufacturers, 203
  government regulations resulting in scarcity of, xv
  Chris Koon and, 11–13, 183–185
  Larry Ley and, 23, 24, 61–68
  Matthew Maniace and, 173, 174
  misprescribing of, 167–168
  NIDA and, 26
  orphan drug status for, 28–29, 108, 203
  portrayal in news coverage of DORN raid, 157
  and press conference on DORN arrests, 156, 157
  scarcity of, 37
  see also buprenorphine; Drug and Opiate Recovery Network (DORN)
Suboxone clinics, 206
  see also Drug and Opiate Recovery Network (DORN)
Suboxone Sublingual Film, 203–204
Substance Abuse and Mental Health Services Administration (SAMHSA), 182
suburbia, and response to addiction crisis, 25–27, 43
suicide, Donavan Doyle's threats/attempts, 78, 115–116, 162
Synanon, 88–89, 91–92
syringe exchange programs, see needle exchange programs

Temple University Hospital-Episcopal Campus, 143–145
temporary workers, 94–95

Index

Tennessee, unpaid labor from rehab participants in, 92–93
Texas, Cenikor facilities in, 84, 90, 182–183
Thaxter, Shaun, 204
THC, 167
"Therapeutic Community model" at Cenikor, 94
Thomas, Derrik, 157–158
treatment, punishment vs., xiii, xiv, 26–27, 43, 153–154
Treuherz, Robert, 167, 168
Trump, Donald, and administration, 226
12-step programs
 during COVID-19 pandemic, 193
 April Lee and, 56, 99, 100, 190
 as model for Drew Pinsky's approach to treatment, 43
 residential programs' prevailing approach, 56
 resistance to Suboxone by, 37
28-day rehab programs
 Katy Jo Dalton and, 33
 Ryan Hampton and, 195
 April Lee and, 56–59

unemployment
 and chronic pain, 6
 correlation with overdose deaths, 7
 during COVID-19 pandemic, 193
 increase in US (1960–2009), 6
United States
 France's approach to addiction treatment compared to, 24–25, 27–28
 health outcomes compared to other developed nations, 118
 overdose deaths since 1999, xiv–xv
unlicensed recovery houses, 100–104
unpaid labor
 James Lucas Austin and, 90
 at Cenikor, 92–93, 97, 128–130, 183–184
 Cenikor and, 182
 as condition of admission to Cenikor, 93–94
 by patients at rehab centers, xv
 temporary workers and, 94–95
 unlicensed recovery houses as source of, 102
urine testing, 118, 135, 173

Veles, Diana, 162–163, 210–212, 216, 218
Vierk, Ron, 159, 202

Wagoner, Marilyn and Don, 62, 157
Wagoner Medical Center (Suboxone clinic), 62, 64, 67–68, 106, 107
Walter, Shoshana, 181–182
Washburn, Kelly, 171–172
weed, *see* marijuana
welfare benefits, 6
welfare reform, 18
Whisenand, Gary, 106–107, 109, 151
white people
 and buprenorphine access, 22, 144
 in drug court, 51
 marginalization caused by addiction, 224–225

Index

overdose deaths in early stages of opioid epidemic, 193
and shift of focus from punishment to treatment, xiv, 26, 43
and Suboxone advertisements, 29–30
see also race, ethnicity, and discrimination
Wichern, Dennis, 151, 152, 154–157
Willet, Warren, 135, 137, 179
Williams, Kedric, 50
Williams Sonoma, 93

work, unpaid, *see* unpaid labor
workers compensation benefits, waiving of, 93–94
working for free, *see* unpaid labor
wrongful-death lawsuits, 164, 169–170, 215

Yale New Haven Hospital, 144
Yvonne (DORN nurse), 62

Zevin, Barry, 223
Zoloft, 167